Edited by David R. Boyd

Best Contemporary Canadian Nature Writing

NORTHERN
WILD

D1566938

David Suzuki Foundation

GREYSTONE BOOKS

Douglas & McIntyre Publishing Group
Vancouver/Toronto

Greystone Books
A division of Douglas & McIntyre Ltd.
2323 Quebec Street, Suite 201
Vancouver, British Columbia v5t 4s7
www.greystonebooks.com

David Suzuki Foundation
2211 West 4th Avenue, Suite 219
Vancouver, British Columbia v6k 4s2

Canadian Cataloguing in Publication Data
Main entry under title:
Northern wild

Co-published by: David Suzuki Foundation
Includes bibliographical references
ISBN 1-55054-824-7

1. Natural history—Canada. I. Boyd, David R. (David Richard)
II. David Suzuki Foundation.
QH106.2.N55N67 2001   508.71   C00-911581-1

Cover design by Peter Cocking
Cover photograph by Darwin Wiggett/First Light
Typesetting by Julie Cochrane
Printed and bound in Canada by Friesens

The quote on page 13 is from Randy Stoltmann, *Written by the Wind: British Columbia Wilderness Adventures* (Victoria, B.C.: Orca, 1993) and is reprinted by permission.

The publisher gratefully acknowledges the assistance of the Canada Council and of the British Columbia Ministry of Tourism, Small Business and Culture. The publisher also acknowledges the financial support of the Government of Canada through the Book Publishing Industry Development Program (BPIDP) for its publishing activities.

This book is dedicated
to the memory of my mother,
who cultivated both my love
of the great Canadian outdoors
and my appreciation for
good writing.

Contents

Foreword

WILDERNESS IS ONE of the defining features of Canada. The summer cottage, canoe trips, and the northern lights are quintessential Canadian experiences. We boast of nature on our licence plates, lure millions of tourists here to experience it, and lionize the artists who capture it. Our flag is graced with a maple leaf, and the beaver and the goose are stamped on numerous Canadian products. What would Canada be without bears, loons, salmon, cedar trees, or fall colours?

Paradoxically, Canada is one of the most urbanized societies in the world. Most Canadians live in large cities in a narrow band hugging the U.S. border. And the sprawl from urban centres swallows farmland, forests, and bogs.

Over the past five centuries, immigrants poured into Canada seeking their destiny. My grandparents were part of that human flood, arriving at the turn of the last century. They were destitute and hoped to make a fortune so that they could return to "civilization," which to them was Japan. When they looked at this land, they saw *opportunity*—a bountiful place that was rich in resources. That continues to be the commanding ethos of our society today.

Now, as Canada's population and technological prowess continue to grow, the impulse to exploit our riches has become increasingly discordant with our love of nature. The resolution of this clash is the challenging issue of our time. Is the fate of Canada's remaining wild areas to rest on economic arguments, or should deeper values inform our decisions?

David Boyd is an environmental lawyer and professor living on Pender Island. He has selected a sample of writings that demonstrate a deep sense of connection with nature that I believe resonates profoundly with most Canadians. In a time when profit, power, and tax cuts dominate our political and economic agendas, these wonderful essays provide nourishment for our souls.

David Suzuki
Chair, David Suzuki Foundation

Acknowledgements

FIRST AND FOREMOST, thanks must go to the twenty outstanding writers featured in this anthology, many of whom waived or reduced their fees since the royalties from this book support the important environmental work of the David Suzuki Foundation. I owe a major debt of gratitude to publisher Rob Sanders at Greystone Books for wholeheartedly supporting this project from day one. My editor, Nancy Flight, was a pleasure to work with and provided invaluable advice as the book evolved. Leanne Denis also helped steer me in the right direction. Finally, thanks to all of my friends, relatives, and colleagues for listening to me rave about Canadian nature writing and for being relentlessly enthusiastic about this book.

Introduction

*To be at home on the planet and welcome here, humanity
must understand and appreciate the primacy of that home,
the Eden we have never left, and the wild that is its emblem.*
— STAN ROWE, *Home Place: Essays on Ecology*

FOR YEARS, CANADIAN wilderness and Canadian nature writers
have given me joy, inspiration, and rejuvenation. Through this
anthology I hope to express my gratitude by paying tribute to
this marvellous land and these outstanding wordsmiths. This
collection celebrates both wild Canada and the eloquent authors
who write what Wallace Stegner has poetically described as the
literature of hope.

The seeds for this book were sown long ago, during my youth
in Calgary. As with so many Canadians, my favourite childhood
memories are of the outdoors—evenings spent poking around
local neighbourhood parks, weekends at my uncle's prairie farm,
and summer holidays exploring the Rocky Mountains. My first
real hike was up to the Plain of Six Glaciers teahouse near Lake
Louise in Banff National Park. It was an exhilarating adventure
—my little brother and I felt like rugged explorers as we climbed
what seemed to us to be a steep and treacherous trail. The

jaw-dropping beauty and knee-wobbling physical grandeur of the Rockies cast a lifelong spell on me.

My other childhood passion was reading. I have vivid memories of books by Farley Mowat, Roderick Haig-Brown, Jack London, and Robert Service—classics such as *Owls in the Family, Never Cry Wolf, The Call of the Wild,* and "The Cremation of Sam McGee."

It is no wonder, then, that in recent years I have become a nature writing afficionado. Perhaps as a consequence of living in the cultural shadow of the United States, most of my early forays into this genre focussed on famous American authors. Nature writing in the United States has a long and illustrious tradition dating back to Henry David Thoreau, Ralph Waldo Emerson, and John Muir. More modern American icons include Aldo Leopold, Rachel Carson, and Edward Abbey, while contemporary greats include Annie Dillard, Barry Lopez, Terry Tempest Williams, David Quammen, Gretel Ehrlich, Gary Snyder, Kathleen Dean Moore, Peter Matthiessen, and many others.

Although I admire these American writers, I wanted to read Canadians writing about Canada. Canadian nature writing also has a long and storied history, yet our writers are much less famous even in Canada than their counterparts to the south. In the 19th century, Canadian nature writers Catharine Parr Traill, Ernest Thompson Seton, and Charles G. D. Roberts broke the trail. In the 20th century, they were joined by Pauline Johnson, Grey Owl, Emily Carr, Roderick Haig-Brown, Gilean Douglas, Bill Reid, Louise de Kirilene Lawrence, Andy Russell, Farley Mowat, and Harold Horwood. Most of these great Canadian nature writers are represented in two historical anthologies: *Treasures of the Place: Three Centuries of Nature Writing in*

Canada, edited by Wayne Grady, and *Living in Harmony: Nature Writing by Women in Canada,* edited by Andrea Pinto Lebowitz.

But what about Canadians writing about nature today? Who are the bright lights and new voices? Although dozens and dozens of anthologies of contemporary American nature writing have been published since 1990, there are no national anthologies of contemporary Canadian nature writing. None. This book attempts to fill that void.

Nature writing, broadly defined, can include just about every imaginable kind of literature. The editor of an anthology must draw some lines. To narrow the search for the best contemporary Canadian nature writing, I considered only writing about Canada by Canadians that was published from 1990 onward. Good coverage of earlier Canadian nature writers is available in the anthologies edited by Wayne Grady and Andrea Pinto Lebowitz. Fiction and poetry are not included in this collection, although many superb Canadian novelists, short-story writers, and poets write powerfully about the land. Canadian fiction already enjoys well-earned fame, and the thought of tracking down and evaluating a decade of Canadian poetry was simply overwhelming.

The most agonizing aspect of compiling a collection of this nature is that many fine writers are left out—for reasons ranging from the editor's eccentricities to the publisher's page limits. Books tend to take on a life of their own, and this anthology was no different. As the book evolved, it became a meditation on the redefinition of our relationship with the wild. Some brilliant Canadian writers whose work could be described as nature writing simply could not be woven in. I encourage interested readers to peruse the works of visionary Canadian environmental philosophers such as Stan Rowe (*Home Place: Essays on Ecology*, 1990), John Livingston (*Rogue Primate: An Exploration of Human Domestication*, 1994), and Neil Evernden (*The Social Creation of Nature*, 1992). As well, there are many outstanding Canadian science writers, such as Adrian Forsyth, Jay Ingram, and David Suzuki. Other noteworthy contemporary Canadian nature writers include Harry Thurston, Candace Savage, John Weier, Ben Parfitt, Catherine Collins, Stephen Hume, Alexandra Morton, Ed Struzik, Bruce Obee, Dawn Hanna, Wayne Grady, Theresa Kishkan, Silver Donald Cameron, Ian and Karen McAllister, Nancy Baron, Monte Hummel, Bart Robinson, Andrew Nikiforuk, Fred Bruemmer, and Rosemary Neering. This list could go on and on—an indication of the extent to which nature writing in Canada is blossoming.

The essays offered in this collection represent my idiosyncratic assessment of the best Canadian nature writing published since 1990. To identify these gems I embarked on a quixotic and exhaustive search. I scanned every issue of *Canadian Geographic*, *Equinox*, *Nature Canada*, *Beautiful British Columbia*, *Atlantic Books Today*, *Brick*, *Explore*, *Kanawa*, *Saturday Night*, *Up Here*, and many other magazines from 1990 to 2000. I surfed the Internet for days, searching through library catalogues from Victoria to Newfoundland. I scoured the shelves of every bookstore that I came across. I cross-examined friends, colleagues, librarians, and bookstore clerks about their favourite nature writers. I read and read and read some more.

In the end, the most difficult choices were not so much about which writers to include but rather which essays. All of the writers featured in this anthology stand out from the crowd. The tremendous diversity of Canadian ecosystems is reflected in the diversity of voices and styles, which include scientific observation, poetic imagination, personal revelation, and irreverent humour.

Some of the best-known authors, such as Wade Davis, Sharon Butala, Sid Marty, Terry Glavin, and David Adams Richards, have won national awards and garnered international recognition for their writing. Reading their work again was a real delight. Yet my greatest pleasure in compiling this collection came from discovering writers that I had never heard of before, such as Beth Powning from New Brunswick, Beth Brant from Ontario, Jamie Bastedo from the Northwest Territories, and Briony Penn from British Columbia. By shining a spotlight on these relatively unsung authors, I hope to share the joy of discovery that accompanied my first encounter with them.

This anthology does not purport to be either exhaustive or definitive. It represents a beginning, a first step in celebrating an underrated element of our cultural landscape.

Look at a child gently holding an unfledged young robin that has fallen from its nest. Look in that child's eyes. The sweet bondage of wildness is recoverable.

— JOHN LIVINGSTON, *Rogue Primate: An Exploration of Human Domestication*

Thirty years ago Margaret Atwood and Northrop Frye used the metaphors of "survival" and the "garrison mentality" to describe the relationship between Canadians and the wild, reflecting our separation from, and our fear of, nature. Since then, the separation and fear have begun to disappear, and along with them much of the early hostility toward the wild. The authors in this anthology exhibit a new land ethic based on wonder, reconciliation, reverence, respect, and responsibility. They also acknowledge the enduring wisdom of traditional aboriginal relationships with the land. These are the common threads that weave this collection of disparate essays into a coherent whole. The revolution in our cultural mindset suggests that we are finally accepting, and indeed even embracing, the wildness that defines Canada.

The first element shared by these essays, a sense of wonder, is something that we all enjoy as children but tend to lose as we grow up. Wonder can be suffocated by the imperatives of choosing a career, finding a mate, raising a family, and striving to become a success (or at least to keep your head above water). The writers in this anthology either never lost their childlike awe or have somehow recaptured it. This sense of wonder is reflected in their relentless curiosity about nature, their open acceptance of the inscrutable mystery of the wild, and their fascination with the interconnectedness of the natural world. Beguiled by the chinook winds that blow from the Rockies, Sid Marty synthesizes history, natural history, cowboy bravado, and Blackfoot mythology to explain the phenomenon in his essay "The Creator Wind." In his piece from *Lines on the Water*, David Adams Richards reveals the magic of the Miramichi River, a place that has enchanted him since early childhood. He is hooked for life. Don Gayton, in "Landscape Mathematics," describes the revelations and synaptic firings provoked by his first encounters with grasslands, encounters that transformed a young man into an ecologist on a lifetime mission to try to decipher the earth's riddles. While on a nocturnal canoe trip in Jasper National Park, Kevin Van Tighem experiences an epiphany, recognizing that "wind and ice, river and mountain, wolf and water: all were part of the same whole." Marty, Adams Richards, Gayton, and Van Tighem are all spellbound by the wonders of the wild.

Reconciliation is the second pervasive theme in this book. All of the writers here seek to transcend the gulf that has grown between humans and nature. In her essay "When Roots Grow Back into the Earth," Heather Menzies describes her family's labour of love in replanting thousands of trees on abandoned farmland in Ontario. For Menzies, the intimacy of planting trees cultivated not only her love for the land but also a feeling of being physically part of it. Sharon Butala develops an unexpected but profound passion for the prairie despite the personal struggle she endures in making it her home. Twenty-five years of living on a farm in a New Brunswick valley enable Beth Powning to learn the language of a land that was foreign to her at first. But now, as Powning writes in her lyrical essay "Home," she "can't imagine ever leaving this place." Basil Johnston's tale "Beyond Yonder: Awuss-woodih" deflates the notion that greener grass grows elsewhere and prompts readers to reconsider the merits of their own landscapes. Our modern proclivity for transience makes it difficult to put down roots, yet that is precisely what most of the writers in this volume have done. Their relationships with the land are based on a philosophy of community, not conquest. The lines between home and wild begin to blur.

The third theme that emerges from these essays is reverence for nature. The authors in this anthology are united by a kind of secular spirituality, worshipping creation no matter who the creator is thought to be. In "The Place Where the X Is,"

David Carpenter displays a religious, albeit humorous, fervour for good fishing spots. Carpenter sings the praises of brook trout and rainbow trout, but beneath his levity lies genuine appreciation. Beth Brant's "Prayer" epitomizes the intimate, spiritual relationship with the land that characterizes traditional aboriginal culture. "Prayer" offers a moving testament to the profound influence great blue herons have had in Brant's life.

The traditional aboriginal world-view resonates throughout the essays in this book to a remarkable extent. David F. Pelly's essay "How Inuit Find Their Way in the Trackless Arctic" chronicles the extraordinary ability of Inuit people to navigate in seemingly impossible conditions—without maps, compasses, or any other aids beyond their own culturally unique way of seeing the world. In "Hunters of the Northern Ice," Wade Davis elaborates on the symbiosis between the Inuit and what many perceive as a barren landscape, providing a stunning example of how people are shaped by the land. Davis observes that "every idea and thought, every notion of culture and society, every impulse, belief, and gesture reflects the consciousness of a people who have not succumbed to the cult of the seed."

The fourth theme of this book, respect for nature and especially wildlife, also reflects traditional aboriginal culture. The authors remind us that Canada is home to more than just rogue primates. There are also bears, wolves, belugas, and salmon, all icons of Canadian wilderness. Many Canadians will never experience the spine-tingling excitement of seeing these creatures in the wild, yet the survival of these species is an integral part of maintaining our Canadian identity. It is satisfying on some atavistic, primordial level to simply know that these magnificent animals are still out there in the wild. Chris Czajkowski and

John and Mary Theberge, who have spent considerable time in the company of bears and wolves, respectively, emphasize that mutual respect is the key to a healthy relationship between humans and wild animals. Today, romantic misconceptions about bears and wolves are likely to be just as destructive as the fear-fuelled vitriol of the past.

The essays in this book highlight not only charismatic megafauna but also enigmatic microfauna and even some enchanting flora. Des Kennedy describes the dramatic transformation in his attitude toward slugs, from revulsion to admiration, as he learns about their natural history and their role in the functioning of British Columbia's rain forest. Jamie Bastedo writes in "The ABCs of Bug Protection" that although northern mosquitoes and blackflies are widely regarded as "an evil scourge," these insects are of colossal ecological importance. Bastedo prescribes tolerance as the secret to "peaceful coexistence with our insect brothers and sisters" and describes a humane device invented by a fellow northerner for removing mosquitoes from tents without harming them. In *A Year on the Wild Side*, Briony Penn speaks for many of the voiceless indigenes of the Pacific coast. Penn's premise is that familiarity breeds community, that learning about other species, such as native blackberries or bigleaf maples, facilitates our connection to them.

The fifth thread running through this book is the concept of responsibility. The writers in this anthology insist that we must acknowledge our role in harming the lands, waters, and wildlife of Canada. Our actions have not yet caught up with our attitudes; despite our oft-professed passion for wild spaces and wild species, we continue to destroy what we love.

Mark Hume's lifelong love affair with rivers has led him to

chronicle many of their stories—those of the Nechako, the Adams, the Khutzeymateen, and the Tatshenshini—but never so personally as in *River of the Angry Moon*, his book about the troubled Bella Coola River. In "December: Moon When the Sun Rests," Hume demonstrates that even those of us who cherish the wild have blood on our hands. Hume's elegiac tone is echoed in Pierre Béland's "Book of the Dead," chronicling the demise of belugas in the St. Lawrence River. Terry Glavin's "Hundreds of Little Jonahs" is similarly sombre but breaks the cycle of despair by showing that just as we are all complicit in harming nature, we can all be part of the healing process. Glavin's cautious optimism derives from his belief that it is the "little things that make a difference, in the long run."

The fundamental reason for preserving whatever wildness remains on land and in water is the symbolism of the act, the implicit recognition of values beyond humanity, something other than ourselves that ought not to be destroyed, an expression of wonder and awe before the marvelous world that created us and that, once gone, we cannot recreate.

— STAN ROWE, *Home Place: Essays on Ecology*

Having worked as an environmental lawyer for many years, I am acutely aware of our society's litany of ecological problems, the daunting dilemmas that gnaw at the consciences of many Canadians. These environmental issues are generally framed in negative terms, focussing on pollution, the destruction of wildlife habitat, and global challenges such as climate change. In the face of this relentless torrent of doom and gloom, I, like many others, seek solace in the wild. Hiking, rafting, skiing, and kayaking trips in untrammelled regions of Canada provide spiritual replenishment.

In recent years I have experienced moments of communion with the natural world that rearranged my neurons and made my spirit sing. Psychologists call these events peak experiences. Being surrounded by a swirling flock of hundreds of thousands of twittering sandpipers on a Pacific coast mud flat. Being watched by a white wolf on the bank of the Taku River. Watching bighorn rams square off and smash their heads together on a windswept grassland plateau. Inhaling the pungent smell of life and death commingling as a million sockeye salmon miraculously make it home to spawn in the Adams River. Listening to the complex underwater language of a family of orcas as they churn through the water around our boat near Kitimat. Waking up under a full moon in the northern Rockies as a herd of caribou wander nonchalantly past my sleeping bag. For me, Canada's wilderness is the perfect antidote for an overdose of civilization.

I am not alone. Across Canada millions of people hear the siren song of the great outdoors every summer. Like pilgrims trekking toward mecca, we stream out of cities toward beaches, trails, campgrounds, lakes, cabins, mountains, and rivers, seeking wild manna for our civilized souls. This annual migration is an integral part of our national identity. We are blessed beyond belief to live at this time in this beautiful place we call Canada.

But Canada is no longer the vast wilderness depicted in our cultural mythology. Much of the once wild landscape has been carved up by roads, clear-cuts, cities, towns, farms, ranches, and seismic lines. In some regions of the country little wild space remains. In other areas there are still sizeable swaths of land where humans have yet to make a mark. Several summers ago my brother and I drove northwest for an hour from Whistler, the bustling West Coast resort town. We parked the car at the end of a logging road, strapped on backpacks, and walked toward the Pacific Ocean for a full three weeks without seeing the slightest sign of humanity, apart from the occasional jet trail in the sky. From high up on glaciers, ridges, and mountains we looked down into gorgeous, healthy rain forest valleys. No roads, no clear-cuts, not a single piece of garbage. Incredibly wild country.

Only five years later Sims Creek, one of the beautiful rain forest watersheds that my brother and I admired from atop a mountain, has been torn open by a logging road and a series of devastating clear-cuts. Wild areas like Sims Creek are disappearing so quickly that we scarcely have time to mourn their passing.

Our society suffers from incremental amnesia, making it impossible to comprehend how much we have lost in the passage of a few short generations. Scarcely more than a century ago, buffalo shook the plains and passenger pigeons darkened the sky. Only decades ago, cod and salmon filled the waters at both ends of Canada. To contemplate these losses is to invite sorrow into your soul. Yet contemplate we must in order to forge the will to do better, to reject the prospect of further losses, and to change our attitudes and actions in the face of seemingly insurmountable odds.

The essays offered here are ultimately more than good writing; they are an impassioned plea, an urgent request that we renew our connections to the natural world and do everything in our power to ensure that we leave a legacy as great as that which we inherited. By celebrating wild Canada we take an important step toward securing its future. As Randy Stoltmann, a young British Columbia writer and wilderness advocate who lost his life in an avalanche, wrote shortly before his death:

> Get to know the land and its wonders for yourself. Care for it as you would a loved one. Share the joy of discovery and the thrill of exploration, have fun and laugh. Hike the forests, climb the peaks, ski the icefields, walk the beaches, canoe and kayak the rivers, lakes and seashore. Or just lie in a meadow, breathe the clean air and renew yourself. Stop. Think. Listen. Hear the roaring vastness of a great valley, or the sigh of wind in the treetops, or the eternal thunder of breakers on the shore. Then go back and speak to the world from your heart.

I urge you to take Randy's advice. The writers in this book already have.

BETH BRANT

Prayer

BETH BRANT is a Mohawk writer from the Bay of Quinte.
She is working on a collection of essays called *Testimony from the
Faithful*, which explores the native connection to the land.
Brant has written numerous books, including *Mohawk Trail,
Food and Spirits: Stories*, and *Writing as Witness: Essays and Talk*.
Brant also edited two groundbreaking collections of native
writing called *A Gathering of Spirit: A Collection by North
American Indian Women* and *I'll Sing 'til the Day I Die:
Conversations with Tyendinaga Elders*. "Prayer" is taken from
Intimate Nature: The Bond between Women and Animals.

I CAN'T REMEMBER the first time I saw you, Great Blue. It seems as though that moment should be imprinted on the cells of my brain that record memory. The other times, the hundreds of times you have crossed my path of vision, sent messages to my heart, are always the first time. The quick intake of my breath, then silence, as I watch you glide across the marsh, or flap your wings for a take-off of indescribable grace; the patient watch on your particular hunting place, or the speed of your beak spearing a fish, a frog, and the easy way it slides down your long, lovely throat.

I have watched you through binoculars, asking a quick forgiveness for this ineffably human way of looking at you.

I have seen you in Michigan, in many provinces of Canada, in California. I have watched you with my lover, with my grandchildren, with special friends. I have met your cousins—Egret, Sandhill Crane, Bittern, Green Heron, Night Heron, Little Blue Heron, Least Bittern. I have watched you build nests, have seen your babies. I have gathered your feathers from the waters where they drifted as you travelled on your journeys. These make a bundle on my altar where I pray.

You have come to me in ordinary times, extraordinary times. Before my surgery in 1987, I saw you. Before my surgery in 1994, I saw many of you. When I was separated from my beloved, two of you flew close over my head as I sat weeping. I am not arrogant enough to believe that you chose to show yourself to relieve my human pain, but I do believe that your presence was a gift, is the gift that keeps me spiritually bound to life.

I am Turtle Clan. That deliberate creature who is comfortable in water and on land. That being who wears a shell for protection and camouflage. But you, Great Blue, are the means by which I fly and dream. You are the way to worship. You are the physical manifestation of my love—you and I become one-in-my-body as my orgasms call forth the spirit of you. You are *there*, in the sky, on the land, stepping through the reeds. You are in me. You are Creator's mark.

Once I saw you dead beside a road. As I prayed over you and plucked some of your feathers, that moment became a story. I clumsily attempt to explain the mystery of my relationship with you. Nothing can explain you. Nothing can describe the way the sun turns your feathers blue as you gaze into the waters. No human being can relate the strength of your neck as it folds into yourself when you reach flight. I cannot tell the story of seeing your eyes meet mine—you were unafraid, but my heart was beating so fast in awe, in fear, in gratitude. I am humble and small in your presence, Great Blue.

Your story is in the air, in sound, in your yellow legs gently walking through the shallow waters. Your story resides in each stick you bring to the dead treetops to make your nest. It lives in the curve of your great wings; it shapes itself in the pale brown ovals of the eggs you lay in your huge stick house. Your story tells itself in the open mouths of your chicks. Your story goes on ceaselessly as you fly to find food, fly home to bring food to those open beaks. You relive your story through generations.

I am blessed to see you. I am blessed to hear your infrequent squawks. I am blessed to come onto your territory and visit with you. You have taught me that it is possible to soar without benefit of wings. That it is possible to live. That it is possible to love. That hope endures with each silent minute searching for sustenance. That faith can be as tangible as a bundle of feathers that lie on my altar. That a story is always in the beating of a heart. That I cry in wonder of you.

You have lived on this Earth and in the skies for centuries beyond imagining. You have completed transformations and resurrections that have brought you into the *here* where I reside. You once lived on an Earth that had no humans. What was your thought the first time you encountered one of my kind?

You do nothing that is not perfect and beautiful. Even your chicks, in their newborn awkwardness, give promise of glory:

the large beaks that seem too big for the delicate neck to hold; the down that sheds and leaves bare patches soon to be filled in by the colours that will become you—grey, brown, blue. Everything about you is a covenant with the rest of creation.

You have become a Clan. Peoples have worshipped you. Peoples have longed to uncover the secrets they think you are hiding beneath your feathers. Peoples have wished in their human souls to *be* you. You are that glimpse into what is possible. Flight. Moving your great wings over trees, over expanses of water, and over those of my kind who look up in awe as we point—"Look, look."

You sojourn in my dreams.

During the winter months there was that one day in late January when I heard your familiar voice and looked up, into the grey, cold sky, and saw you flying overhead—alone. I wondered what had kept you behind in this cold place. Your body was almost etched into the air, a solitary being. I felt the immense solitude of your journey. I heard a kind of music in my heart. I smelled the air—snow, cold, perhaps the hint of thaw. I cried, "Thank you, thank you." I lifted my arms as if to embrace you. A portrait of a woman gone mad from winter—standing in her backyard, turning in circles, shouting her thanks, arms reaching for possibility. I fell in the snow; sparrows eating from the bird feeder flew away in distress as I laughed and ate snow. I laughed, pulling myself up, returning to the warm kitchen.

You have brought me so much. What can I bring you? Assurances that your territories will not be polluted and blasphemed by the corruptness of man? Promises I cannot keep? I *will* bring you this: As each of our grandchildren come into the age of seeing with their hearts, I will point you out to them. I will say your name with reverence. I will draw in my breath as we watch you fly. They in turn will know what prayer is—the hushed moment of discovery. The quiet flame of regeneration. They will love you and treasure the completeness that is you. They will honour you in their lives. This I promise you.

Nia:wen.

WADE DAVIS
Hunters of the Northern Ice

WADE DAVIS is an internationally renowned ethnobotanist
and author who splits his time among Vancouver, the Spatsizi
Plateau, and Washington, D.C., when he is not exploring
remote corners of the globe. "Hunters of the Northern Ice"
is from *The Clouded Leopard: Travels to Landscapes of Spirit and Desire.*
Born and raised in British Columbia, Davis is also the author of
*Rainforest: Ancient Realm of the Pacific Northwest, One River:
Explorations and Discoveries in the Amazon Rain Forest*
(nominated for a Governor General's award in 1996), *Nomads of
the Dawn: The Penan of the Borneo Rain Forest, Shadows in the Sun:
Essays on the Spirit of Place,* and *The Serpent and the Rainbow.*

OLAYUK NARQITARVIK is a hunter. As a boy of twelve he killed a
polar bear at close quarters, thrusting a harpoon into its soft
underbelly as it lunged toward him. That same year he took his
first whale. In winter darkness, when temperatures fall so low
that breath cracks in the wind, he leaves his family each day to
follow the leads in the new ice and kneel motionless, for hours
at a time, over the breathing holes of ringed seals. The slightest
shift in weight will reveal his presence; in perfect stillness he

squats, knowing full well that as he hunts he is hunted. Polar bear tracks run away from every hole. If a seal does not appear, Olayuk may roll over, mimicking the creature to try to attract a bear so that predator may be reduced to prey.

Ipeelie Koonoo is Olayuk's stepfather, second husband to his mother. Revered as an elder, he too is a hunter. When he killed his first bear at nine, with a harpoon made for him the night before by a favourite uncle, he could not stop smiling. His first seal was taken when he was still too small to lift it from the ice. But he knew that the animal had chosen to die, betrayed by its thirst for fresh water. So he followed his uncle's teachings and dripped fresh water into its mouth to placate its spirit. If animals are not properly treated, they will not allow themselves to he taken. But if they are not hunted, the Inuit believe, they will suffer, and their numbers will decrease. Thus the hunt is a reflection of balance, a measure of the interdependence of all life in the Arctic, a polar desert cloaked in darkness nine months of the year and bathed in intense luminosity for the short weeks of *upinngaaq*, the summer season of renewal and rebirth.

Simon Qamanirq is both artist and hunter, the youngest of the three men, nephew of Olayuk's wife, Martha, the matriarch of the extended family. On his accordion, he plays Scottish reels adapted from those of ancient mariners and whalers, and with his firm hands turns soapstone into exquisite figurines of animals, all depicted so powerfully that they seem to move within the stone. "You can't be a carver," he explains, "if you are not a hunter." For some time, Simon lived down south, attended vocational school, and played drums in an Inuit rock-and-roll band named "The Harpoons." But he grew tired of the confused ways of people whose "heads were full of a thousand words." So he returned north. "I got nothing more interesting than hunting," he says. "Down in Canada I'm always cold. My body needs blood. Even their meat has no blood."

Three men, three generations of Inuit hunters. Seeking caribou on the open tundra during the cold months of fall, taking narwhal from the ice in July, they replicate through movement a seasonal round that recalls a distant time when all our ancestors were nomads. In living by the hunt, they remain apart, utterly different. Every idea and thought, every notion of culture and society, every impulse, belief, and gesture reflects the consciousness of a people who have not succumbed to the cult of the seed. Ideas that we take for granted—private ownership of objects and land, laws and institutions that place one person above another in a hierarchy of power—are not just exotic to the Inuit, they are anathema. If implemented, they would doom a way of life. This is something the Inuit know. "We hunt," Olayuk explains, "because we are hunters."

For most of the year, these men and their families live in the small community of Arctic Bay, a fiercely self-sufficient and independent clan, survivors of a century that has seen untold hardships unleashed upon their people. But for a brief time in June, in the fortnight leading up to the solstice, they make camp on a gravel beach at Cape Crauford, on the western shore of Admiralty Inlet, the largest fjord on Earth, a vast inland sea that cleaves the northern shore of Baffin Island 800 kilometres north of the Arctic Circle. There, beneath the dark cliffs of the Brodeur Peninsula, on a promontory overlooking Lancaster Sound, the richest body of water in the Arctic, they invite outsiders into their world.

The journey north begins before dawn in Ottawa and ends nine hours later on the seasonal ice off the shore of Olayuk's camp. It is a five-hour flight just to the weather station and settlement of Resolute Bay, the highest point in the Arctic serviced by commercial jets, where we switch from a 727 to a de Havilland Twin Otter. North of Resolute lie another 1600 kilometres of Canada. It is a place, the pilot remarks, where Canada could hide Britain and the English would never find it.

We fly across Barrow Strait, then over Lancaster Sound. From the air, the ice fuses with the snow-covered land. Ringed seals appear as dark specks on the ice. There are no polar bears to be seen, only their silent tracks wandering from seal hole to seal hole. At the mouth of Prince Regent Inlet, east of Somerset Island, the ice gives way abruptly to the black sea. Beyond the floe edge, scores of white beluga whales move gracefully through the water. A small mesalike island rises out of the sea. The plane banks steeply past the soaring cliffs, and in its wake tens of thousands of birds lift into the air. The Prince Leopold sanctuary is just 78 kilometres square, but on it nest nearly two hundred thousand pairs of migratory birds: thick-billed murres, northern fulmars, and black-legged kittiwakes. Baffin Island lies ahead, and within minutes the plane roars over the beach at Cape Crauford, turns into the wind, and lands on skis on a smooth stretch of ice 800 metres offshore.

In the brilliant sunlight we stand about, nineteen strangers drawn together by the promise of the journey. As an anthropologist, I want to take a firsthand look at ecotourism in action. The leader of the expedition is Johnny Mikes, outfitter and legendary river guide from British Columbia. It was Mikes who first encouraged Olayuk's family to establish a guiding

operation. On a warm day in September 1989, while on a kayaking expedition in Admiralty Inlet, Mikes stumbled upon a bay
where hundreds of narwhals were feeding in the shallows. On
the shore was an Inuit encampment, with narwhals hauled up
on the beach. Olayuk's brother Moses had just killed a bearded
seal, and in the bloodstained waters Greenland sharks lingered.
Mikes had never seen the raw edge of nature so exposed. As he
spent time with the Inuit, he came to understand that for them
blood on snow is not a sign of death but an affirmation of life. It
was something he thought others should experience. And then
Moses introduced him to Olayuk, and Olayuk told him about
the floe edge and the ice in June.

There are places and moments on Earth where natural phenomena occur of such stunning magnitude and beauty that they
shatter all notions of a world of human scale. It is such an event
that draws Olayuk and his family to their June camp at Cape
Crauford.

Every winter in the Arctic, virtually all of the sea between the
islands of the Canadian archipelago lies frozen, a single horizon
of ice that joins the polar icecap and eventually covers 15.5 million square kilometres, twice the area of the United States. As
temperatures drop to as low as minus 60 degrees Celsius, of
marine mammals only the ringed seals remain, dependent on
breathing holes scratched through the ice. Polar bears survive by
stalking the seals throughout the long Arctic night. Other
marine mammals—belugas, bowhead whales, walrus, and narwhals—head out through Lancaster Sound to the open waters
of Baffin Bay and Davis Strait, between Canada and Greenland.

Only small populations overwinter, surviving in rare pockets of open water kept ice-free by the action of winds and currents.

In spring the animals return, wave upon wave, hovering against the retreating ice edge. The winter population of a hundred thousand mammals soars in the summer to 17 million. Foraging in the rich waters, they await a chance to disperse to feeding grounds scattered throughout the Arctic. In the long hours of the midnight sun, brown algae bloom beneath the ice, billions of shrimp and amphipods flourish, and millions of arctic cod thrive upon the zooplankton. A quarter of a million harp, bearded, and ringed seals feed on the fish, as do thousands of belugas and narwhals. They, in turn, fall prey to roving pods of killer whales. A third of the belugas in North America gather here, and three of every four narwhals on Earth.

By June, the waters of Lancaster Sound are free of ice. But those of Admiralty Inlet, 48 kilometres wide at the mouth, remain frozen. From the camp at Cape Crauford, using snowmobiles and sleds, it is possible to travel along the floe edge, where the ice meets the sea, and listen as the breath of whales mingles with the wind.

Snowmobiles and a dozen Inuit kids descend on the plane. An old Inuk man motions us to split up and pile our gear and ourselves onto one of the sleds, which he calls *qamatiks*. He speaks no English, and the soft sounds of Inuktitut, the Inuit language, delight and astonish.

The camp is a line of canvas outfitter tents, arrayed in military precision along the high shore. At one end is the cooktent, at the other the guides' tents. The foreshore is a clutter of sleds and snowmobiles. Tethered on the ice are three dog teams. They yelp and howl, and the air is pungent with the scent of seal meat and excrement. One of the young Inuit, Olayuk's son Eric, explains his preference for snowmobiles: "They are fast, they don't eat meat, and they don't stink."

We divide ourselves up two to a tent and stretch our bedrolls on caribou hides on the ground. Johnny Mikes then distributes insulated boots and bright orange survival suits. They are awkward and stiff, but essential. Chances of survival in Arctic waters plummet after a minute of exposure. In the cooktent we are introduced to the Inuit—Olayuk, Ipeelie, Simon, Olayuk's brother-in-law Abraham, and, most important of all, Olayuk's wife, Martha, and her older sister, Koonoo Muckpaloo, who run the kitchen. Both are beautiful women, especially Martha, whose face is radiant and kind, quick to laugh. Someone asks Olayuk how many children they have. He looks pensive and begins to count on his fingers. "Ten," he concludes. Martha elbows him and spits out a quick phrase. Olayuk looks sheepish. "Eleven," he adds.

Over a dinner of narwhal soup, bannock, arctic char, and caribou, I learn that Olayuk and Martha were the first of their generation to marry for love. They planned to elope and were willing to court death by setting off over the ice, when finally the families agreed to the match. They are still in love. One sees it in their every gesture: Martha carefully drawing a comb through his thin beard, Olayuk gently nestling her hand in his. Martha is asked whether it bothers her to be cooking dinner at such a late hour. "I am used to it," she responds, "my husband is a hunter." Olayuk is asked how many seals a polar bear kills in a week. "That depends," he explains, "on how good a hunter he is."

There is no night and no morning, only the ceaseless sun. At some point we sleep, with blinders and earplugs. The camp never rests. Winter is for sleep, and the summers are ephemeral. We wake and head off in five sleds, travelling south up Admiralty Inlet to get around a body of water before returning north to reach the edge of the floe. The ice by the shore is a tangle of pressure ridges, but farther on it becomes smooth, glasslike. The spartan landscape rolls on, empty and desolate, and all one can think of is survival. On the horizon, islands, ice, and sky meld one into the other, and the black sea is a dim mirage.

A dense fog descends, muffling the roar of the engines as the snowmobiles drag us, three or four to a sled, over the ice. The drivers push on, watching for patterns in the ice, small ridges of hard snow that run parallel to the prevailing winds and reveal where you are. When clouds obscure the sun, Simon explains, the Inuit study the reflection of the ice on the underside of low clouds. Open water appears black, the sea ice white, and ground covered in snow and traces of open tundra appear darker than the sea but lighter than snowless land. Upon the clouds lies a map of the land. Not one of our guides can remember ever having been lost.

A pair of ringed seals are killed to feed the dogs back at camp, and moments later we reach the edge of the floe. Olayuk peers out over the water, sensing the wind in his face. It's from the north, which is good. Should a fissure appear in the ice behind us, a southerly wind could push our entire party out to sea, without our knowing it. Just two weeks before, a party of schoolchildren and teachers had misread a lead in the ice, and were set adrift on an ice floe. It was a new moon, with high tides and gale force winds that prevented rescue. For eight days they drifted, reaching all the way to Baffin Bay before finally being saved by military helicopters. There was no panic. The elders prepared food and kept the children calm with stories.

The only sign of life at the edge of the ice is a cackle of glaucous and Thayer gulls, fighting over the carcass of a narwhal killed by a hunter. One of the guides slits open the narwhal's stomach and examines the contents—chitonous beaks of squids and octopus, the carapaces of crustaceans, the ear bones and eye lenses of fish. The ligaments running the length of the back are salvaged for rope. The deep red meat is too rich to be eaten. The skin and blubber, a delicacy eaten raw, has already been harvested.

Suddenly, a shout from the floe edge. I look up to see the marbled backs of four female narwhals barely crest the surface before slipping once again into the dark sea. As we wait, hoping the animals will return, Mikes asks Olayuk to say a few words about his life. A thin, somewhat reluctant account follows. Clearly, Olayuk finds the moment awkward. Later, Abraham, university educated and remarkable in his ability to move freely between worlds, explains Olayuk's reticence. "In your culture, the goal is to excel and stand out, flaunting your excellence in public. Here, the greater your skills, the more you want to fade into the background. You must never reveal what you know, for knowledge is power. If you step forward, you show yourself to your enemies. In the old days it might be a shaman who waited outside a camp and watched before casting spells on the strongest man. This is something the whites have never understood. The only time you can reveal your stories is when you no longer have the power. In old age."

The next evening we encounter a polar bear and give chase on the ice. After long hours of searching in vain for wildlife, the drivers are eager to get as close as possible to the animal. The bear is run ragged. No one objects. For a brief moment, each client succumbs to the thrill of the hunt. "If you think that was fun," Abraham later tells the one vegetarian on the trip, "you ought to try it with a tag" (that is, a hunting permit).

When asked who had first seen the bear, Abraham replies, "Simon did. Well, actually, it was Olayuk, and Simon saw it in his eyes. Olayuk said nothing."

There are ancient graves above the camp, stone mounds erected centuries ago. The bones from those that have been breached lie covered in lichen and moss. Around the gravesite is a circle of life—purple gentians and dwarf willows, small plant communities established long ago on the rich nutrients of the dead. A ring of flowers around an eider's nest, a seedling growing out of the droppings of a gull, lichen slowly eating away at rock, two centimetres of soil taking a century to accumulate. One marvels at the art of survival. Bears hunting seals, foxes following the bears and feeding on excrement. Inuit cutting open animals, feeding on clam siphons found in walrus stomachs, lichens and plants concentrated in the gut of caribou, mother's milk in the belly of a baby seal, a delicacy much loved by the elders. Meat taken in August is stored in skins and bladders, cached in rock cairns where it ferments to the consistency and taste of blue cheese to be eaten in winter.

Beyond the graves, 800 metres from the shore, the land rises to a high escarpment 400 metres or more above the sea. An hour of scrambling on steep scree takes me to the ridge and a promontory overlooking all of Lancaster Sound. The sense of isolation and wonder is overwhelming. Gravel terraces on the shore reveal the beach lines of ancient seas. Icebergs calved from the glaciers of Devon Island, and the sea ice covering the mouth of the inlet, are awash in soft pastels—pinks, turquoise, and opal. On the underside of distant clouds are streaks of dazzling brightness. Every horizon shimmers with mirages. Low islands seem towering cliffs, ice floes appear as crystal spires. The land seduces with its strange beauty. In the entire annals of European exploration, few places were sought with more passion, few destinations were the cause of more tragedy and pain.

The Northwest Passage, which begins at the mouth of Lancaster Sound, was always less a route than an illusive dream. Hopes of fame and riches drove those who sought it, and certain death found the many who came ill-prepared for the Arctic night. By 1631, the voyages of Martin Frobisher, John Davis, William Baffin, and Luke Foxe had made clear that no practical commercial sea route to the Orient existed south of the Arctic Circle. Incredibly, by the early nineteenth century these journeys had passed into the realm of myth and the discoveries had become suspect. Brilliant feats of navigation and cartography were supplanted by fantasies of a northern polar sea, ice-free water at the top of the world.

The real impetus for seeking the Northwest Passage was provided by Napoleon. In the wake of his defeat, the British navy reduced its conscripted force from 140,000 to 19,000. But it was unthinkable in class-conscious England to lay off a single officer. Thus by 1818 there was one officer for every three seamen. The only way for advancement was to accomplish some stunning feat of exploration. And so they sailed for the Arctic. Edward Parry and John Ross's was the first of dozens of expeditions to be flung against the ice, each met by Inuit who spoke to the ships as if they were gods. The entire endeavour, spanning the better part of half a century and culminating in the search for John Franklin and his gallant crew, was coloured by a single theme: those who ignored the example of the Inuit perished, whereas those who mimicked their ways not only survived but accomplished unparalleled feats of endurance and exploration.

The British mostly failed. They wore tight woollens, which turned sweat to ice. The Inuit wore caribou skins, loose, with one layer of hair toward the body, another turned out to the wind. The British slept in cloth bags, which froze stiff with ice. The Inuit used the heat of one another's naked bodies on sleeping platforms of ice covered with caribou hides, in snow houses that could be assembled in an hour. The British ate salt pork and, to prevent scurvy, carried lime juice in glass jars that broke with the first frost. The Inuit ate narwhal skin and the contents of caribou guts, both astonishingly rich in vitamin C. Most disastrous of all, the British scorned the use of dogs. They preferred to harness their young men in leather and force them to haul ridiculously heavy sleds made of iron and oak. When the last of Franklin's men died, at Starvation Cove on the Adelaide Peninsula, their sledge alone weighed 300 kilograms. On it was a 360-kilogram boat loaded with silver dinner plates, cigar cases, a copy of *The Vicar of Wakefield*—in short, everything deemed essential for a gentle traveller of the Victorian age. All of this they planned to haul hundreds of kilometres overland in the hope of reaching some remote trading post in the endless boreal forests of Canada. Like so many of their kind, they died, as one explorer remarked, because they brought their environment with them. They were unwilling to adapt to another.

At one end of camp is a recently erected wooden cross marking the grave of a woman who died delivering a child in the midst of winter. Asked about her fate, Olayuk responds, "She decided to have a baby." This lack of sentiment confused and horrified the early British explorers. To them, the Inuit were brutal and callous, utterly devoid of human kindness. How else to explain a language that has no words for hello or good-bye, or thank you? Or a people who would abandon an elder to die, or allow the body of the newly dead to be dug up and gnawed by dogs? What the English failed to grasp was that in the Arctic no other attitude was possible. The Inuit, a people of patience and resilience, laughed in the face of starvation and confronted tragedy with a fatalistic indifference because they had no choice. Death and privation were everyday events. In our camp is an old woman who remembers the last time her people were forced to eat human flesh. It occurred in the late 1930s, during a season when "the world became silent." All of the animals were gone. So one of her extended family had designated himself to die, and he was killed. "Someone must survive," she said, "and someone must die." After the event, the women in the group cut off their long braids, a symbol for all others that they had been obliged to sacrifice their kin.

Fear of going native, of succumbing to such impulses, blinded the British to the genius of the Inuit. In dismissing them as savages, they failed to grasp that there could be no better measure of intelligence than the ability to thrive in the Arctic with a technology limited to what could be made with ivory and bone, antler, soapstone, slate, animal skins, and bits of driftwood that were as precious as gold. The Inuit did not endure the cold, they took advantage of it. Three arctic char placed end to end, wrapped and frozen in hide, the bottom greased by the stomach contents of a caribou and coated with a thin film of ice, became the runner of a sled. A sled could be made from the carcass of a caribou, a knife from human excrement. There is a well-known account of an old man who refused to move into a settlement. Over the objections of his family, he made plans to stay on the ice. To stop him, they took away all of his tools. So in the midst of a winter gale, he stepped out of their igloo, defecated, and honed the feces into a frozen blade, which he sharpened with a spray of saliva. With the knife he killed a dog. Using its rib cage as a sled and its hide to harness another dog, he disappeared into the darkness.

Sitting with Ipeelie by his tent early one morning, I thought of the Inuit ability to adapt. His gear was scattered about, some of it draped over the cross of the young mother who had died. He was cleaning the motor of his snowmobile with the feather of an ivory gull. Earlier that day on the ice his clutch had failed, and he needed to drill a hole in a piece of steel he intended to use as a replacement. Placing the metal on the ice, bracing it with his feet, he took his rifle and casually blew a circle in the steel.

Gradually and effortlessly, we work toward a nocturnal schedule, when the light is soft and the animals more active. Out on the ice by late afternoon, long pounding runs in the sleds across the edge of the floe, midnight by amber sea cliffs on the far side of the inlet, where northern fulmars nest by the tens of thousands. Breakfast at noon, dinner at four in the morning, a few hours of sleep in between. There is a hallucinatory quality to the endless sun. All notions of a diurnal cycle of light and darkness fade away, and everyone is cast adrift from time. By the third morning, not one of my companions is certain of the date, and estimates of the hour vary to an astonishing degree.

The wildlife sightings are far fewer than expected. In the first seven days of a nine-day sojourn on the ice, we see birds and ringed seals by the score, but only one other polar bear, four narwhals, one bearded seal, and a fleeting glimpse of walrus and belugas. The numbers are there, but the landscape is so vast that it absorbs the multitudes. The other clients don't seem to object. A psychiatrist from Seattle speaks of the land in religious terms and is content to sit on his collapsible seat for hours at a time, glassing the sea for birds. Others are brash and irritating and find it impossible to be quiet, a trait that makes them appear willfully dense. At one point, during a discussion of Inuit clothing, Martha passes around a dark sealskin boot with a beautiful design of an eagle sewn into the hide. One especially garrulous woman examines the stitching and asks, "How do you find fur with such an interesting pattern on it?" Later in the evening, talk passes to all the places she has been—an impressive list that includes the Amazon, the Galápagos, Nepal, Antarctica, and now the Arctic. When she mentions Borneo, a place I know well, I ask what she did there. After a confused moment, she says, "I don't really remember. But it was all very interesting."

Such conversation is discouraging and gives the impression of travel reduced to commodity, with the experience mattering less than the credential of having been somewhere. By the economics of our times, anyone can purchase instant passage to virtually any place on the planet. Ecotourism has become a cover for a form of tourism that simply increases the penetration of the hinterland. But have any of us earned the right to be there? Whatever the shortcomings of the early explorers, they gave something of themselves and paid a real price for their experiences.

One night I escaped the camp shortly after midnight and returned to the mountain ridge, where I walked for several hours. Gazing out over the sound, I thought of what some of the early explorers had endured. One who stands out is Frederick Cook, an American physician and explorer who tried to reach the North Pole. In 1908, lost in the barrens, he and two companions walked 800 kilometres, living on meat scraped from the carcasses of their dogs. When forced to winter on the northern shore of Devon Island, a mere 160 kilometres from our camp at Cape Crauford, he had only four rounds of ammunition left for his rifle, half a sled, a torn silk tent, and the tattered clothes on his back. For five months of darkness they lived in a shallow cave hollowed by hand from the earth. With tools carved from bone, they killed what they could, using blubber to fire torches to thrust into the jaws of the bears who stalked them. At the first sign of light in February, they made their escape. Living on rotten seal meat and gnawing the skin of their boots, they walked some 500 kilometres across the frozen wastes of Baffin Bay to rescue in Greenland.

Another astonishing story of survival is the ordeal of the Danish explorer Peter Freuchen. In 1923, while on expedition on the west coast of Baffin Island, Freuchen became separated from his party in a blinding blizzard. Seeking shelter, he dug a shallow trench in the snow and pulled his sled over top. Exhausted, he collapsed in sleep. On waking, he had no feeling in his left foot.

When he tried to move, he found that his sled was frozen above him. He considered sacrificing one of his hands, deliberately allowing it to freeze in order to use it as a spade. But he feared it would break too easily. Instead, he chewed on a piece of bear-skin, which froze hard as iron. Using this as a tool, he managed to scrape a small opening in the snow. He stuck out his head, and the moisture around his mouth froze his face fast to the metal runner of the sled. He tore it away, leaving a mass of hair and blood. Breaking free at last, he crawled deliriously through the storm and, by chance, was saved by an Inuit hunting party. When his foot thawed, gangrene set in, and the flesh around his toes fell away until the bones protruded. The Inuk shaman treating him wanted to remove the toes with his teeth to prevent dark spirits from entering the body. Freuchen chose instead to knock them off himself with a hammer.

Someone has brought a copy of *New Age Journal* on the trip. In it is an advertisement for post cards featuring the faces of endangered species, prominent among them the harp seal. There are 5 million harp seals in the eastern Arctic, and their numbers have never been higher in this century. There are 7 million ringed seals, and it is upon this species that the Inuit have traditionally relied. When in 1983 the Europeans banned the import of seal-skins, they did not distinguish one species from the other, and Inuit families on Baffin Island saw their *per capita* annual income drop from $16,000 to nothing. Simon asks, "How can they love a seal more than a human being?"

One evening, after a long day on the ice, there is a demonstration of dogsled-mushing. Everyone is to have a ride. Though the sound of runners passing over ice and snow is sublime, the event is a fiasco. Harnesses become tangled, dogs bellow and snarl at their drivers, riders are left behind on their duffs as sleds dash off in all directions. It is a far cry from the days when a dogsled musher, with a quick snap of the whip, would cut off the tip of a stubborn dog's ear and bring the team into line. On the way back to camp, some of the clients grumble about "loss of tradition." One asks Abraham if the people ever wear their traditional clothes. Abraham gestures to the modern coat on his back. "Yes," he says pointedly, "I wear my parka all the time."

For the Inuit, the first fundamental break with their past occurred in the early years of this century. Along with European diseases that left only one in ten alive came missionaries whose primary goal was the destruction of the power and authority of the shaman, the cultural pivot, the heart of the Inuit relationship to the universe. The missionaries discouraged even the use of traditional names, songs, and the language itself. The last avowed shaman in Olayuk's community of Arctic Bay died in 1964.

By then the seduction of modern trade goods had drawn many of the people away from the land. As Inuit concentrated in communities, encouraged by Canadian authorities to relocate, new problems arose. In the late 1950s, the wife of a Royal Canadian Mounted Police constable was mauled and killed by a sled dog. Thereafter, all dogs had to be tethered outside the settlements. Any dog found without a vaccination certificate for rabies was summarily shot. A distemper outbreak rationalized wholesale slaughter. In exchange, the RCMP offered snowmobiles. The first arrived in Baffin in 1962. No technology since the introduction of the rifle did more to transform Inuit life.

In 1955, the decision was made to screen all Inuit for tuberculosis. Medical teams accompanied by RCMP constables dropped by helicopter into every nomadic encampment, whisking away every man, woman, and child for a compulsory X-ray examination on a hospital ship named the *C. D. Howe*. Anyone who showed signs of the disease was held forcibly on board and sent south to sanitaria in Montreal or Winnipeg. One out of five Inuit suffered such a fate. Although the intentions of the medical authorities were good, the consequences for those ripped from their families were devastating.

Other initiatives were less benign, even in conception. As recently as the 1950s, the Canadian government felt compelled to bolster its claims in the North American Arctic by actively promoting settlement. Inuit were moved to uninhabited islands. Others found work constructing the DEW (Distant Early Warning) Line and other Cold War installations. Family allowance payments were provided but made contingent on the children's attending school. Nomadic camps disappeared as parents moved into communities to be with their young. Along with the schools came nursing stations, churches, and welfare. The government conducted a census, identified each Inuk by number, issued identification tags, and ultimately conducted Operation Surname, a bizarre effort to assign last names to individuals who had never had them. More than a few Inuit dogs were recorded as Canadian citizens.

After half a century of profound change, what, indeed, is tradition? How can we expect a people not to adapt? The Inuit language is alive. The men are still hunters. They use snares, make snow houses, know the power of medicinal herbs. They also own boats, snowmobiles, television sets, and satellite phones. Some drink, some attend church. As anthropologist Hugh Brody points out, what must be defended is not the traditional as opposed to the modern but, rather, the right of a free indigenous people to choose the components of their lives.

Canada has at long last recognized this challenge by negotiating an astonishing land-claims settlement with the Inuit of the eastern Arctic. On April 1, 1999, an Inuit homeland known as Nunavut will be carved out of the Northwest Territories. Including all of Baffin Island and stretching from Manitoba to Ellesmere Island, with a population of just twenty-six thousand, the area will be almost as large as Alaska and California combined. In addition to annual payments of $840 million over fourteen years to fund start-up costs and infrastructure and to replace current federal benefits, the Inuit will receive direct title to over 350,000 square kilometres, an area larger than New Mexico. Within Nunavut, all political control will effectively be ceded to a new government completely staffed and administered by Inuit. It is arguably the most remarkable experiment in Native self-government anywhere to be found.

In the meantime, like any other people, the Inuit will grow and change. The threat to their culture is not the delight that Olayuk's young daughters show as they turn up their Walkman and blast their ears with the latest rock and roll but rather the underwater noise from ships' engines and propellers that chase away the narwhals, or the plans to grant a score of oil and gas drilling permits in the mouth of Lancaster Sound. Or the global spread of contaminants that raise the levels of industrial toxins in the milk of Inuit mothers five times above those of white women further south. Or Ipeelie's lament that the weather has become wilder and the sun hotter each year, so that for the first time

Inuit are suffering from skin ailments caused by the sky. These are things that do threaten the Inuit, just as they threaten us.

Day by day the ice melts. Blue pools yield to a dark bay, the bay fills with broken ice, and the leads in the ice spread to broad channels. The frozen airstrip where we landed but a week ago is now open water, and it is here, a day before our scheduled departure, that the narwhals and belugas finally arrive. Olayuk sees them first, and Abraham rustles up the camp to a fever pitch. Movement over the ice, first by sled and later on foot, is precarious. Olayuk walks ahead, testing the path with a harpoon. It is at precisely the time when the ice is most dangerous that the Inuit hunt narwhals. As we move cautiously forward, with a blazing noonday sun overhead and the ice bending under our weight, someone asks Simon what it is like to camp out on the floe for days at a time when everything is in flux. "You wake up in the morning," he replies, "and run like hell."

A hush falls upon the group as we hear the first sighs of the belugas as they breach and see the vapour of their breath. There are hundreds of the beautiful creatures, white as pearls, moving in small groups, ebbing and flowing with the current. The narwhals swim among them, diving in unison to great depths, driving schools of cod to the surface at such a rate that the fish lose consciousness and lie stunned upon the surface of the water. A feeding frenzy is under way, though it occurs in slow motion, as each massive animal rises and falls with astonishing agility and grace. Only the frantic flight of gulls as they dip and dive toward the water betrays the excitement of the hunt.

A smile comes to Olayuk's face as the tusk of a male narwhal breaks the surface at our feet. It appears like a creature from a bestiary, and in an instant one understands how it inspired the legend of the unicorn. Throughout the Middle Ages, narwhal ivory sold for twenty times its weight in gold. In all of Europe, only fifty complete tusks were known, and they were a source of endless mystery. The beautiful animals still are. Nearly blind, their entire sensory world is based on sonar reflection, a clatter of clicks by which they communicate. Of their behaviour and ecology, the patterns of their migration, we understand little, for they live most of the year beneath the polar ice. No one knows where they go or what they eat in winter. There is something wonderful in this, a chance to be with a creature that has defied science and all our obsessions with systematizing the world.

Olayuk knows only that the narwhals come in the spring, as they always have and always will. From him, we have learned something of a hunter's patience and are grateful to encounter the animals before leaving. Patience is perhaps the most enduring trait of the Inuit. There is a story from Greenland about a group of Inuit who walked a great distance to gather wild grass in one of the few verdant valleys of the island. When they arrived, the grass had yet to sprout, so they watched and waited until it grew. I see patience now in Olayuk's face, as he observes the arrival of the first wave of a migration that is one of the highlights of his life. I ask him if he will hunt tomorrow, after we are gone. His eyes sparkle. "Oh yes," he says. "We will be here."

BRIONY PENN

Huckleberry August: Chaos and Harmony in the Classic Patch

BRIONY PENN lives on Saltspring Island in the midst of what she refers to as the Salish Sea, that body of salt water separating Vancouver Island and the Gulf Islands from the mainland coast. "Huckleberry August" and "Maple Leaf Rag" are essays from Penn's first book, *A Year on the Wild Side*. Penn is a writer, illustrator, and lecturer with a Ph.D. in geography.

I SEEM TO SPEND these long summer evenings at a berry patch along the edge of our road. I stand in it for at least half an hour a day. I notice the odd motorist passing by, narrowing their eyes then accelerating quickly past. I wave and beckon them with my red-stained hands and they accelerate even faster. It is a pity because they might enjoy the odd foray into the patch.

I go there because my ears are filled with the hum of crickets and the chatter of birds, my eyes move hazily from one red or purple jewel to the next, and my stomach has the rare delight of being filled with the fruit of our forest, instead of the fruit of yet another banana republic. Our patch is still what would be termed a classic coastal Douglas-fir forest berry patch. This is not the rampant patch one finds overtaking vacant city lots, composed of those interlopers, the Himalayan and the Evergreen Blackberry. These two species are definite challengers in taste and quantity—but for diversity, subtlety, and seasonal duration, nothing can beat our classic native berry species.

A classic patch is one which begins with the first blossoming of the Salmonberries in March and extends into the middle of November with the last of the huckleberries and Bunchberries. Over the last five months, I have been able to complement most evening meals with a modest dessert of sweet and succulent berries of varying size, hue, and flavour. Day after day, month after month, I march down to the patch, open my mouth, and drop a few in.

I know it is April when the big pink flowers of the Salmonberry wave in my face and the Swainson's Thrush calls to ripen the first berries to orange and red. I know it is May when the delicate white Thimbleberry flowers are dropping off and the blood-red berries are starting to come out. In June, I can glean the last of the Salmonberries, the best of the Thimbleberries, and the first of the Blackcap, our native raspberry. By July, I am scouring the ground cover for Trailing Blackberries (our native blackberry, which far exceeds in flavour the exotic species) and Wild Strawberries. For bulk I'll fill up on Salal berries and for pure sweet, I'll go for the gooseberries. There are two gooseberries, the Wild and the Gummy Gooseberry. Both produce large red berries. The Gummy berries are hairy. By August the Red Huckleberries are out as well and I go searching the northerly, damper patches for the late bloomers. The rest of the autumn I can rely on consistent crops of the Red and Evergreen Huckleberries and Bunchberries until the first frost. Thereupon

I cease my visits to the patch and go hibernate like all good berry-eaters.

I like my berry patch because it is a reassuring place to be. Anxieties about war and famine are forgotten in this patch. Sedatives by the thousands are out there for modern anxieties, but I prefer the berry patch. It all stems from an influential time in my life when I encountered the Berry People. They hung out in a barn in the 1960s and attempted to live entirely off berries. They ate them, drank their juice, tie-dyed their clothes purple, and fuelled a car off berry methane gas. They lasted quite a while before the glamour of a subsistence lifestyle wore off and they retired to their condos in Vancouver with terminal stomach aches and permanently dyed fingers. Back then it was the closest thing to a subsistence culture I had experienced. Later, I was to work with some First Nations Chilcotin people who put the Berry People in their rightful roles as rank amateurs.

Of course the Berry People are gone now and so are most vestiges of true aboriginal way-of-life in this region, but we still have some berry patches left. Not many, but enough to complement a few diets. For an uncertain future this is a reassuring thought. I only have to think of friends in what was once Yugoslavia, supplementing their diet with local berries as the food ran out. Who would have thought that my sophisticated Croatian friends studying law, then wind-surfing on their holidays, would have to reach to their aboriginal roots to survive. So I think of them in my berry patch.

Another reassurance that this patch provides is something to do with the whole biodiversity argument. They say that many of the commercial raspberries, strawberries, and gooseberries were hybridized from our native species. In my little thicket of tangled berries, one species entwined with another, tumbling over rotting logs, insects and birds humming around, I know the combination is right for enduring the hazards of nature. It is unlikely that there will be a large-scale insect devastation or blight in this patch because it is chaos. Equilibrium is reached by virtue of thousands of years of confusion. When the commercial hybrids have foundered from over-specialization, the scientists will come back to this thicket.

My final comfort comes from a Chilcotin legend about the repercussions of over-fulfilling one's desires—a tale to be told in the patch. Raven once stole the only Salmonberries on earth from a sacred patch guarded by the people. He laughed so loud, thinking himself clever to steal them, that the berries all fell from his mouth and scattered over the land, springing up as new bushes wherever they fell. Standing amongst the Salmonberries, I felt it was fitting that as a tribute to our cleverness at manipulating the world, we might be left with the odd patch of berries. As those motorists zoom disdainfully by me, I'll have the last laugh.

Maple Leaf Rag: Leaf Me Alone

SEX AND POLITICS were the only conversation topics I used to avoid at polite parties. But now I am adding leaves to that list. Leaves are not inherently controversial; it is just that they evoke complicated emotions. First, there's the tension between those who like the leaf on the flag and those who don't—and that is getting more complicated, especially in Quebec. And then there is the division between those who want to get rid of leaves and those who leave them on the ground for posterity—and that is getting more divisive every day.

I have always taken the word "leaves" in its literal sense, as in "leave them where they are." I'm a dead give-away as a leaf leaver; I have leaves pinned to my chest and gumboots stuck to my feet and I hiss whenever I see a leafblower. As far as the maple leaf on the Canadian flag goes, I feel quite proud that as a nation we aspire to a humble leaf instead of a distant galaxy of stars or some rampant lion. But I didn't know I felt so strongly about the subject until I was caught by a surprise question at a party. "Don't you find these enormous leaves are a real nuisance to rake up and get rid of?" a woman innocently asked, pointing to the baroque canopy of gold, red, and orange maple leaves draped around us.

She was from California, and they are a bit funny down there. They invented pink stucco and talk about nothing but sex at parties. But something snapped when she raised the question and I ended up in a tirade against everything from free trade to the extinction of amphibians. There were probably a few invectives thrown at leafblowers too. It was quite a performance. She quickly moved on to the next guest.

In hindsight, things could have been handled much better. She probably didn't know they were maple leaves pinned to my Canadian heart. She certainly didn't know it was a Bigleaf Maple, the biggest-leafed maple in Canada, that every west coaster boasts about and presses between two sheets of wax paper in kindergarten. She probably wasn't used to real autumns where the days are so moist and tranquil that you slide through them like a Banana Slug over Skunk Cabbage. I could also forgive her for not recognizing the signs of a person who leaves leaves. I had left my gumboots and my religion at the door.

Now I have had time to calm down and prepare what I would like to have said. "Funny big leaves aren't they? Whenever I used to see the pictures of Adam, I wondered what would have happened if he had worn a Bigleaf Maple. Eve would never have been tempted and everyone would be in the Garden of Eden instead of just us lotus eaters on the coast. The biggest one ever found was a metre wide, hanging off a tree as huge as a heron's wingspan. We also have the smallest maple leaves in Canada. You hardly notice the Douglas Maples all year until now, when they turn scarlet and leap right out of the bush at you. When you get the two together you have perfection. That is why we are having a party here—a maple party. It is a quaint west coast custom.

"If you stay here a while you'll get to love them. Did you know that this month was called 'time of the changing of the colours of the leaves' in one of the Salish languages? Our maples are subtle here in their changes. Easterners say that our maples can't hold a candle to theirs but I'm not so sure. Although I bet they have maple parties too. It is probably a quaint trans-Canadian custom.

"And the leaves are so useful. You can leap in them, use the stems to whip up Soopalallie-berry ice cream, and steam a fish in them. You can even stick them on a flag and wave them. In November of 1964, Canadians proposed the maple leaf flag for the first time. We debated over including the *fleur-de-lis* and

Union Jack, but in the end, a simple autumnal leaf seemed just right. They flutter down around every Canadian from the Pacific to the Atlantic regardless of religion, language, cultural origin, and politics. And then they quietly rot into the earth.

"In fact, what leaves are best designed for is decomposing—tons of organic matter creeps slowly into the earth via an army of bacteria and minibeasties. Then next spring, there will be a rich layer of humus cloaked with a delicate lace shawl of skeleton leaves that will fly up into the air with the equinoctial gales. Speaking of gales, November was called, by that same Salish nation, 'month of the shaking of the leaves.' It's a signal that the golden time is over . . ."

I wouldn't be able to trust myself to go further. It is an emotional subject, these leaves. I am sort of attached to the ideas of Canada and rich soil and tranquillity and having golden piles of leaves to leap into. Next party I go to, I'll just stick to the weather.

SID MARTY

The Creator Wind

SID MARTY worked as a warden in Banff National Park for many years before becoming a writer. The author of *Men for the Mountains* and *A Grand and Fabulous Notion: The First Century of Canada's Parks*, Marty lives in Alberta's foothills, just to the east of the Rocky Mountains. His most recent books are *Switchbacks: True Stories from the Canadian Rockies* and *Sky Humour*, a volume of poetry. "The Creator Wind" is from *Leaning on the Wind: Under the Spell of the Great Chinook*, which was nominated for a Governor General's award in 1995.

OVER THE CASTELLATED crest of the Rocky Mountains, the sky is a blue ribbon, its bottom sawtoothed with limestone ridges and towers; its upper band formed of a bow in the clouds, the bow curved as the planet, stretching from Peace River in northern Alberta some 680 miles to Sun River, Montana, stretching on to Denver. The arch is so sharply delineated for miles at a time that it gives the cloud a solidity it cannot possibly possess, as if this curved border were carved out of ivory instead of vapour.

This is the Chinook Arch, the totem of a famous transformer, a warm Pacific wind that brings temporary spring in the midst of winter to the high border country of Alberta and Montana, the western edge of the ancient Buffalo Ground.

It is winter, and the peaks of the front ranges, from 8000 to 10,000 feet in altitude, are corniced with snow that will endure, in the colder temperatures of those altitudes, until spring. The snow is carved by the wind's rough cat's tongue; burnished by the bronze-tongued sun. Today the peaks are backlit and bathed in sunlight, while clouds cast shadows over the Porcupine Hills, and over these lion-coloured hills of home.

Meteorologists classify this region as "part of the northern cool temperate belt," though there is nothing "temperate" about our climate that I can see. I was raised in Medicine Hat, where the temperature extremes can go from 108 degrees Fahrenheit in July to 51 degrees below zero in January. We south Albertans are not lulled to torpor by summer temperatures that could fry an egg on a human forehead, because it can snow in this country in every month except July. And I'm not ruling out July, either. Killing frosts in July and August along the foothills where I live stunt a gardening season that is only 100 days long to begin with.

The oldtimers described the Canadian climate as "eight months of winter and four months of rough sledding." But in Chinook Country, we don't have a climate—we have weather; a circus of weather, a Guinness record book of weather. The heaviest snowfall to hit Alberta in one day—44 inches—was recorded ten miles north of our house, at the Livingstone Fire Lookout Tower. And it did not fall in winter; it fell on June 29, 1963. Or consider that in 1992, Great Falls, Montana, proclaimed *August* to be the snowiest month of that year. More snow (eight inches) fell on August 23 than had fallen in the previous winter months of 1992. On the other hand, a record high was reached for winter, January 20, 1982, of 67°F. And sometimes the summer growing season will stretch out to 110 frost-free days, leaving disgruntled local gardeners wishing they had planted tomatoes or squash.

Craziness.

When it comes to weather here, the saying is, "If you don't like it, wait five minutes and it will change." The warm wind, in its gentler moods, brings us spring in the midst of winter, but King Winter rules the plains. We must be prepared for the frigid despot's return at any moment. Dark clouds will suddenly advance over the plains, as another arctic cold front pushes in from Lake Athabasca. The temperatures can seesaw with outrageous rapidity. Down in Havre, Montana, 225 miles southeast of us, the citizens once contended with four separate chinooks in five days, the temperature gyrating between –1 and 50°F as King Winter and Chinook battled for the field.

Cresting the mountains at 10,000 to 14,000 feet and higher, on average the wind strikes forty-five or more days each winter on the foothills and prairie that lie at the mountain foot from Pincher Creek, Alberta, south to Livingston, Montana, the area known to Montana meteorologists as the Northern Chinook Zone. The chinook zone stretches eastward from the mountain foot to an invisible boundary varying in width from approximately 180 to 240 miles. Where I live, we expect winds of 60 m.p.h. or higher at least once a month from November to February. And these winds mostly bring a whiteout of blowing, thawing snow, not a blackout of blowing dirt.

The Creator Wind begets many facts and as many fictions.

Fact: The most rapid temperature change in the United States —from –32°F to 15°F in seven minutes, in Great Falls, Montana, January 11, 1980—was caused by a warm chinook wind. Fiction: The fastest Montana wind speed, 82 m.p.h., was recorded at

Great Falls, on December 10, 1956. This record has been broken many times in the Browning and Livingston vicinities, but there were no National Weather Service stations to officially measure it. Environment Canada has clocked the chinook at Pincher Creek, Alberta, at 84.9 m.p.h. and the maximum gust at 109.74 m.p.h. Nobody who has lived in the Pincher Creek area (including this writer) believes those records, either. They are too slow. The wind in the nearby Crowsnest Pass, the wind-tunnel of Canada, was once clocked at 135 m.p.h. by the staff of the old Saratoga gas plant.

"She's blowing a steady ninety," as one Montanan put it to me, "and she's whuppin' about one-twenty." Now that's more like it.

This Wheelhouse of mine is wired to the wind. I have an anemometer on the roof and a temperature sensor outside, both hooked up to a small Davis Weather Monitor on my desk, which records wind speed, temperatures, and barometric pressure. It is blowing a "fresh gale" as I write this—according to the old Beaufort Scale, the equivalent of 39 to 46 m.p.h. It blew harder yesterday, gusting to 72 m.p.h. and raising the temperature, gradually this time, from –22 to 9°C. There were two feet of snow on the ground and on the roof of this shack yesterday morning, but by noon it was melting so rapidly that a spume of water blew in sheets from the trailing edge of my roof. Soon enough, water began dribbling through a crack in the ceiling right over "Alberta," which is the trade name embossed on the potbellied stove I use for heating. Water droplets hissed on the stove lid. The same old well-tarred leak had opened up again.

Out I went, down to the stable to fetch the ladder and the tar bucket. I had to walk backwards into the wind in order to carry the ladder back. It is long and heavy, but the wind carried part of it for me. I held one end, and the wind blowing under it lifted up the other. I might have been wise, and just put the bucket under that leak. Not me. I like to tar things—it's part of my naval heritage as a former Royal Canadian Sea Cadet. I clambered up, shovel in hand, and began to push the wet snow off the roof as fast as I could. But the wind came back, blew the ladder down, and knocked me to my knees. If I hadn't grabbed the chimney, it would have knocked me off the roof, too.

Sitting shivering in a puddle of slush, I contemplated the fifteen-foot drop into the mud and slush below. I knew that Frank Halek, the Local Oracle, would be passing by on the road any moment, heading home for his dinner, driving his battered green 4×4 half-ton one-quarter full of binder twine, old hay, and cowshit. And Frank, hawk-eyed, would no doubt spot me perched on the roof, outlined against the clouds as some kind of gigantic, soggy raven: he would know immediately what had happened. Ignoring my frantic semaphore signs for him to piss off and mind his own business, he would back up at high speed to my driveway. And I would peer helplessly through the tops of the aspen trees, watching him roar up my drive. I would hear him cackling before he even got out of the truck. He would walk up through the trees laughing, fighting the wind, up through the slop and muck in his tall, insulated green rubber gumboots. And he would stand there in his tattered parka and coveralls, laughing and shaking his head in disbelief. He would savour the ridiculous spectacle for a few moments before he picked up the ladder for me.

I would never live it down.

Next to the alphabet, the parachute roll is the most useful

thing a kid learns in the Royal Canadian Sea Cadets. I hit the muck, knees flexed, and immediately tucked my head in and rolled forward, taking the impact along right forearm and shoulder. I got a nice swath of slush and muck from head to toe, before I got to my feet again.

When I was a boy, a Montana uncle told me soberly that the wind was heated up by friction as it slid over the tops of the mountains. It seemed a reasonable explanation to my credulous ears back then. Now, however, I know that the chinook is a foehn-type wind, a moving mass of air whose temperature is warmed in passing over an incline, though not quite as described by my uncle. The foehn is a famous dry south wind of southern Germany and Switzerland. (The telltale cap cloud that forms over the mountain tops during such winds is known as the "Foehn Wall.") Such winds are found in many places in the world. The zonda of Argentina, the Mediterranean sirocco and the sharav wind of Israel are other examples. Another well-known foehn on this continent is the Santa Ana of California. This is the one that fans up brushfires and blows sand into the swimming pools down in Santa Barbara.

The physical descriptions of chinook wind creation and its effects become complicated: there is no room here to discuss the role of the jet stream (to give one example) in steering chinook direction. There are different degrees of chinooks, but I will aim for a more general explanation of what causes the major sustained chinook, when the whole troposphere begins to flow over the Rocky Mountains. That is the one that Westerners love to brag about.

Despite its tropical effect on the Chinook Country psyche,

the wind owes its origin to a low-pressure system occurring off the Gulf of Alaska and a low-pressure zone east of the Rockies. A cyclonic (counterclockwise) motion of air around the Alaska low eventually drives the southwest wind into Montana and Alberta. The Montana chinook expert Warren Harding, a former weather observer in Alaska, once told me that the Alaska low "throws off wind like a big wheel throwing off mud." Eventually this moist Pacific air begins rising up the west slope of the Coast Ranges. "By definition," Harding explained, "when a surface and upper ridge of high pressure approaches a mountain range, the lee side trough will start to form—that is, the pressure starts to fall on the east slope."

Air flows from areas of high pressure to areas of low pressure. The air rises and partially subsides several times, lifted orographically by the interior mountain ranges of the northwest before it rises for the final time up the west slope of the Rockies. The cooling effect as it rises causes a loss of moisture (water vapour) to precipitation when the dew point is reached, and that is why most of the precipitation will fall on the west side of the Rocky Mountains. (This is also why the eastern plains, in the "rain shadow" of the mountains, are so arid.) The cooling effect of altitude rise is much greater in drier air, but in this wet air, the cooling is tempered by the principle of the latent heat of condensation. That is because energy from the sun (heat) was originally stored in the water vapour contained within that rising air. As this vapour condenses, it releases energy (heat) to the surrounding air. The air, drier now, subsides on the eastern side of the mountains, drawn into the trough of low pressure. As it plunges down, it is warmed further through compression, like the air in a bicycle pump. Since the air is drier, it gains heat at the dry adiabatic lapse rate of 5.5°F per 1000 feet. There is a dramatic net gain in temperature from the windward to the leeward side of the Rockies.

Meanwhile, on the east side of the mountains, the snow-covered plains, all unsuspecting of these physical forces, may be gripped by temperatures that are well below zero, as in the case of Great Falls mentioned above. So the warm air descends on this cold air mass like warm water on an ice cube. The variation between wind and surface temperatures accounts for the wild temperature swings during chinook conditions. There can be an eerie precision about the contact zone between chinook air and arctic air. I have driven to Pincher Creek at −30°F when, at a certain point on the prairie, the car enters the descending wave of chinook air. Instantly, the entire surface of the frozen vehicle, including every inch of glass, is covered with an impenetrable glaze, so that I have to roll a window down in order to see the white line. This can be a terrifying experience—especially if your last glimpse of the road contained an oncoming semitrailer truck.

Now take this winter. The weatherman may claim that five feet of snow have fallen so far this season, but why is there so little trace of it, save for a few white streaks in the creek bottoms and in the poplar forests along the Oldman River? Right now Alberta farmers in Pincher Creek and Fort Macleod, Montanans down in Havre and Cutbank, are staring glumly out of their picture windows at their fields. They are depressed, and it is not because of all the positive ions released by this witch's wind (a phenomenon I will deal with later).

There is no reserve of moisture in these dark brown and shallow black soils to germinate the spring grain crop. The snow, melting into the soil under the warm wind, might have provided enough reserve to at least get the crops started. So where *is* all this moisture? It has been "chinooked." This hound of a wind has not only melted the snow, it has lapped it up, and evaporated it not only from the surface but from deep within the topsoil.

When Chinook comes calling, it brings a desert thirst along. It could vacuum the milk from a cow's udder, drink the coffee from your cup, suck the alcohol out of your shoe polish. This is not only a winter phenomenon. Although it is also known as the Snow-Eater, the chinook wind blows both winter and summer, and it dries up the soil in both seasons. Since the 1880s, its furnace breath has burned out many a grain farmer's green crops before they had a chance to ripen.

The medium that crops grow in is topsoil, the thinnest and most productive layer of the earth's skin, full of micro-organisms that make life possible. In southern Alberta, it has taken 10,000 years for this loam to attain depths of from one to 20 inches. In 1985–1986, the black blizzards carried off five million tons of this precious resource from 988,000 acres of farm land.

There have been many years in the history of the arid Palliser's Triangle when drought conditions were accompanied by dry west winds. In 1920, my grandparents' era, one million acres of topsoil was blown out by the wind, and, in 1934, so much soil blew off from the western states and provinces (300 million tons by one estimate) that clouds of dirt covered New York City. Dirt at 10,000 feet altitude forced aircraft to change course.

The irrigation skills that Mormon settlers brought with them to the Cardston area, along with modern dryland farming techniques and equipment invented by dryland farmers, have helped to green in parts of the Triangle. In fact, it contains some of the

finest grain-growing topsoils on the continent, and 40 percent
of the region's arable land. It produces more wheat than any other
region of Canada—75 percent—when enough rain falls to grow
the crops, that is.

The story of the chinook began long before white contact,
and the first European explorers noted the phenomenon long
before the word "chinook" came into currency. Two early explorers, Peter Fidler of the Hudson's Bay Company, and his
rival, Alexander Mackenzie of the North West Company, were
embraced by the same warm chinook in 1793, though they could
not have known it at the time. They were separated by five hundred miles of virgin wilderness, but thanks to their scrupulous
journal-keeping, we are able to compare their experiences centuries later.

Mackenzie was embarked on the history-making journey that
would make him the first white man to cross the continent and
reach the Pacific Ocean. Fidler had been sent south from Cum-
berland House on the North Saskatchewan River to explore the
country and establish trade with the Blackfoot.

On December 7, 1792, Fidler encountered "Light Airs from
the Westwards" and found the day "clear & hot at 2½ PM," he
wrote, "Thermometer 58 which at this season of the year is remarkably warm." The light airs soon turned into full gales that
blew tents away and fanned campfires into prairie fires—wildfires in the wintertime!

Mackenzie meanwhile had embarked from Fort Chipewyan
on Lake Athabasca bound for the headwaters of the Peace River,
where he arrived in November, and went into winter quarters at
Fort Fork. He found the weather so cold that axe blades shattered against the firewood. On December 28, five hundred miles

south, Fidler noted gale conditions. On December 29, the chinook finally bulled its way through the arctic cold front surrounding Mackenzie. He notes, "the wind being at North-East, and the weather calm and cloudy, a rumbling noise was heard in the air like distant thunder, when the sky cleared away in the South-West; from whence there blew a perfect hurricane, which lasted till eight. Soon after it commenced, the atmosphere became so warm that it dissolved all the snow on the ground; even the ice was covered with water, and had the same appearance as when it is breaking up in the spring. From eight to nine the weather became calm, but immediately after a wind arose from the North-East with equal violence, with clouds, rain, and hail, which continued through the night and till the evening of the next day, when it turned to snow."

What Mackenzie and Fidler described in 1793 is the very same battle of winds, the same arid climatic conditions that Albertans are familiar with today. If not for the current controls we have over wildfires, if not for all the roads and summerfallow providing fire breaks and access for firefighters, I could look out my east windows on many a day and see the same clouds of smoke from distant prairie fires that Fidler saw two hundred years ago.

Fidler was a shrewd observer of natural history on the buffalo ground. "These fires burning off the old grass," he noted on January 15, 1793, "in the ensuing Spring and Summer makes excellent fine sweet food for the Horses & Buffalo, &c."

Fire, whether caused by men or by lightning, was driven by the Creator Wind to renew the grass, to keep down encroachment by willows and aspen trees. Aspens are shallow-rooted, easily damaged by fire. The roots of native grasses, however, go deep into the earth, making fine networks in the soil. Better yet for surviving droughts, the hair-like filaments of some native grasses, if unravelled, would stretch for miles. Fire, wind, and rain nurtured the earth that fed the buffalo, whose flesh fed the people, and whose entire body, hide and skeleton, furnished a hundred different objects of use, from bowstrings through to teepee covers, and from moccasins to natural glue.

Apparently it was a Euro-white who affixed an Indian name on this wind. The Chinook people, namesakes of the wind, dwelt in fur-trade days near the mouth of the Columbia River. The name was said to have originated as a joke made about 1840 by a Mr. Birnie, a Hudson's Bay factor in Oregon. A warm northwest wind used to blow toward his fort from the camps of the Chinook Indians between Fort Ellice and Cape Disappointment. He called this wind "the chinook," and it is possible that the name arose not only from the warmth of the wind but from its perfume, because the Chinook villages were fishing villages.

The tribes living in Chinook Country had their own names for the wind. To the North Peigan, for example, it was `aisiksop`u, the oily wind, though according to two white authors who lived with the Peigan in early Montana, it was known there as the "Black Wind." Either description seems credible: the wind first turned the ground greasy with mud and slush, but might later turn the air black with dust. The Peigan or Piikani, my closest Indian neighbours, seemed to attribute the wind to the work of the Blackfoot trickster-creator figure Napi, or Old Man. The expression was *"Napiua aisiksopumstau"*—the Old Man makes the oily wind.

Everywhere you look in Chinook Country, you will see the marks of the wind upon the earth. It is there in the permanent lean of the aspen groves, those white tree trunks all leaning northward as living wind-vanes indicating the prevailing southwest winds. It is there as a current of energy wavering through the grain fields and through the sweep of remaining prairie grass. The wind keeps aspens, willows, and rose bushes penned up in hollows behind the little drumlin hills left behind by the Great Ice. Those that try to root themselves in the open it attacks, blasting the leaves with flung dirt, tearing off the new leaves. It will thaw out the roots in midwinter so the sap begins to run. Then the frost comes back with an arctic cold front, freezing the tender buds, injuring the roots, and sometimes killing the tree. Acres of conifers in Waterton National Park have had their green needles turned to a ruddy orange by this windburn. Trees killed by this process in winter are standing tinder for a summer lightning strike; the west wind waits to fan the strike into a forest fire.

What the wind likes is a clean slate of grass to slide over. What the wind hates is anything that obstructs its passage, anything that overturns the sod. So it is always at war with man's constructions, always testing these impertinent windbreaks.

The wind takes physical shape in a thousand hoodoos carved in the sandstone rimrock of the Porcupine Hills, and all the outlying ridges on the tops of the Rocky Mountain foothills. It is seen especially at that haunted, that joyful home of the First Nations, Writing On Stone, just north of Montana's Sweetgrass Hills. There the wind has made not only hoodoos but windows in the rimrocks, side streets, cliff dwellings for no one to inhabit but rattlers and coyotes above the Milk River.

By whatever name, this fierce wind is what keeps those wide open spaces open.

The Pleistocene, the Age of Ice, marks also the dawn of man. No one knows when the first people, those Paleo-Indians of unspecified Eurasian stock, made their way to the New World. That they followed an intermittently open ice-free corridor to reach the New World has long been an accepted theory of archaeologists, though when the corridor was open for business and when it was plugged with ice remains a matter of debate.

The corridor stretched from Alaska, through the Liard River of the Yukon and down through Alberta to the Marias River of Montana, closely following the edge of the mountains, along the line where the continental glaciers and the cordilleran glaciers met, and later receded. This line would eventually be known to the oldtimers as the Old North Trail.

Across this land bridge came mastodons and mammoths, came members of the deer family. They shared the boggy wet grasslands at the margins of the ice sheets with New World animals, horses and camels. The horses and camels were slated for extinction here, and survival in the east. Horses would not return to this continent until the coming of the Spanish *conquistadores.*

No one knows how old the chinook is, but since it is a mountain wind, formed from air moving over an incline, it must have been conjured up inchoately from the sea when the mountains rose from the highlands. I have hinted at the creative power of this wind as a transformer of landscapes. A geographer, Ronald L. Ives, once went much further. Writing in *Annals of the Association of American Geographers* (1950), Ives suggested that the chinook wind, combined with the rain shadow effect of the mountains, created an ice-free corridor between the continental and cordilleran glaciers.

Looking at the distribution of loess (glacial silt) across the plains, and examining the fretting of rocks by the wind, Ives concluded, "Wind motion during much of the Pleistocene, was in the same general directions as wind motion today." He found further evidence of ancient chinook winds in the patterns of ancient glaciation on the windward and leeward side of the mountains, patterns still found today, and consistent with chinook wind and rain shadow effects.

Ives was writing about Colorado, but the thrust of his argument seems to apply to the entire range of the chinook wind. (I have but to climb the hill behind the Wheelhouse to see this same aeolian fretting in the sandstone outcrops there.) It seems likely that when the first people were ready to follow the corridor south into the unknown, the chinook was there to greet them.

The existing fauna of the Great Plains is only a shadow of what it was before white contact, and that richer fauna but a shadow of the species that roamed this country as recently as 15,000 years ago. As biologist Valerius Geist has pointed out, there was no historic grazer to compare with the prehistoric American mammoth, elephant, or long-horned bison that were at home on these plains; no predator as fierce as the dire wolf, the sabre-toothed tiger, or a sort of "running bear" large enough and fast enough to kill elephants. Only fossils remain to testify to that diversity, and one singular beast, the pronghorn antelope, which can reach a sprint of 65 m.p.h., hopelessly outgunning the poor little coyote, which alone remains to uphold wolfish tradition on the prairie.

Similarly, the history of Canada's first Paleo-Indian people may never be more than a fragmented record of artifacts discovered at widely dispersed sites throughout the continent. The precise cultural and racial linkages between those first-comers and those we think of as their descendants, who roamed the buffalo plains with only dogs as beasts of burden in the days before white contact, are open to debate. The stone age life was hand to mouth. But days of famine, or omnivorous days of snaring rabbits and digging out camass bulbs and bitterroot with a forked stick, suddenly turned to feasting when buffalo, run into box canyons or decoyed over a *piskun* (jump), were crippled or trapped, and could more easily be killed with stone-tipped spears or war clubs. They must have been a lean, athletic race, these hunters and gatherers, like the tribes who succeeded them. Their everyday life was a pentathlon.

When the first whites arrived in Chinook Country, they found that a vast expanse of territory, stretching south of the North Saskatchewan River to the Yellowstone, and from the Rocky Mountain foothills east to the Cypress Hills and the mouth of the Milk River, was controlled by the Blackfoot, a nation of fierce Algonquian-speaking nomads. The irresistible forces of British and American expansionism collided with the immovable object of Blackfoot territorial imperative; the white flood was pushed off course, forced to make historic detours. This equestrian, warrior nation would resist and redirect the thrust of settlement for fifty years, and many whites would leave their bones on the buffalo ground for the sin of underestimating Blackfoot power.

DAVID ADAMS RICHARDS

From *Lines on the Water: A Fisherman's Life on the Miramichi*

DAVID ADAMS RICHARDS is a critically acclaimed Canadian novelist whose books, including *Mercy Among the Children,* *For Those Who Hunt the Wounded Down,* *The Bay of Love and Sorrows, Hope in the Desperate Hour, Blood Ties,* and *Evening Snow Will Bring Such Peace* have garnered two Governor General's awards. Excerpted here is the first chapter from his memoir *Lines on the Water: A Fisherman's Life on the Miramichi,* which won the Governor General's award for nonfiction in 1998.

AS A BOY, I DREAMED of fishing before I went, and went fishing before I caught anything, and knew fishermen before I became one. As a child, I dreamed of finding remarkable fish so close to me that they would be easy to catch. And no one, in my dreams, had ever found these fish before me.

I remember the water as dark and clear at the same time—and by clear I suppose I mean clean. Sometimes it looked like gold or copper, and at dusk the eddies splashed silver-toned, and babbled like all the musical instruments of the world. I still think of it this way now, years later.

As a child I had the idea that trout were golden, or green, in deep pools hidden away under the moss of a riverbank. And that some day I would walk in the right direction, take all the right paths to the river, and find them there.

In fact, trout, I learned, were far more textured and a better colour than just golds and greens. They were the colour of nature itself—as naturally outfitted in their coat of thin slime as God could manage. They were hidden around bends and in the deep shaded pools of my youth.

I had the impression from those Mother Goose stories that all fish could talk. I still do.

My first fishing foray was along the bank of a small brook to the northwest of Newcastle, on the Miramichi. A sparkling old brook that Lord Beaverbrook took his name from.

My older brother and a friend took me along with them, on a cool blowy day. We had small cane rods and old manual reels, with hooks and sinkers and worms, the kind all kids used. The kind my wife used as a child on the Bartibog River thirteen miles downriver from my town of Newcastle, and her brothers used also, at the same time that I was trudging with my brother.

It was a Saturday in May of 1955 and I was not yet five years of age. Fishing even then could take me out of myself, far away from the worry of my life, such as it was, and into another life, better and more complete.

We had packed a lunch and had got to the brook about ten in the morning. Just as we entered the woods, I saw the brook, which seemed to be no deeper in places than my shoe. In we went (a certain distance) until the sounds of the town below us were left behind.

Leaning across the brook was a maple, with its branches dipping into the water. At the upper end of the tree, the current swept about a boulder, and gently tailed away into a deep pocket about a foot from the branches. The place was shaded, and sunlight filtered through the trees on the water beyond us. The boys were in a hurry and moved on to that place where all the fish *really* are. And I lagged behind. I was never any good at keeping up, having a lame left side, so most of the time my older brother made auxiliary rules for me—rules that by and large excluded me.

"You can fish there," he said.

I nodded. "Where?"

"There, see. Look—right there. Water. Fish. Go at her. We'll be back."

I nodded.

I sat down on the moss and looked about, and could see that my brother and his friend were going away from me. I was alone. So I took out my sandwich and ate it. (It was in one pocket, my worms were in the other. My brother doled the worms out to me a few at a time.)

I was not supposed to be, from our mother's instructions, alone.

"For Mary in heaven's sake, don't leave your little brother alone in those woods." I could hear her words.

I could also hear my brother and our friend moving away, and leaving me where I was. In this little place we were out of sight of one another after about twenty feet.

I had not yet learned to tie my sneakers; they had been tied for me by my brother in a hurry, for the second time, at the railway track, and here again they were loose. So I took them off. And then I rolled up my pants.

I had four worms in my pocket. They smelled of the dark earth near my grandmother's back garden where they had come from, and all worms smell of earth, and therefore all earth smells of trout.

I spiked a worm on my small hook the best I could. I had a plug-shot sinker about six inches up my line, which my father had squeezed for me the night before. But my line was kinked and old, and probably half-rotted, from years laid away.

I grabbed the rod in one hand, the line in the other, and tossed it at the boulder. It hit the boulder and slid underneath the water. I could see it roll one time on the pebbled bottom, and then it was lost to my sight under the brown cool current. The sun was at my back splaying down through the trees. I was standing on the mossy bank. There was a young twisted maple on my right.

Almost immediately I felt a tug on the line. Suddenly it all came to me—this is what fish do—this was their age-old secret.

The line tightened, the old rod bent, and a trout—the first trout of my life—came splashing and rolling to the top of the water. It was a trout about eight inches long, with a plump belly.

"I got it," I whispered. "I got it. I got it."

But no one heard me: "I got it, I got it."

For one moment I looked at the trout, and the trout looked at me. It seemed to be telling me something. I wasn't sure what. It is something I have been trying to hear ever since.

When I lifted it over the bank, and around the maple, it spit the hook, but it was safe in my possession a foot or two from the water.

For a moment no one came, and I was left to stare at it. The worm had changed colour in the water. The trout was wet and it had the most beautiful glimmering orange speckles I ever saw. It reminded me, or was to remind me as I got older, of spring, of Easter Sunday, of the smell of snow being warmed away by the sun.

My brother's friend came back. He looked at it, amazed that I had actually caught something. Picking up a stick, and hunching over it he shouted, "Get out of the way—I'll kill it."

And he slammed the stick down beside it. The stick missed the fish, hit a leafed branch of that maple that the fish was lying across, and catapulted the trout back into the brook.

I looked at him, he looked at me.

"Ya lost him," he said.

My brother came up, yelling, "Did you get a fish?"

"He lost him," my brother's friend said, standing.

"Oh ya lost him," my brother said, half derisively, and I think a little happily.

I fished fanatically for the time remaining, positive that this was an easy thing to do. But nothing else tugged at my line. And as the day wore on I became less enthusiastic.

We went home a couple of hours later. The sun glanced off the steel railway tracks, and I walked back over the ties in my bare feet because I had lost my sneakers. My socks were stuffed into my pockets. The air now smelled of steely soot and bark, and the town's houses stretched below the ball fields.

The houses in our town were for the most part the homes of working men. The war was over, and it was the age of the baby boomers, of which I was one. Old pictures in front of those houses, faded with time, show seven or eight children, all smiling curiously at the camera. And I reflect that we baby boomers, born after a war that left so many dead, were much like the salmon spawn born near the brown streams and great river. We were born to reaffirm life and the destiny of the human race.

When we got home, my brother showed his trout to my mother, and my mother looked at me.

"Didn't you get anything, dear?"

"I caught a trout—a large trout. It—it—I—"

"Ya lost him, Davy boy," my brother said, slapping me on the back.

"Oh well," my mother said. "That's all right, there will always be a next time."

And that was the start of my fishing life.

That was long ago, when fishing was innocent and benevolent. I have learned since that I would have to argue my way through life—that I was going to become a person who could never leave to rest the *idea* of why things were the way they were. And fishing was to become part of this idea, just as hunting was. Why would the fish take one day, and not the next? What was the reason for someone's confidence one year, and their lack of it the next season, when conditions seemed to be exactly the same?

Or the great waters—the south branch of the Sevogle that flows into the main Sevogle, that flows into the Norwest Miramichi, itself a tributary of the great river. What infinite source propelled each separate individual fish to return on those days, at that moment, when my Copper Killer, or Green Butt Butterfly—or anyone else's—was skirting the pool at exactly the right angle at that same moment, and *when* was it all announced and inscribed in the heavens—as insignificant as it is—as foreordained.

When I was seven we moved to a different side of town where we fished a different stream. Here grass fires burned in the April sun. Here the sky was destined to meet the horizon beyond the pulp fields and tracks, where the woods stretched away toward the hinterland of the north, arteried by small dark-wood roads for pulp trucks. Boys not much older than I would leave school to work cutting pulpwood, or try to make money any way they could to help their families.

When we lived in the centre of town, we might have been described as city dwellers. But here we had different friends, far more ambitious and competent woods travellers. We were closer to the main Miramichi River. We would jump ice floes in the spring, with kitchen forks tied to sticks, spearing the tommie cod under the ice, as the sun melted these floes beneath our feet. Or we would wait along the side of the bank and throw hooks baited with carpet lint at the smelts that ran close to shore.

I grew up with poor boys who knew when the smelt run was on, and when the tommie cod came, because much more than me, they needed these things for their families to eat. We were wasteful—they were not. To them, fishing, and their fathers' hunting, had a whole different perspective. Some I grew up with ate more deer meat than beef, and relied upon it. And when they went fishing, it was less a sport than part of their diets. I remember a child who fell off an ice floe and started crying, not because he fell in, but because he'd lost the tommie cod he had promised his mom he would bring home.

As we started off to fish in June, the year I was eight, I did not know that out in that great river was the next generation of salmon moving up. They travelled in waves and waves of fish—

perhaps seven to ten feet under the water and no more than fifty or sixty yards from the shore—absolutely unconcerned with me, or the fact that I would be fishing their descendants in the years to come; that they were the ancestors of fish I would some day see rise for my fly on the Renous or Little Souwest; that they were the progeny of fish that had moved up these rivers in the time of Caesar and Hannibal—the glacier fish (as David Carroll calls them), the salmon.

By late May to late June we would be fishing in the cool brooks and streams beyond town. We would sometimes jump a freight train leaving the Newcastle station, and ride it about a mile, as far as the Mill Cove turn.

I was with my brother and two of our friends, one who had the nomenclature Killer, and that morning we had walked down to the Mill Cove brook past the ancient crooked bridge, past the turn where the headless nun (a seventeenth-century French nun) would sometimes appear to unsuspecting lovers (almost always nearing the moment of climax) to ask them if they would be so kind as to help her find her head, which was chopped off by the Micmac, so that she could go back to France and rest in peace.

We passed the Cove, splendid in the early sunshine, where a small boy we knew had drowned the year before, in a neat little shirt and tie he had worn for a Sunday outing—when they found him, there were still sinkers and hooks in his shirt pocket. Then crossing the bridge, we turned to our left and went up the rocky brook.

The brooks we fished always had the same makeup. They

were two to three feet deep, maybe four in the hidden pools, and sometimes no more than five to eight feet wide. They meandered and babbled through a green windy valley toward the great Miramichi, overgrown with alders and tangled with blow downs, which crossed them haphazardly, and for the most part the paths to and from them were paths made by children.

All during our youth we invented ourselves as cavemen, as Neanderthals. We had our own spots, caves along the side of the embankment, places on the streams that allowed us the luxury of this. This part of the spirit can never die if you are going to be self-reliant. If you think it can, try to excise it away from children, from one generation to the next.

Each year of our early youth we revisited spots on this Mill Cove stream that were rich with the memories of the year before. The dreams of children are poignant because they are so easily dashed.

That day, long ago now, we had gone to the left bank. It was hard going all the way. Many times we'd have to crawl through alders and thickets to get to a spot. Or cross the windfalls from one side to the other. And the spot where we were going was not much more than a small rip in the texture of the stream, about four feet long, just beneath the bank that we were walking on. Yet out of these small tiny pockets in this most unassuming remote northern stream came wonderful trout—ten inches long and more—which to boys of eight and nine years old were God-given.

There were four trout taken that day. It was a warm day and we were walking back and forth on the windfalls that crossed the brook, wearing sneakers and short-sleeved shirts. It was almost time to go when we decided to cross, once more, a windfall to the right because there was a pocket further down the brook that Jimmy remembered, which we hadn't been to yet.

"It's right over there. I caught a trout there last year this same time," he yelled.

We put our rods in one hand and started to cross the windfall that was angled higher on the right bank than the left. Jimmy went across first and then my brother, then Terry, and then me. I am fairly clumsy and have fallen in many times. When I hear of old river guides on the Miramichi who've done handstands going down through the rapids in a canoe, I can only say I've unintentionally done that as well.

I started inching along the windfall and glanced up to see the rest of the boys already on the other side and moving along the bank. The water babbled swiftly beneath me. I took one more step, and then another, and suddenly found myself under the windfall I had been crossing, and underwater as well.

The log was directly above me and I couldn't stand up. There was a rock in front of me so I couldn't go ahead, and one of the tree limbs from the windfall was preventing me from going backwards. Even when I lifted my head I couldn't clear the water.

I just had to hold my breath and watch the boys walk away. I was literally between a rock and a hard place and I must have looked something like a trout. I can tell you there was no panic. But I sure thought I was in a bad spot. With the sound the brook made, the boys had no idea I had fallen in.

But then Terry said something to me, and when I didn't answer he turned. I wasn't on the log, but he could see something under it.

They ran back and hauled me out. They were all quite pleased they had saved my life. So was I.

The pool Jimmy wanted to fish was half full of sand and silt. The year had changed it, and aged it forever. That's why he hadn't initially found it.

We went home. It was June 1959.

This was the day of the Escuminac disaster, when men drifting nets for salmon got caught in a storm as fierce as any seen at sea. Their boats were twenty-five feet long, the waves they faced were eighty feet tall. But so many of them would not leave other boats in trouble, and continued to circle back for friends being swallowed up, cutting their nets so their drifters wouldn't sink, but being swept away, tying their sons to masts before losing their own lives. Handing lifelines to friends instead of keeping them for themselves. If this sounds heroic, it was. It was.

That night I slept through the death of thirty-five men out in the bay.

Just after this experience, I went with my brother to dig worms in an old garden. We were going downriver to fish on the Church River, which we did every summer, until I was about eleven, with our father. My brother took the pitchfork and started to dig, while I shook the sod and picked up the worms. I happened to drop a piece of nice plump sod over my left foot. I stood there counting up the three or four worms we had managed to capture.

"This looks like a good place here," my brother said, and he drove the pitchfork into the sod above my foot. I looked down at it, in a peculiar way, I suppose, and then he jumped on his pitchfork to get some depth.

And then he lifted the fork, and me, and my foot up with it. One of the tongs had gone right through the top of my foot, and I landed about four yards away.

Mr. Simms, the man who came to our aid, and carried me to the doctors, and who'd known about my near-death experience in the Mill Cove, made the observation: "Fishing's pretty darn hard on you, Davy, isn't it."

I suppose those were the truest words about me he ever spoke.

SHARON BUTALA

The Subtlety of Land

SHARON BUTALA lives on a ranch near Eastend, Saskatchewan,
and is one of Canada's best-known writers. Butala's novels include
The Garden of Eden, The Gates of the Sun, Luna, and *The Fourth
Archangel.* Her most recent book is *Wild Stone Heart:
An Apprentice in the Fields.* "The Subtlety of Land" is from
The Perfection of the Morning: An Apprenticeship in Nature,
nominated for a 1994 Governor General's award.

SOME YEARS LATER, when I was an established author, I said to
a Toronto reporter who had asked me a question about him,
"My husband is a true rural man."

"What does that mean?" the reporter asked, his voice full of
skepticism.

"It means," I said, "that he understands the world in terms of
wild things." I was a little surprised myself at my answer, having
been called upon to explain something that until that moment
had seemed self-evident, and realizing that, caught off guard,
I had hit on the heart of the matter.

The reporter's pencil stopped moving, his eyes shifted away
from me, he reflected, his eyes shifted back to me, and without
writing anything down he changed the subject. When I told this

story to a writer-naturalist friend, he said, laughing, that for the reporter my answer "does not compute."

A true rural person must be somebody born and raised on the land, outside of towns, and far from most other people. That being a given, then it follows that such life experience must result in an intrinsic understanding of the world different from that of someone raised in the cement, asphalt, glass, and crowds of the city. Peter's thinking about the world was different from mine in ways that went beyond our different sexes or our different lifestyles. Where I had been trained to understand human nature from Freud and pop psychology, and the functioning of the world from classes in political economy and in history, that is, from formal education, Peter's starting point was what he had all his life lived in the midst of—it was Nature.

As years on the ranch passed, though, I began to learn from Nature too; I began to catch a glimpse of the world as he saw it through my own life in Nature. When that began to happen, a new understanding slowly, very slowly, began to dawn on me about what a life in Nature teaches one. I began to see that there might be more at the root of this difference in understanding of how the world works than I had guessed at, thinking it had to do only with simple, surface matters, like understanding cattle behaviour well enough to predict their next move, or knowing the habits of antelope, or reading the sky with accuracy. I didn't yet have any idea what this deeper knowledge might be, but I watched Peter closely and tried to see what he saw.

While he was doing the spring irrigation at the hay farm, he would sometimes come across fawns only a few days old lying in the hay where they'd been left by their mothers who had gone off to forage. More than once he came to the house to get me so I could see the little spotted creature for myself.

"Watch," he would say. "When they're this young they don't even move when you come near them." Then he would bend down, pick up the trusting fawn in his arms, carry it to the closest grass-covered dike, and place it gently down where the irrigation water couldn't reach it. I worried about the mother locating her baby, but he said, with the confidence born of experience, "Don't worry. It won't take her a minute to find him." When we went back hours later the fawn would always be gone. These and other incidents reminded me over and over again that Peter, and other rural people who knew no other landscape, had formed his attitude to the prairie and his understanding of its weather, its growth patterns, and its animals by a lifetime of immersion in it.

In my reading and occasionally in conversation with urban visitors, I read or hear people either saying directly or implying indirectly that *true rural* people don't notice or appreciate the beauty in which they live. Although I don't say so, the arrogance and ignorance of such remarks always makes me angry, implying as it does that rural people lack humanity, are somehow an inferior branch of the human species, that beauty is beyond their ken. It is one thing to come from the city and be overwhelmed by the beauty of Nature and to speak of it, and another thing entirely to have lived in it so long that it has seeped into your bones and your blood and is inseparable from your own being, so that it is part of you and requires no mention or hymns of praise.

Peter preferred to do our annual spring and fall cattle drives on horseback, a trek which took three days. Bringing the cattle down to the valley around Christmastime could be very unpleasant and then it was often hard to get help, so that we sometimes made that move with only Peter, me, and one other person. But three days out on the prairie during a warm spring were paradise; we never had any trouble rounding up enough riders then. If the spring move was usually a joy, the best part of it was the eight to ten miles of unbroken prairie without even any true roads through it that we used to cross each time.

I knew the first time Peter took me across those miles of prairie that I loved to be there far from towns or even houses, on native shortgrass that had never been broken, where the grass hadn't been overgrazed and was full of birds' nests in the spring, and long-eared jackrabbits as big as small dogs, antelope in the distance, and coyotes that often followed us singing all the way.

Of course, unless she's a dyed-in-the-wool, bona fide horse-and-cattlewoman herself, when it's time to move cattle, and especially if there are adolescent sons on the place, the rancher's wife usually gets stuck driving the truck. The rancher is the one with the understanding of the cattle, knowledge of the route, and the cattle-management skills. As boss and owner, he has to ride. If there are adolescents along, it's taken for granted that they'll ride because they have to learn, which has a high priority on Saskatchewan ranches, and because it's so much fun and nobody wants to deprive kids of a little harmless fun.

The rancher's wife packs the meals, stows them in the truck, serves them when the time comes, and packs up after. She carries drinking water and coffee and the extra jackets or the ones taken off when the day gets too warm. She carries tack, fencing pliers, and other tools, and sometimes, if the move is just before calving begins, she'll have a newborn in the back of the truck and often several of them, each one marked in some way—maybe a coloured string around its neck—so it can be returned to the right mother every few hours. As the drive wears on, she's likely to have exhausted adolescents in the cab with her, while their horses are either driven ahead or led by one of the men from his own horse. Usually, at some point, somebody will take pity on her and spell her off for an hour or so, so that she can get out into the fresh air and ride a little herself.

When you move cattle you move, depending on the weather, at the leisurely pace of about two miles an hour. For long stretches you don't need to speak at all, and you can ride a mile or more away from any other rider if you want to. As you ride, the prairie slowly seeps into you. I have never felt such pure, unadulterated joy in simple existence as I have felt at moments out on the prairie during the spring move.

Ordinarily I wouldn't get to ride until we were close to the ranch and our helpers went home. Then Peter and I changed our headquarters from the hay farm to the ranch house and we'd ride horses out to the cattle to bring them the rest of the way home. Occasionally, he'd have someone along who didn't ride and who would drive the truck so that I could ride. Most of the time, though, I reluctantly drove the truck and kept my fingers crossed for a chance either to ride or, as I sometimes did, to walk leading Peter's horse—for me to ride him was unthinkable, the very thought making my stomach turn over and my knees quake—while Peter spelled me off in the driver's seat.

Nowadays we calve at the hay farm instead of at the ranch, mostly because it's easier to keep an eye on the cows, but also because there's shelter for them here during the inevitable calf-killing spring storms. Often, too, in spring there is no water in the ditches or fields along the way and, of course, the cattle must have water each day, moving or not. If we calve at the hay farm—Peter not being a believer in early calving—by the time we're ready to move in late April most of the farmers along the route have seeded their crops. The traditional mistrust between farmers and ranchers being what it is, it would be dangerous if one cow strayed one foot from the road allowances, those which, usually without bothering to get permission from the munici- pality, farmers haven't plowed up and seeded to wheat. And cows being what they are, you never know when one might take it into her head to head out, calf at her side, racing for Alaska or Mexico across a newly seeded field with a couple of cowboys in hot pursuit. Guns have been pointed on such occasions. Now- adays, it hardly seems worth the risk.

During one of the last spring moves we made, Peter had had more people along than he'd expected and before we'd gone very far he'd given one of the kids my horse, which he'd been leading, to ride. Not long after that, he'd given my saddle—the only one with stirrups that could be shortened enough for small people— to another teenager to use. I had reconciled myself to not being able to ride on this move. I could still look at the landscape, I could roll down the window and smell the sweet air and feel the breeze and the sun on my face, and occasionally I could stop, get out, and stroll around a bit in the grass.

We always made it a practice to stop for a meal when we reached that stretch of pure unbroken prairie. The riders would dismount and hobble their horses or tie them to the fence, I'd park the truck, Peter would throw down a couple of hay bales for a table or for people to sit on, and I'd put out the lunch. We'd sit in the sun and eat sandwiches, and his mother's baked beans, the pot wrapped in layers of newspapers to keep it warm, and drink coffee from thermoses. Long before we reached there I'd have begun to look forward to that moment.

I discovered what the annual day spent crossing these acres of prairie meant to me when, as we were about to begin that part of the trip, a circumstance arose—I don't even remember what it was—that meant somebody had to drive one of the men the twenty or so miles around the fields, down the roads, and wait with him there at the corrals for the riders and cattle to arrive. Since Peter could hardly order anybody else to do it, and nobody volunteered, it was taken for granted that as his wife I would leave the drive and take this man where he needed to go.

I wanted to protest, but I couldn't bring myself to do it in front of so many people, especially since arguing or complaining is just not done on a trip like that. It would be a little like a sailor telling the captain of a ship that he didn't feel like taking the watch that night. My true feelings were too private to speak out loud, and I couldn't come up with any practical reason why I shouldn't have to that didn't hint of adolescent pique or, not knowing how the others felt about the prairie—but the fact that nobody volunteered to go should have given me a hint—that I could be sure anybody but Peter would understand. And everyone else was a volunteer; I was official staff. I knew I wouldn't be able to go back and catch up with the drive, either. For me, for that year, the drive was over.

I got back in the truck and started driving, trying to smile, trying to make conversation, while all the time I was fighting back tears. I wanted so badly to spend that last few hours on the prairie, the only time we ever went through those fields, that I had an actual pain in my chest as I drove away and that stayed with me till I went to bed that night.

I said about that incident much later to a friend, "If everything happens to teach you something, why was that taken away from me? What was I supposed to learn from that?" and answered myself, "To teach me how much the wild prairie means to me." Years later, I was able to go further: to understand how precious it is, how unique, how deeply it might affect one, changing even one's understanding of life.

Sometimes I think I'm still not over that loss. Especially since, during the good times, farmers bought all that land the rest of the gang travelled over on horseback that day, and plowed it up to turn it into a farm. Now, ten years later, the farming operation is failing, but you can't turn plowed-up shortgrass prairie back into the original terrain. It's gone forever, or given a human life span, as good as forever, along with the wildlife that lived on it.

It occurs to me now to wonder if perhaps the very real—and surprising even to me—sorrow I felt that day as I drove away, and all the rest of the day and for days afterward, wasn't perhaps intuitive, if perhaps a part of me knew that I would never again experience the sweetness of that air, the sun warm on my face and hands, the view so vast the soul felt free, because by the next spring or the spring after that it would be gone forever.

As the years passed, I felt more and more that the best comfort I had was in being in the landscape. I was only mildly curious about how the prairie was formed, and when and how it was evolving, and I certainly had none of the interests of ecologists or environmentalists. I was merely looking at the prairie as a human being, savouring it for its beauty which engaged all the senses and brought with it a feeling of well-being, contentment, and often even joy.

My approach was to simply wander in it with no particular destination, to lie in the sun and bury my nose in the sweet-smelling grasses and forbs such as sage, to admire the colours and textures of the sedges, shrubs, and succulents which make up the mixed grass prairie, or to sit on a slope looking out across miles of prairie to the horizon, watching the shifting of shadows and light across it, thinking no thoughts that, a moment later, I would remember. I was there only to enjoy the prairie. I asked for nothing more, not thinking there was anything more.

I had only the most cursory interest in the names of the plants, although Peter's mother taught me a few of those which flowered: scarlet mallow, three-flowered avens, gumbo prim-rose, golden bean, which she called "buffalo bean," and which someone else told me she knew as the wild sweet pea. I could hardly miss the wild rose or the prairie sunflower, and I knew a few others such as the wild licorice and the wild morning glory and anemones which grow along the riverbank, from my child-hood in the north. Peter showed me the greasewood, badger bush, and club moss and pointed out the two species of cactus—the prickly pear and the pincushion—and much later I learned from a rancher's wife (herself a rancher and also a poet) that if you had the patience to gather the berries, you could make cactus-berry jelly. I taught myself a few: the many types of cinquefoil and sage, and milkweed, and the Canada thistle with its purple flower that a saddle horse—"Watch this," Peter said—would clip tidily off with its bared teeth, never touching a barb. I longed to see a field of wild prairie lilies as I had in my childhood in the north, but I never have, not even a single flower growing wild in the grass.

Because we had a hay farm, I learned to identify a number of grasses—timothy, bromegrass, foxtail—and legumes—clover, alfalfa—which I saw every day, some of which were imported species, crested wheat grass, Russian wild rye, and many of which, like reed canary grass, were very beautiful. I attended three day-long range schools with Peter, one in the Bears Paw Mountains of Montana, but I did so chiefly for the adventure and to spend an entire day on the prairie instead of only a few hours. At these schools I learned to identify death camas when I saw it, and a few of the many native species of grass—needle-and-thread grass, June grass, blue grama, or buffalo grass—and a forb or two.

Other seasons brought different pleasures. All one snowy winter I walked a mile down the riverbed every morning with the dog trotting ahead, flushing out cattle from the banks or far back around the last curve where the fenceline crossed and stopped them, then chasing them up to the feed-grounds where Peter and his hired man were throwing out hay, grain bales, and grain itself. For two winters the snow was so deep that it muffled sound so that the cattle which had sought shelter in these snug places couldn't hear the tractor and didn't come out for feed. Or sometimes, looking back, I think Peter came and got me each morning to make that walk out of understanding that I needed to feel useful, a part of the operation, and that if I spent all of each day inside that tiny log house I would soon be "bushed," develop cabin fever, be impossible to live with—that I might leave.

I remember those walks each morning as among the best of my life. I would head down the riverbed, following in the tracks of the cattle where the snow was too deep to walk comfortably in. The banks of the river are high and steep, and the winds had pushed the snow into deep banks that overhung the edges of the cliffsides in fat lips of snow that looked like waves on the ocean and from which long icicles sometimes hung. Looking up from the snowy riverbed, I saw white walls of snow and then the snowy billows and beyond them the brilliant sky. I saw the places where partridges snuggled up for the night to keep warm and followed the tracks of coyotes and foxes and animals whose tracks I didn't recognize. I was picking up knowledge, hardly even noticing that was what I was doing. Running to cut off a cow, I fell headlong in the snow and, with no one watching me, lay there laughing, blinking up at the sky, losing myself in its blue depths.

For most people the worse the weather is, the more likely they are to stay indoors; not so for old-fashioned ranchers—for them the worse the weather, the more likely the rancher is to be out in it, in the midst of blizzards searching for cattle out on the prairie and chasing them down into the shelter of deep coulees, or home to the windbreaks and corrals. On such days I went along with Peter and learned again that the human limits of endurance are much greater than day-to-day life has us believe; that is, I became less afraid of the weather at the same time as I became a good deal more respectful of it.

One of the first Christmas gifts Peter gave me was a pair of cross-country skis, and as long as there was enough snow, which there usually isn't in this desert country, I'd be out on the prairie in the winter, too, skiing. I began to take my skis and go out into the hills during storms, having discovered that I liked storms for the way they changed the appearance of familiar places and for the sense of mystery they brought to them.

Memories of my childhood came back to me: playing in the bush with my friends, with my sisters and cousins in our grand-mother's garden, skating on frozen sloughs in winter till the pain from the cold became so bad even we kids couldn't stand it any-more and went home, the winter we had built a snow fort that lasted for months as we added on and made it more and more substantial so that it stood well into spring. I felt like a child again, had fleeting moments when I remembered how wonder-ful the world itself had once seemed, and how it was to be cared for, worry-free, and living in the body again and not just the mind.

And I was recreating myself as a writer. I not only was medi-tative by nature, this having been developed in me as the result of being an extremely shy and retiring child in a big family, I had also developed in me the seeds of the observer. It was a lucky thing, although I'd never have admitted it then, to have arrived a stranger in a strange land, when I was no longer young, with a touch of the observer's cold eye already in my makeup.

I found myself observing the very people with whom I seemed to have so little in common. I saw the people of my new community as different from those of the rest of the province, and I was surprised to discover that they themselves seemed to define themselves as different, although nobody ever explicitly said so, in that they often had closer links both in terms of lifestyle and in family ties to Alberta and to Montana than they did to Saskatchewan. Many of the families had begun as Americans and had close relatives on the farms and ranches over the border and in Alberta, and when young people went off to higher education or trade schools or to jobs, when I first came here, they were much more likely to go to Alberta than to Saskatoon or even Regina. As a group they seemed to me often to think more like western Americans or like Albertans, with that essentially conservative, independent cast of mind, than they did like the good-old-Tommy-Douglas-prairie-socialist school of thought to which I belonged and which had always seemed to me to define Saskatchewan.

I soon discovered, in my attempt to tell the story of these people and this place, that my fund of facts, of precise knowledge, was inadequate to the task I'd set myself. Each story, each book, each play would become an exercise in information gathering. When Peter couldn't answer my questions I turned to books. Peter took me to meet old people, old men who'd pioneered in the area, and I listened to their stories and made notes, and where it was possible, which was practically never, I tried to match their memories to the scant written history I could find.

I carried a notebook everywhere. Chasing cows home on bitter winter days, I'd stop the truck, get out, draw a little diagram of the way an animal had pushed away the snow from a sage bush, write a description of the bush and the snow and the droppings the animal had left, the colours, the place where the sun was in the sky on that day at that time and how the cattle looked. I wrote the last few pages of *The Gates of the Sun* sitting on a straw bale in the back of the pickup in a neighbour's field while I waited for Peter to finish baling the straw, pausing in my scribbling only to ask questions of Peter and the neighbour, when they stopped for coffee, about what was a native species, whether bird, animal, or plant, and what wasn't. It constantly amazed me how much the men knew.

With every story and every book I was forced to search out new information. My fund of information, of facts, obtained in all these ways—my own observations, Peter's answers to my incessant questions, the stories of old people, books—was growing. Without intending to or even really wanting to, I was becoming knowledgeable about the history of the area and its plant and animal life. Although I will never know all there is to know—Peter still knows a thousand times more than I do—having begun by being transported by its beauty, and then being overwhelmed by my sense of loneliness and purposelessness, I was at last starting to feel at home in the terrain, at home in the landscape. Of course, I didn't see this as it was happening, but by learning to name things in my new environment, by discovering the scheme of the place and the way the parts fit together, I was making them my own, and by this I was slowly healing myself.

Years later when I was the expert instead of the neophyte, a friend and I were out walking in the rain. In this semiarid country where rain is rare and precious, walking in it is exhilarating, imbued even with a touch of magic. We came to a place where a pair of great horned owls sat watching us, and as my friend went closer to see them better, I sat in the grass in my leaky boots and a borrowed yellow rain jacket which came to my knees, not minding the wet, looking out over the misty fields, noticing how everything smelled different because of the moisture, how colours had changed and intensified.

I thought of how my friend and I had moved over the wet

ground, where we had gone and not gone, what we had found ourselves doing, and suddenly I realized that it was the land—Nature—that had guided our steps, made our choices for us, and not the other way around. That is, because we were friends and rambling in the countryside for the pleasure of each other's company and for the pleasure of being out-of-doors, having no set plan or goal, we had gone where the shape of the land had suggested itself to us; we had done what the land had made available to us. If it was too muddy or wet in one place, we went somewhere else; if a hill was too steep, we went around; there was no way to cross the river without swimming and it was too cold to swim, so we followed its course instead and sat on its bank.

I thought, then said, "This land makes Crees of us all." By this, I meant that it appeared to me that the Crees, for example, developed the culture they developed because it was the best fit between themselves and the land. And it was the *land* that taught them that. They adapted to the land, and not the other way around as we Europeans so stupidly did, trying to force this arid western land to be, as government propaganda had for seventy-five years and more put it, "the breadbasket of the world."

I began to think about the ways in which land affects the individual, or at least this particular landscape, the Great Plains of North America. I began to see that in our human arrogance we assume we can affect the land but it can't affect us—except in practical ways: hurricanes, floods, drought—when there are plenty of ways we might find that the land—Nature—is affecting us without our being aware of it. In considering the differences between Peter and myself, I had not imagined or considered the possibility that he had been shaped by the land, by Nature, that in subtle ways we've never identified nor even really talked about, his psyche itself had been shaped by Nature not merely by *his* observations of it but by its subtle, never described or even consciously realized, influence on *him*.

The Great Plains landscape is an elemental one. There is little natural water in the form of lakes or rivers or even ponds, no forests, no mountains—just miles and miles of land and a sky across which weather visibly, majestically passes. One winter visitor to this place said it reminded him of the high Arctic where he had once lived, and several others, Wallace Stegner included, spoke of the plains of Africa. The landscape is so huge that our imaginations can't contain it or outstrip it, and the climate is concomitantly arbitrary and severe.

It is geology stripped bare, leaving behind only a vast sky and land stretched out in long, sweeping lines that blend into the distant horizon with a line that is sometimes so clear and sharp it is surreal, and sometimes exists at the edge of metaphysics, oscillating in heat waves or, summer or winter, blending into mirages and the realm of dreams and visions which wavers just the other side of the horizon. The Great Plains are a land for visionaries, they induce visions, they are themselves visions, the line between fact and dream is so blurred. What other landscape around the world produces the mystic psyche so powerfully? Sky and land, that is all, and grass, and what Nature leaves bare the human psyche fills.

It was not until I moved into the country to live that my significant dreaming really began. I did not think about this fact, but if I had, I am sure I would have explained it as a by-product of the radical change in my way of life. Eventually it was suggested to me by an eminent western Canadian writer in whom I had confided that perhaps living in this ancient, skeletal landscape had brought on these dreams. At the time I reserved judgement, but a few years later, in another context, another western Canadian writer told me how she had, after years of living in the city where she didn't believe she had dreamt at all, moved out into the country and suddenly began having vivid, meaningful dreams. She attributed these to the influence of the landscape in which she now made her home.

In the context of these remarks it seems to me very significant that dreams have always held an important place in Aboriginal cultures of the Great Plains of North America, as they have in many other such cultures around the world. Aboriginal people take the content of their dreams as simply another source of information about the world, a guide for action, and as prophecy, either in their individual lives or as directives to their communities. In these cultures it is considered extremely foolish, a great insult, even a sin, to ignore an important dream.

Prophetic dreams are accepted at face value and are used as a basis for action. A South Dakota writer living near Rapid City told me that a few years ago Chief Crazy Horse—whose name I'm told should more accurately be translated as "Enchanted Horse," or "Vision Horse"—appeared in dreams to the elders of his nation to warn them about an imminent flood on a branch of the Cheyenne River. The flood did occur and it killed more than a hundred of his people who lived along its banks. Hugh Brody, in *Maps and Dreams*, describes a hunting culture, the Beaver Indians of northeastern British Columbia, where the best hunters are guided by dreams to their kill; the very best hunter-dreamers have even dreamt the way to heaven and then, awaking, have drawn the map.

Although I sometimes go for long stretches without any dreams that seem important to me, a few years ago I began to have the occasional prophetic dream myself. I dreamt the San Francisco earthquake a couple of weeks before it happened. Since I'd never been to San Francisco, I thought the city in the dream was Vancouver and the broken bridge, the Lions Gate. Although it was a powerful enough dream to tell people about it, I certainly never took it as prophecy until I saw the broken span of the bridge on television. It was identical to the one in my dream, where it had been the main icon. I dreamt of the Japanese airplane that lost its rudder and, after weaving drunkenly through the air for half an hour, crashed into a mountain. I was in bed dreaming it as it was happening. When I got up the first thing Peter did was to tell me about this terrible event that had just happened in Japan. I even dreamt of the death of one of the Russian Communist leaders a few days before he died. It may be that I've had more prophetic dreams than I know but simply haven't remembered. Actually I think this may be true of everyone, but most people don't record their dreams as I usually do, and so forget them.

I have described the dream I had in which a giant eagle and a giant owl appeared to me. It became for me a life-dream, a significant dream that launched me on a journey through comparative religion, mythology, the study of dreams, psychoanalysis, and finally into the study of the nature of the female. At an archetypal level, it is a dream about masculine power, symbolized by the soaring eagle, and feminine power, symbolized by the owl standing near me on the ground. In beauty and power they are exactly equal, but I, a woman, had spent my life to this point following the eagle—that is, accepting masculine interpretations of life in general and, of my own life, accepting masculine goals and taking masculine desires for my own—instead of cleaving to the owl, searching out and coming to terms with my own feminine soul.

My search for understanding of the dream led me into and through my novel *Luna*—the story of the lives of contemporary ranch and farm women and how they live, feel about, and understand their rural, agricultural, traditional lives—and from there into my short story collection *Fever*, a much more personal and urbanized study of the same issues. It's been a good dozen years since I had that dream and I still run across further ways to interpret it. Not only have I accepted it as guidance in the direction my life has taken, it is, to a degree, the foundation on which I have built the rest of my life.

I think that significant dreaming is one way in which Nature influences and changes the individual, developing in her/him an awareness of Nature as more than mere locale, or a setting, a context, as more than beauty, as more than something that is merely Other.

It was in Joseph Campbell's *Primitive Mythology* that I first heard of Aboriginal dreamtime, and, not long after, in a much more firsthand and compelling way in *The Lost World of the Kalahari* by Laurens van der Post. All peoples of the earth have creation stories of one kind or another. The stories of pre-scientific peoples tell variously of a time when the world was in the process of being created along with the creatures on it. This was a timeless time, a time before time, when animals, plants, and people could become one another and the formations of the earth were taking shape. It is called, in mythologies around the world, dreamtime, and out of it spring stories and legends about archetypal creatures, sometimes gods, whose manifestations remain now in the fallen time.

It seems, too, that on some level this timeless time still exists in another realm, and those people peculiarly blessed—including, but never exclusively, shamans—may still go there. In this realm many strange things can happen: animals can converse with humans and vice versa; the dead may appear and speak, or creatures from the dreamtime thought by some of us to be merely metaphoric. The earth becomes more beautiful, approaches, even achieves, perfection, and everything in it and on it is imbued with meaning. And especially the sense of the ticking of time vanishes.

I believe that since Aboriginal people around the world have nontechnological cultures and live in and by Nature—or at least, once did when their cultures were developing—and these cultures had developed the concept of dreamtime and took dreaming very seriously whether in New Zealand, Australia, the Kalahari Desert of Africa, or the Great Plains of North America, that surely it was Nature which, whether with will and intention or not, taught, allowed, gave them dreams as an instrument of knowledge.

I began to see from my own experience living in it that the land and the wild creatures who live in it and on it, and the turning of the earth, the rising and setting of the sun and the moon, and the constant passing of weather across its surface—that is,

Nature—influenced rural people to make them what they are, more than even they knew.

Close proximity to a natural environment—being in Nature—alters all of us in ways which remain pretty much unexplored, even undescribed in our culture. I am suggesting that these ways in which such a closeness affects us, from dreams to more subtle and less describable phenomena, are real, and that we should stop thinking, with our inflated human egos, that all the influence is the other way around. We might try to shift our thinking in this direction so that we stop blithely improving the natural world around us, and begin to learn, as Aboriginal people have, what Nature in her subtle but powerful manner has to teach us about how to live.

More and more I am coming to believe that our alienation from the natural world is at root of much that has gone so wrong in the modern world, and that if Nature has anything to teach us at all, her first lesson is in humility.

DAVID F. PELLY

How Inuit Find Their Way
in the Trackless Arctic

DAVID F. PELLY has spent considerable time
living in the Canadian Arctic. Pelly is the author of
Thelon: A River Sanctuary. His essay "How Inuit Find
Their Way in the Trackless Arctic" appeared
in *Canadian Geographic* in 1991.

BEFORE THE STORM BEGAN, I did not really know Tulurialik at
all. It was my first winter trip "out on the land," as the Inuit say.
Tulurialik planned to check his trapline one last time before the
season ended and invited me to join him. Travelling by snowmobile over the trackless tundra, I marvelled as time after time
he pulled up beside an insignificant hump in the snow and
thrust his snowknife beneath the crust to exhume a steel foxtrap.
I was witnessing, for the first time, two amazing processes: an
Inuk's navigation over great distances of seemingly featureless
terrain and the acute visual perception that enabled him to recognize a precise spot on the snow.

Those observations were still whirling around in my head
four days later, as we sat in our igloo patiently waiting out the
blizzard that had begun late on that first day. For four days the

wind blew fiercely and swirling snow obscured visibility beyond a few metres. Confined to our tiny igloo, Tulurialik and I
became good friends. Finally, sensing that we had both been
cooped up long enough, he suggested that we "go outside for
some fresh air."

We emerged to face a raging blizzard. I took four steps into
the wind, stopped, and turned to look back. Already Tulurialik
and the igloo were lost to sight. I retraced my steps downwind
and found him calmly brushing accumulated snow from the
snowmobile. I was certain of one thing: if he was going somewhere on that machine, I was going with him. We got on and
tore away across the bumpy ridges of windswept snow. Without
the clue of gravity, it would have been impossible to tell which
way was up in the boil of wind and snow that surrounded us.
Five minutes later, Tulurialik stopped our snowmobile, dis-
mounted, and began walking into the storm. I followed hurriedly. When he halted, he turned to inform me that we were
standing on the island where his wife was born fifty years ago.
Though I believed him, I had no way of identifying the spot as
any different from the surrounding river.

On the return trip to our igloo Tulurialik again sped across
the frozen river through whirling snow, this time for at least ten
minutes before stopping. Even I sensed that we had missed the
igloo. Tulurialik, however, was unperturbed. He joked about
"being lost"—a state he understood in my terms but which was
not real for him. He remained confident, driving on farther in
the same straight line. In a few minutes, he stopped and pointed
at a bare tip of rock protruding from the snow. "I remember that
rock," he assured me. Then he wheeled the snowmobile around
and headed back at an acute angle to our last course. I did not

see our igloo emerge from the whiteout until we came to rest beside it.

At the time, I had little idea of the extraordinary navigational technique I was witnessing. In fact, I was just happy to be inside again, sitting on the comfortable bed of caribou skins, waiting for some water to boil. As we sipped our hot tea, Tulurialik explained that he had kept going in a straight line even after we were "lost" because he was confident he would encounter some familiar landmark to give him his bearings. He had indeed noticed that small protruding rock as we passed it four days earlier, and he remembered it. If not the rock, there would have been something else. As he offered all this matter-of-factly, I realized that the process was as natural to him as the way I find a parking place in downtown Toronto is to me.

When we missed the igloo on the first pass, my immediate reaction was to turn back. His was different. It was some while before I understood why. Like most wilderness travellers, I carry a map and remain conscious of my location. I view the land around as an area, for the moment as *my area*. An Inuk travels differently. He naturally adopts a linear approach, rather than an areal one. To him it is a linear world.

Dr. Robert Rundstrom, a geographer who has studied Inuit spatial concepts, ventured an explanation. "Given the nature of the Barren Grounds terrain, linear conceptualization of the territory may be the easiest way to bring a sense of order to an otherwise chaotic landscape, an order which allows human beings to think and act as a successful part of that landscape."

The Inuit are right, of course. If you could rise up above the Barrens and look down, you would see a landscape full of lines —rivers, eskers, and caribou paths—all running with some regularity in a pattern across the tundra. To get this linear view, areal thinkers have to detach themselves from the landscape. Inuit instinctively adopt this perspective at ground level, with themselves in it. It is a key to their survival.

It follows that a hunter would not seek his prey by going back and forth over an area, but rather by travelling along a line, searching for another line—tracks—that will lead him to his object. Similarly, if "lost," the linear thinker would logically travel in a straight line until he intersects evidence of another, more familiar, line. In a linear world, it is inevitable that he will, in time, be rewarded.

Tulurialik was. He found a path leading to our igloo. To me it was confoundingly impressive (areal thinker that I am). To him it was entirely logical, though he followed this instinct without so much as a moment's thought. That explains his actions, but there remains his recognition of the telltale rock.

It is not surprising that Inuit exhibit superior visual acuity. They are traditional hunters, after all, dependent on an ability to find their prey in a vast landscape. Only a few decades ago, the observation and retention of information about the land and its animals was fundamental to survival. From a young age, Inuit are encouraged by their elders to watch the land around them. Tulurialik was raised as a hunter. Now, as he approaches fifty, it remains his central role in life.

All these instincts are at work as an Inuk navigates his way across the open spaces of the Arctic. Much of it appears desolate and empty, without features that catch the eye. Often it rolls on, mile after mile, toward a distant horizon where, at times, the sky is indistinguishable from the snow-covered land. There is no perspective. Navigation is not easy. But, for the Inuk, there are clues.

Vilhjálmur Stefánsson, the renowned arctic explorer who perhaps experienced more of Inuit life than any white man before him, described the arctic sky. "When clouds of a uniform colour hang low there is reflected in them a map of the earth below them. Snow-free land and open water are shown in black on the clouds; the pure white sea ice appears in white, and land covered with snow soiled by blown sand (and tiny pieces of plant matter) is reflected darker than the sea but lighter than snowless land. This sky map is of great use to sledge travellers always."

As is the wind. It blows nearly all the time. As the prevailing wind sweeps across the frozen, flat expanse of sea or tundra, it carves out a pattern in the ice-crusted snow. The *sastrugi*, small ridges of hard snow running parallel to the prevailing winds, are more reliable than a compass needle for the traveller seeking direction. In severe weather, maintaining the relative alignment of the *sastrugi* to the line of travel is one of the few resources left to a hunter unable to see more than a few metres in front of him.

Directional navigation is one thing, but without maps, there remains a more basic problem—knowing the right way to go in the first place. "Before I left on my first time to go from Arvilikyoak (Pelly Bay) to Ukhuktuk (Gjoa Haven), I went to my father-in-law," explained Okpik, now a veteran hunter in that coastal region near Boothia Peninsula. At the time Okpik was a young man who had never before ventured along the coast to the west. His father-in-law sat down and outlined the 300-kilometre route to him, in minute detail, without using a map. He described every landmark along the way with its name and story. To this day, Okpik knows that route, though he knows it as a line, a trail.

Okpik remembers his route in a litany of place names, each one descriptive. A map of the Northwest Territories indicating all the traditional place names would be crowded. In the mind of a hunter contemplating a route, the place names are focal points. The names themselves suggest the nature of the terrain, and the relation of the place to its surroundings. The community of Baker Lake, that name styled after an Englishman with little significance for the local people, is known by the Inuit as Qamanituaq, "where the river widens into a lake," which describes exactly its location. Place names, to a large extent, define a trail.

During a 500-kilometre trip by dogsled along the Arctic coast, I asked Okpik to draw me a map of where we were going. He took my blank sheet of paper and began by placing on it several large dots. Each one, it became apparent, represented for him a specific location along the trail, and each one had a place name. Once all his dots were assembled in what seemed to him to be the correct relative positions, he connected them with a line, and handed me the completed map. No landmarks off the route were, apparently, of any consequence. The map was route-oriented, drawn to illustrate our trail rather than all his geographical knowledge of the area.

This is not to suggest inaccuracy. Mapping in the Inuit way serves its purpose effectively, insofar as it provides information useful for navigation. Several of the early explorers' accounts attest to that.

In July 1822, during his explorations along the coast of Melville Peninsula in search of the Northwest Passage, William E.

Parry wrote: "I cannot delay any longer to remark how valuable the geographical information received from the Esquimaux had now proved to us." At least some of that information came from a woman named Iligliuk. Subsequent explorers became more and more dependent for their success upon native knowledge of the land.

Joseph B. Tyrrell, in 1894, was the first white man to descend the Kazan River into the central Barrens. He employed native guides, either Chipewyan or Inuit, all the way. On August 26, with the season advancing quickly toward winter, he made a decision to alter his plans based on information given him by local Inuit. He recorded the event in his journal:

> This morning we brought the rest of the things over the portage, and as we were about to start a (son) of Pasamut came up from the Eskimos just below us, and drew a map of the river for us showing that it ran into Chesterfield Inlet. This at once decided us not to go on, as we would have no chance of getting to Churchill in open water that way. But Mr. Ferguson and I went down in a light canoe to the Eskimo camp and then got Pasamut to draw us a map of the country. We found that the river runs down into Chesterfield Inlet, but there is a route by a portage out of this river into another which flows into the Bay opposite Sea Horse (Walrus) Island. We decided to try that.

In all there are extant about a hundred Inuit maps drawn for European explorers. The praise for their accuracy, though widespread, was not universal. There is one map collected during the search for Franklin which, though it claims to depict the coast east of Point Barrow, is nothing like the actual landform. Skill level varied, but more often than not, the explorers relied heavily on their Inuit cartographers. Knud Rasmussen, leader of the 1921–24 Fifth Thule Expedition, navigated nearly 300 kilometres up the Kazan Valley from Baker Lake to Yathkyed Lake using a map made by Pukerluk. In his account of the trip, Rasmussen describes the process:

> These two men (Pukerluk and Kijokut) drew a large number of maps for me and, despite the fact that they were quite unaccustomed to the use of pencil and paper, it was astonishing to see their ability to reproduce the peculiarities of the landscape in a few strokes.

Today's documentary evidence of Inuit mapping is composed entirely of maps drawn for explorers, but that should not suggest that Inuit never drew maps for themselves. They did, but usually in sand or snow. Often I have travelled with Inuit who carry no map. They may have had one drawn for them before leaving, but it was not intended for navigation along the trail. The user simply absorbed the information, to be recalled in his mind as he travelled, a task made easier by the use of descriptive place names.

There is no record of pre-20th-century Inuit maps drawn on animal skins. Preservation was not the priority; a transfer of information was. The act, not the product, was important. Perhaps nothing demonstrates this so profoundly as the image of an old Greenland Eskimo, Uutaaq, tracing routes with his finger in the air while describing, years later, his attempts to reach the Pole with Robert Peary in 1909. No map could be less permanent.

Inuit maps are a logical extension of their culture. Travel was inborn to these erstwhile nomadic hunters, and such travel implied far-ranging knowledge of the land. Both the manner and the quality of mapping suit a people who have lived intimately with the land around them. The same could be said of Inuit art as we know it today. Both echo the environment with a degree of precision that suggests unusual sensitivity. As geographer Robert Rundstrom points out, "The persistence and flourishing of Inuit culture in the arctic environment was assisted by development of extraordinary abilities to mime aspects of that environment." He cites the way Inuit hunters can adopt the posture and movements of their prey, both caribou and seal. In the days before rifles, such skills were fundamental to success. The ability to mimic, whether by lying on the ice like a seal or by drawing landforms in the snow, was an essential survival skill.

The environment and the Inuit relationship to it are both reflected in the maps collected by explorers. In most, the scale varies from one area to another. One map drawn by Pukerluk shows the area of concern—the valley from Baker Lake upstream to Yathkyed Lake—disproportionately larger than other features included in the drawing. This may be simply because of space available on the paper, but it is more likely a result of other factors. Pukerluk must have known that territory better than any other. He may have chosen to emphasize it for purposes of navigational ease. Yathkyed Lake was the destination, and it may therefore have been assigned appropriate prominence. In any case, he felt no compulsion to maintain a consistent scale.

Scale variations may also stem from the inconsistent nature of the terrain. Some areas take longer to traverse than others, and this greater time and energy may be reflected in a larger representation of space on a map image. Traditionally, for Inuit, travel was not measured in units of distance, such as miles or kilometres. A journey was described as so many "sleeps." That has not changed a great deal. As we set out on our dogsled trip along the Arctic coast, Okpik was unable to tell me how many kilometres we would travel. But he was quite happy discussing our approximate destination for each day, given agreeable weather.

Surrounded by the hills of Boothia Peninsula, Okpik directed his dogs to take us into a sinuous valley that climbed slowly higher and higher. The dogs twisted and turned and pulled until finally we were on top of a ridge. Okpik stood up high, looking for one of the landmarks that had been described to him. He declined my offer of the topographical map in my knapsack. He had a mental map in his head, essentially a list of landmarks. He pointed along the coast. When the landmarks no longer fit his mental image he admitted confusion, but still he continued looking for new clues. Finally he understood where he was, and reversed direction to regain the proper trail. That evening we built our igloo exactly where he had predicted we would be. We had accomplished the day's journey; the number of kilometres and the exact route were not important.

To the Inuit traveller, time is a fundamental dimension of distance; for example, what is two days' travel in winter may take a week in summer. Distance is also an amalgam of many other variables: weather, snow conditions, hunting success, terrain, etc. This complexity is depicted in the maps, and might be mistaken for inconsistency. In fact, it is reality. Reality in mapping, I have learned from Inuit travelling companions, is more than a geometric interpretation of the land. That reality, in their world, embraces both space and time.

Tavalok is a young man, nearly twenty, living on King William Island. He is just beginning to apply his instincts, his power of visual acuity, his ability to map in his mind the landscape through which he travels. I watched once as he looked out across his land. At his feet were the lines of *sastrugi* that helped to guide us there. In the distance beyond him was an infinity of whiteness, a combination of white sky and white land that stretched forever. He must have been imagining the trail that we would follow.

Tavalok spoke to me of plans for a hunt. "I will go across the sea," he said, pointing roughly south toward the mainland, "to the place where there are always caribou." He could dream about these hunting places, and about the trails that lead to them. But they remained distinct points, never to be joined in a continuum that would define the area or even the coastline across the sea from his home.

He knew in his mind the place where he would go. It existed at the end of a trail leading out from his base. He would carry no map. He knew the way, even though the frozen sea looked featureless to me. Similarly, Tavalok knows other places, at the ends of other trails, where he might go on other trips. They exist on his mental map of the space and time that define his reality.

CHRIS CZAJKOWSKI

Bear Facts #1

CHRIS CZAJKOWSKI has carved out a unique niche
for herself, building a cabin at Nimpo Lake in British Columbia's
remote Coast Mountains and writing three books about her
experiences living in the bush. Her earlier books are *Cabin at
Singing River: Building a House in the Wilderness* and *Diary of a
Wilderness Dweller*. "Bear Facts #1" is from Czajkowski's most
recent book, *Nuk Tessli: The Life of a Wilderness Dweller*.

Bears and humans have never gotten along very well . . .
— BEN GADD, *Handbook of the Canadian Rockies*

THE FIRST TIME the bear broke into my cabin was in the spring
of 1991. I had been outside since the beginning of April, tree-
planting in the East Kootenays, that section of British Columbia
that separates Alberta from Montana. Spectacular scenery there,
too, if you could ignore the hideous clear-cuts which overran
much of the terrain. But the Rockies are a very different range to
my own granite Coast Mountains with their steep, forested
plunges to the sea.

When I left my truck at the end of the logging road, prior to
hiking back to my cabin, it was already the second half of June.

At Nimpo Lake, twenty-six air miles north, the ice had gone out six weeks before; it had likely left my place three or four weeks later. There would be a lot of snow still in the alpine areas, and the creeks and rivers would be raging.

Usually I am alone for this first spring hike over the mountains, but this time another hiker was tagging along. An avid canoeist, he had done very little backpacking but was amply fit enough to revel in the sweeping views and bursts of early flowers that coloured the two long days of our trip. It was an exhilarating time: rich, blue spring sky; blinding white snow; the newly naked tundra a roar of snowmelt. As we descended through the upper reaches of the forest to my lake the west wind flexed his muscles and tossed spurts of foam over the long ultramarine swells of the water. It would not have been wise to cross directly to the cabins in these conditions, so we opted for the long way round, down to the foot of the lake behind Crescent Island where the water would be calm and we could avoid going broadside to the waves. Along the main body of the lake, the big swells pushed us from behind, slewing the stern of the little boat with each thrust. White horses pawed the swells alongside and the water sang and hissed with the wind. The lagoon behind the island was smooth enough to have only a riffle marring the surface, but at its end we had to swing back into the wind and paddle like souls demented, knees braced wide, until we slid into the last few yards of shelter beside the wharf.

And thus the first look at the cabin since April. The roof was still on and the chimney still snug in the wire bracing I had rigged up after the snow had swept it to the ground one year. Everything seemed orderly and in place.

The door is enclosed by a porch around the end furthest from the wharf, where it is most sheltered from the west wind and the drifting winter snow. The first intimation that something might be amiss was not evident until we rounded the corner. Skis and poles were tossed about the porch and several boxes of odds and ends like string and cans (which *might* be useful one day) had been raked from their shelves. Nothing, however, seemed seriously out of place—there is always a mess of some sort to deal with when I come home in the spring—and it could well have been the work of squirrels, who lose no time in appropriating the place when I am gone. But squirrels could not have made the deep, V-shaped groove next to the homemade wooden bolt that fastened the door. The bolt was still wired in place; I slid it across and swung the door open.

Two of the cabin's windows face west. They are out of sight from any of the angles a human might use to approach the cabin, but that was the way the bear had come in. Both shutters were off, the screens were ripped, and one of the windows had disintegrated into a powdering of glass dust and slivers. Bedding, books, kitchenware, and furnishings were tossed and tangled like a garbage dump. My feet crunched on cutlery, splintered wood, and broken glass. Wind swirled papers, pine needles, and shrivelled alder leaves.

I'd had firsthand experience of a couple of other bear breakins during the thirteen years I have lived in the wilderness and had been dutifully impressed with not only the destructive power of these animals but also their purposefulness in making an entry. Once they get the idea they want to be inside, there is very little that will stop them. So I had resigned myself to this probability and had tried to design my cabins accordingly. I'd heard of such strategies as making door and window mats of beds of nails; but my cabins had a lot more windows than the average wilderness shelter and the ground beneath them was very rocky and uneven and would have required a complicated structure to hold the boards. They would also have looked very ugly. Shutters were another suggestion, and in fact the west windows had possessed them; not, however, against the vagaries of animals but to protect the glass from snow that piles up on that side. The shutters worked well enough for their purpose, but their attachment was flimsy and it was this that Mr. Bear had casually swiped away. I could have tried spiking their seating and the surrounds of the windows with a barrage of outward-pointing nails, but to make that kind of structure strong enough, it would have to be permanent, and I simply did not want to live in a place bristling with hardware like a porcupine with a Rambo fixation.

The attic, therefore, had been designed to store food and breakables—not that I could hope to build the top of the cabin any more solidly than the bottom, but, I reasoned, to break in upstairs, a bear would have to climb the walls and hang on with at least three limbs and so would have a lot less agility and power at his disposal. The downstairs door had been lightly constructed in the hopes that it would present the easiest target for a break-in, for that would be the simplest to repair. The windows were the next simplest (they would not be difficult to mend although the replacement of glass posed logistical problems); the walls and roof would be the hardest to fix.

But I had not been smart enough. I had made the mistake of leaving flour on the ground floor. Experience had shown me bears were drawn primarily to strongly aromatic items: rotting fish, meat both fresh and old, garbage, even gas. But flour?

Behind the stove had been two stone crocks and a white plastic bucket with a close-fitting lid, the kind you acquire if you have friends in the restaurant business. Whole-wheat flour had been packed into the larger crock; white in the smaller one; and rye flour in the bucket. I had deemed them too heavy to lug upstairs, and in any case had presumed them to be safe.

The bear, however, had been delighted. Every container had been licked squeaky clean. The five-gallon crock still stood behind the stove where I had left it, but the smaller one, its opening presumably too small for the bear to get his nose into, had been packed out through the broken window and dropped on a rock. Both halves were as sparklingly immaculate as a wine glass in a dishwasher advertisement. The lid of the bucket had been pried loose but oddly enough without the tiniest scratch, even though I always had found it a real chore to get off. And this despite the fact that most of the pots and metal containers under the kitchen bench had been gouged and pierced; some of the lighter vessels were as crushed as discarded chocolate wrappers. Bears are renowned for their strength and powers of destruction, but I have noticed before how they also have a great deal of delicacy and finesse when they wish.

The floorboards covering the root cellar had been tossed aside, as had the layer of sheep fleeces laid over the contents to protect them from freezing. (It had still been full winter when I had left.) Interestingly, although the bear had stirred the potatoes, carrots, jars, and cans into a jumbled heap, he had not attempted to take a bite out of anything, which was very fortunate: if he had broached a can of fruit, everything would have been ravaged. Among the mess there was, however, another manifestation of the bear's dexterity.

It is not a very convenient root cellar, being simply a hole under the floor. It protects the food from the cold well enough, but access is only from the top and to haul anything out I must lie on my stomach and reach down. I was pawing about among the root vegetables and cans and fleece in an effort to survey the damage when my hand touched a clammy, flaccid, finger-length object which, when unearthed, appeared to be covered in a matted grey pelt. *Dead mouse!* said my brain and I dropped it at once. There were more of them, peeping among the debris. They were not mice at all—they were dill pickles gone mouldy. Somehow the hear had unscrewed the lid of the jar and the pickles had been released to make their contribution to the root cellar's ecology.

A few ornaments were broken and books chewed (in particular a large thesaurus which had impressive tooth holes an inch deep near its spine), but thankfully the stove and chimney were intact, so I did not have soot to add to the disaster as had once happened in another cabin I'd been tenanting. The attic was inviolate, so most of my food was untouched; the only real damage had been to the window.

The bear had obviously not been quite sure what to make of this strange, insubstantial barrier. If he was the same animal who had repeatedly broken into the trap cabins in the area, glass was something he would not have experienced, as their small openings had been covered with plastic film when in use and metal from flattened tin cans or heavy slabs of wood bristling with spikes when the trapping season had ended. (Not that this had stopped Mr. Bear: he had torn the metal coverings like paper and split and splintered thick limbs like matchwood, had even, on one occasion, ripped apart a wall in his efforts to get inside.

And for what? A crunch or two at a coffee can whose contents he didn't like—the brown grains had simply spilled through the holes—and an unproductive lick at a frypan which might have had the remnants of a smell. Bears, it would appear, develop their own brand of cabin fever.)

All my windows were old and multi-paned, but it was not the feeble dividers which had presented the bear with his challenge. It was the glass which had given him pause. Having watched bears at work, I could imagine him examining the peculiar, cold, hard, invisible barrier, his head swaying back and forth, trying to figure the best way to deal with it. In the end, judging by the spray of glass fragments, the animal must have launched himself through the window with considerable force: shards were showered clear across the room.

Then he had apparently turned his attention to the food, but, appetite satisfied, it was the glass that once more gained his attention. Every single window pane—and there were thirty-eight of them still intact—every single pane had been investigated with a slobbery, floury nose. Every piece of glass was smeared, from corner to corner, with an encrusted film of dried, floury glue.

Well! I would have had to clean the cabin after a three-month absence anyway, and the broken window was a nuisance as it would be some weeks before I would be able to organize new glazing, but otherwise there was not a lot of harm done. The two west windows were the same size and as I liked to look out of the broken one while I sat on the seat, I switched the good one into its space and put builder's plastic over the other. In inclement weather the shutter would have to go back on as well; it would make the back of the cabin a little dark, but at this time of year the days were long and I was not planning on spending a lot of time inside anyway.

The guest cabin was untouched, presumably because no food had been stored there. My client made himself at home while I cleaned up and did not seem worried or put out by the bear's record of achievements. He lived in a rural area in the Kootenays and seemed familiar with nature and much of her machinations, so I gave his indifference little thought. My guiding assignment had finished with our arrival and the client was now going to rent the guest cabin and amuse himself for a while. He was a solitary man who enjoyed his own company, so I asked him how he would feel if I left him alone for a couple of days while I built a bridge along the trail toward the road. It was a job I wanted to do as soon as possible to take advantage of the high water I would need to float the logs to the site. Also, as I expected to spend a lot of time in the water, the hot sunny weather we were having was ideal. The rapturous gleam in the client's eyes was answer enough and, as I also love to be alone—everything seems more intense and tangible then—I had no problem understanding his enthusiasm at seeing the back of me.

I use a variety of routes to travel to Nimpo Lake, but, no matter which way I go, I have to cross at least one river on the way. So far, my preferred summer route involved wading a tributary which was shallow but about a hundred yards wide; even so, during spring runoff the central channel was too deep and slippery to be negotiated safely, especially when carrying a pack. The previous fall I had explored upstream about half a mile from the ford and found a series of islands and stepping stones which spanned almost the whole width of the river with the exception of a single, deep, narrow channel. Prominent rocks that flanked this channel looked as though they might be suitable to hold two foot-logs clear of the water.

With the help of the dogs, I backpacked a small chain saw, gas, axe, come-along, ropes, a roll of heavy-gauge wire, pliers, a few large spikes, and food and camping gear for a couple of days. The river crossing was about two hours' hike away from home and about five hundred feet higher, which meant the forest was even sparser and scrubbier than that around the cabin: it took some time to find trees tall enough to span the gap.

I had moved all the logs for the two cabins with a come-along, so I knew that it could be done, but it was incredibly labour-intensive to fall and trim two trees, winch them inch by inch to the water, then prod and float them across a wide, shallow part of the river to the narrow channel. At the last, the current was a help, but it was also a hindrance as I could no longer stand in the water and the force kept trying to slide the logs where I did not want them to go. With only one winch and one set of ropes (I could not have carried any more) I had to yank at one end of the log, disengage the apparatus and haul it across the river (in a circuitous wade that took me well beyond the reach of the current), link everything up again, and pull at the other end, sometimes only an inch or two, before I had to take everything apart again and haul the equipment back. For most of the two days I was up to my waist in water, but the weather was glorious, and the task, although frustratingly slow, was a challenge for my meagre engineering skills. Once the grunt work was over I quite enjoyed it: I was also very much relishing my first dose of solitude in nearly three months.

It was late morning on the third day when I arrived back

home. As my canoe slid into the quiet stretch of water by the wharf I was a little disconcerted to find the boat that the client had used had been pulled up so sloppily onto the wharf it was teetering on its keel. It was neither overturned nor tied and a gust of wind might easily have toppled it into the water. I would not have expected a man with my client's canoeing experience to leave it that way.

I made both boats secure, tramped along the wooden walkway to the back porch of my cabin, and opened the door.

The bear had been back.

He had used the same hole to gain entry, and as I had so thoughtfully switched windows for him, I now had a second pile of broken glass. This time, however, there seemed to have been no hesitation on the bear's part as to how he should deal with it; an upraised paw swept downward, and all six panes and the divisions that separated them had been reduced to neat heaps of slivers and chunks of putty on both sides of the sill.

The somewhat rickety table I had cobbled together and which had survived the first intrusion lay pretty much in its component parts. There had been no food at all downstairs—but the bear had discovered solar power. Two six-volt batteries for a small photovoltaic system had been flown in the previous winter. They were stored under a bench. The bear had dumped one of them and a brown stain ran across the wide, home-made floorboards and under my bed. A hand-stitched rug my mother had made was bleached and holed in the middle and a couple of brown blotches, distinctly bearpaw-shaped, lay on the floor beside it.

The acid had soaked into some cardboard boxes that had been stuffed under the bed. The bear apparently liked his snacks spiked, for he had packed one of the cartons out of the window and eaten it—very carefully—leaving the contents, mostly unresolved manuscripts, in an undisturbed pile among the rocks. Fortunately, there had been no rain and little wind, or all the papers would have been lost. There seemed to be little other real damage, but the mess, as before, was appalling.

And where, in the meantime, was the client?

The guest cabin is only a stone's throw from my own, but the two are hidden from each other by trees and boulders. I stepped over the rocky trail between them; the cabin looked deserted. There was no smoke coming from the chimney; the door was fastened securely; and the shutters were bolted tight against the windows. I pulled open the door—and there the client sat, crouched by the table in the gloom. He was absolutely petrified.

He had been paddling on the lake for most of the previous day (I could well imagine his euphoria in that perfect summer weather: *This is it! The real wilderness! I am finally here!*) and he had decided to leave the canoe in an inlet a few minutes' walk from home. Halfway along the trail back to the cabin, he met the bear.

He couldn't possibly have known at that point that the bear had broken into my place again, but just seeing the bear caused him to panic. He tore back to the canoe, paddled round to the wharf, hauled the boat out of the water, ran back to his cabin, and locked himself in.

And there he had stayed for eighteen miserable hours.

He had read every book about the wilderness that he could lay his hands on and I don't doubt that there would have been bear stories in all of them. His home was surrounded by brushy ranchland tight up against the Kootenays and he seemed to know his local wildlife quite well, but apparently bears had never been an issue. The evidence of the first break-in fazed him not one bit. This was a secondhand experience; someone else's concern. To him the wilderness was a starry-eyed vision of Disneyland where everything is picture-book perfect and emotions are inspired by violins. Now his ideal was shattered; his golden dream of the wilderness tarnished. For the first time in his existence, he had known real fear. That four-legged, furry denizen of the bush he had met on the trail had been the first bear he had ever actually encountered in his life.

Like many people, he had been in love with the romance of wilderness rather than the wilderness itself. And I certainly cannot deny that romance constitutes a large part of why I am here. Nature is fascinating, beautiful, and uplifting to the soul. It is exciting, exquisite, and miraculous. But it is also dirty, uncomfortable, itchy, and cold, full of disinterested murder and terror, unnecessary cruelty, misery, and waste. To accept the wilderness you have to understand that both sides are valid, both are part of the intricate relationships that give us our water, air, all life-support systems, and sanity. To deny one side of nature is to abrogate the other, and to understand the essence of these natural laws provides insight into our own behaviour as a species. We are part of nature and nature is part of us. To ignore that is to ignore reality, and I am afraid that is what most people do.

JOHN B. THEBERGE

with Mary T. Theberge

Amber Fire

JOHN AND MARY THEBERGE are among the world's
leading authorities on wolves. John and Mary have
collaborated on many articles as well as three books: *Wolves
and Wilderness, Legacy: The Natural History of Toronto,*
and *Kluane: Pinnacle of the Yukon.* "Amber Fire" is excerpted
from the Theberges' most recent work, *Wolf Country:
Eleven Years Tracking the Algonquin Wolves.*

AUGUST 1987. The first of over 150 wolves to oblige us with data,
albeit unwittingly, lay sprawled out full length under a spruce
tree. A light, all-day rain had petered out; the wet bush hung
suspended in early-evening hush. From a distance a hermit
thrush played taps.

The wolf raised her head, struggled to rise, fell back. A few
minutes passed. Phantom-like, a gray jay glided in, perplexed by
the scene, and landed above the wolf. Cocking its head sideways,
the bird uttered a confused-sounding squawk. Again the wolf
lifted her head, this time trying to focus on the sound. Again her
head fell back.

More time passed. We sat as motionless as we could on the mossy ground a few metres away and watched. Then, thirty-five minutes later, the wolf lifted her head for the third time, groggy from the drug, but more alert—she was remembering. She looked for us, found us, our eyes met and locked. She held her gaze for a full minute, two minutes, an eternity. Wolf—human—each searching for meaning in the eyes of the other. Eyes so alike—iris, pupil, cornea, lens, size, musculature, movement. But eyes so different, reflecting two different social orders that began diverging, like two continents drifting apart, hundreds of thousands of years ago. One species possesses great physical prowess—speed and endurance, night vision, a keen sense of smell. The other possesses an unprecedented mental capability.

Burning in those amber wolf eyes was the vital force of wilderness itself, a force that left our eyes some four thousand years ago as human civilization first began to separate man from nature. Locked in neural connections behind those eyes were ecological secrets we no longer remember, shared with the pines who whisper them from ridge to ridge, and the beavers who tell them in their lodges late at night. As a summit predator, the wolf ties species together, binds them into a marvellous functioning whole, provides the ecosystem glue.

Burning in those amber eyes, too, were deep and unsettling questions. They were about the capacity to hate another species, about persecution and population genocide. They asked what kind of future we were creating for wolves and wilderness, indeed for species, ecosystems, the very biosphere itself. They were embarrassing questions; they made us ashamed. They brought tears to our eyes, changed the buoyancy of success into a poignancy of self-recrimination. Did we have to do this, to capture and lay at our feet the very spirit of wildness? We tried to look elsewhere, at the trampled ferns, the open drug kit, the poke stick with syringe attached, but always our eyes came back to the wolf, because we could feel her eyes on us.

We had trapped the wolf in a foothold trap designed for scientific research. In Canada, commercial trappers trap a few thousand wolves every year. Those wolves not already dead from starvation and freezing must look up into the eyes of the trapper, as this wolf did. For them, the look is brief. The trapper puts rifle to wolf forehead and shoots. As a bucket of water douses a campfire, so the amber fire in a wolf's eyes goes out.

It has been said that wolf eyes are mirrors; what different people see in them is simply a reflection of themselves. Could they reflect even more, not just a person's attitude toward wolves, but toward the environment, wild lands, nature itself?

We named the wolf Nahma 1. She was the first wolf to be radio-collared in a pack whose territory centred on Nahma Lake. We did not call her Jane or Sue: it was enough to put a collar on her without further humanization. She was a yearling as shown by the limited wear on her incisor teeth, a medium-sized wolf with a slender build and long legs. She was tawny with black guard hairs along her back and flanks, reddish tinges behind the ears, and darker legs—a typical Algonquin wolf. She weighed twenty-seven kilograms (sixty pounds) by the bathroom scale, part of our handling gear.

Fifty-five minutes after injection she was on her feet, wobbly, and gone. We collected our equipment and left. Her radio signal showed that she had not gone far. Probably she was asleep again under a tree.

We hiked back along an abandoned railway bed once used to haul logs out of this hill country. Now healing, alders crowded the embankment's shoulders, moss and grasses buried the cinders, and wolf feet used the path for a trail. Our truck was parked at a washout two kilometres away. We felt encouraged, especially Jenny, whose trap set had caught the wolf. With our two student crews, we had been trying to radio-collar wolves for five weeks without success. Finally we had a wolf to follow.

When we returned the next day, we heard her signal weakly from the washout. Squadrons of deer flies accompanied us on our walk along the old railway, and cicadas hummed in the maples. Nahma 1 was up on a hill above what we suspected was the grassy rendezvous site where her packmates waited. From a strategic knoll beside a lily-covered beaver pond, we sat on a log and listened to her signal. Its irregularity told us she was moving. Five minutes passed, ten minutes. She was working her way downhill toward the rendezvous site on a trajectory that would have her pass within two hundred metres of us. We moved into the denseness of a hemlock stand and turned the volume of the signal down. Now she was close, now she was past, like a ship going by in the mist. Forest phantom.

In a few minutes she would be at the meadow's edge. We left the hemlock grove and followed, to be within hearing when she reached her pack. She was in the opening now, walking fast to its far end, maybe even loping. A whine and a soft bark of greeting floated through the trees.

We stayed, listening to the now steady beat of Nahma 1's signal as she slept among her packmates. At dusk we heard what we had waited for, first a single wolf voice lifting from the other end of the meadow, then another, and a third—the wolves were spread out. The howls of the third wolf came from exactly where she was.

On a map, Nahma Lake does not take up much space. From the ground it is almost obscured by big, rolling hardwood hills over which broad-winged hawks ride the summer thermals and in whose forests red-eyed vireos sing all day. The surrounding country is laced with bogs and streams. The loggers pulled out a few years previously, leaving old roads in the process of regenerating to one-moose-wide trails through raspberry vines and brush. Good wolf country.

Our interest in this northwest side of the park was to compare the ecology of wolves where white-tailed deer were scarce with the rest of the park, where deer were more plentiful. This was to be the basis of Graham Forbes' Ph.D. thesis research. Partly because we could occasionally use a log cabin we had built nearby, Mary and I centred our work there; the student crews worked farther east.

A week before we caught Nahma 1, Mary, Jenny, and I had canoed Nahma Lake and part of Craig Lake in a heavy afternoon wind, returning in the calm after dark. We had heard wolves, faint and far away, so far that we decided to search elsewhere for a more accessible pack. So we drove thirty kilometres to a system of logging roads near the ranger station of Kiosk. No sooner had we arrived than the chief ranger there received a strange report. Back near Nahma Lake a wolf had approached some campers to within a few metres. It had stayed only briefly, then walked away.

So we returned to Nahma Lake, this time walking the overgrown railway by flashlight, pausing every kilometre to howl.

Wolves respond to human howls commonly enough that howling is a useful research tool. We have used it more consistently over more years than other wolf researchers. The human howl does not have to be good, just loud. At each stop we howl three times with only short pauses between, then wait for about two minutes and do it again. On only our third stop, a pack with pups answered.

The next evening we returned to howl at them again, wanting confirmation that they were not simply on the move. The forest was calm, out of breath after a hot, hazy humid day. No leaves rustled. No birds sang. Too much effort. We walked for half an hour along the old railway, surrounded by mosquitoes. A woodcock flew off the trail ahead, the whir of its wings making us jump. Firefly flashes loosely defined the edges of the wet meadow where we expected the wolves to be. Pups answered our howl, but no adults; rarely do we hear pups only.

Because the howl had given us the information we wanted, we started back without disturbing them further. When we were almost to our truck by the washout, we howled one last time, wondering where the adults might be. A deep-throated wolf answered from a hundred metres down a stream, five or six long, beautiful, night-splitting howls, each like the other, dropping in pitch suddenly near the end. Following are my notes made later that night:

We sat on the old railroad and made no noise. In five minutes I howled again. Now it was closer and gave shorter, softer howls. A few minutes later we heard sticks breaking in the alders right beside us, and the wolf began to whine. Mary whined back and it whined some more. Then it gave some very short howls, one to two seconds long, deep in pitch, low in volume—obvious short-range communication. For an amazing one and a half hours the wolf stayed no more than four metres from us in the alders. We kept the flashlight off, wanting to see how events would turn out, periodically giving short little howls or whines that the wolf answered. It seemed like it wanted to join us but just couldn't get up the nerve to take those last few steps up onto the embankment.

Finally I stood up to ease my cramped legs. We heard the wolf move back a few metres (maybe to ease its cramped legs too). Then we made our way very slowly to the truck, thinking that the wolf might come out on the road, but instead its howls began to fade. At the truck, we howled again, and now from a more distant ridge it gave us a final serenade of longer, louder breaking howls like the ones it began with.

Friendly, curious, perhaps it was the same wolf that had approached the campers a few days earlier. We had never experienced such a prolonged, close-range acceptance by, and back-and-forth communication with, a wild wolf.

A year later, the event was almost repeated. That summer the Nahma pack had not used the same rendezvous site, although wolf tracks along the old railway told that pack members occasionally swung through. One August evening, three wolves answered us, one beginning its howls with a bark, or trailing an initial series of barks into a howl, typical of a wolf disturbed at close range. We checked the receiver; the radio-collared wolf was not one of them. Three minutes later, while we were sitting on the embankment writing notes by flashlight, we heard the bark-howler again, this time even closer. Another wolf howled from the edge of a pond less than a hundred metres away. Moments later, one wolf, very close to us, began to whine. Mary whined back. We heard a wolf splash across the outlet creek and rattle stones as it climbed a bank a few strides directly behind us. We waited, breathless, not wanting to turn around for fear that movement would frighten it. Mist was rising from the moonlit surface of the pond. A few migrant passerine birds peeped overhead. Nothing happened; silence.

We waited for a full thirty minutes, then I howled, expecting to find that they were long gone. Two wolves answered from the outlet creek. What had they been doing all that time? Maybe they were exhibiting passive defence, staying between us and pups somewhere nearby. Or maybe they were just waiting for us to leave—so we did.

Through a long journey of over one million years, wolves have lived with humans or our immediate ancestors first in Africa, then Asia, Europe, and for the last forty thousand years or so in North America. As two species of large mammals, often hunting the same prey, it was inevitable that some ecological relationship would evolve between us.

If we had been equals in communication and reason, like early hominid species living at the same place and time, we might have become two warring species. But war requires a disagreement shared and communicated by members of each side, reciprocated hate, the ability to remember past wrongs, and the desire to retaliate. Wolves simply do not possess this emotional or intellectual equipment. So, while humans have waged war on wolves, wolves have exercised their only biological option, which is to behave as a hunted species. As such, wolves who react with fear have had an obvious selective advantage—they have been harder to exterminate.

How much fear is locked into the genetic makeup of a wolf? How much can be modified by experience? The Nahma pack provided us with other evidence that illustrated the various ways wolves regard us. One frosty October afternoon that first year, Nahma 1's signal was coming in loudly as we walked along the same old railway bed toward the now-abandoned rendezvous site. The signal from a radio transmitter is most audible when the wolf is in direct "line of sight." Trees have little effect, but just one or two high hills are enough to block it out.

She was close, so we turned toward some alders where the signal was loudest. Suddenly, there she was, standing face on, watching us. She trotted a few steps, seemingly not alarmed, then disappeared in the brush. Judging by her signal, she stayed within fifty metres or so for the next ten minutes. We sat on a mossy bank waiting to see what she would do. She may have been doing the same thing. Then she left. Curious, cautious, unafraid.

Other wolves from other packs exhibited similar curiosity. The Brûlé Lake wolf, for example, routinely urinated on vehicle tires and on occasion walked down an abandoned railway in full daylight and in full view of people. We received so many reports about that wolf that Graham thought he could radio-collar it by immobilizing it with our dart pistol. One afternoon he sat on the old railway waiting for the wolf to show up. It did, walking straight toward him. He didn't know whether to grab the camera or the pistol. As the wolf walked by, he took eye-level, full-frame pictures. Then as he reached for the pistol, the wolf galloped out of range.

And a wolf in the Lavieille pack was curious too. One night in a logging clearing, student assistant Carolyn Callaghan and Jenny howled and received no reply. Then while they were writing up their notes, a wolf walked through the sweet ferns into the headlights of their truck and just stood there. They howled softly to it, which seemed to increase its curiosity. After a while they carefully climbed out the truck window, not wanting to open the squeaky door, and sat on the ground near the wolf. Cautiously it circled them, staying about ten metres away. Finally, as in our encounter with the Nahma wolf, humans broke off the engagement, not the wolf.

At the park museum for a few consecutive winters before our study began, a wolf became habituated to humans and fed from the ground-level bird feeder attached to the window of the staff house. Nicknamed "Rosy" by park interpreters, it was the subject of several stories told by naturalists. Back when I was a student, another wolf raised ire at a children's camp in the park for its habit of tearing clothes off a clothesline.

It was not curiosity that Nahma 1 exhibited toward us early in the summer of 1988 when we found her at Mujekiwis Lake. It was dramatically different behaviour. On this occasion, she was the most aggressive wolf we have faced. That summer, the wolves were not around Nahma Lake. Graham's flights showed their movements centred on a big beaver pond–marsh complex near Mujekiwis Lake about nine kilometres away. We set out with two objectives: to radio-collar more wolves in that pack and to collect wolf droppings (scats) from a spring den and early-summer rendezvous site. The scats would provide evidence about the importance of moose calves in wolf diets when calves are small and vulnerable.

I flew with Graham to plot a route into Mujekiwis Lake. We took off in a float plane from Kawawaymog Lake, and in only a few minutes we were over the pond-marsh complex with Nahma 1's signal booming up to the antennas attached to the wing struts. Down below was a typical rendezvous site with a wet, post-beaver-dam meadow, an eye of water still in the centre, and tall grasses and alders around its edges. It was a good place for pups to explore and adults to watch for an unwary deer or moose coming to drink. Down below, too, stretched beautiful Mujekiwis Lake with rocky, pine-clad points, no canoes or people, and the Nipissing River to the south meandering out in wide sedge flats. The river was the obvious route in.

No people; no wonder! If you spot Mujekiwis Lake on the map of Algonquin Park, don't go there. Not unless it is early spring after a huge snow melt and it has rained for a week. Conditions were the opposite. The mighty Nipissing River, up there near its source, turned out to be a thin veneer of water on mud. We (Mary, Michelle, and I) put in, paddled, poled, hauled out around a beaver dam, put in again, got stuck, got off, got stuck again . . . with supplies for a week, twenty-five heavy traps, drug kit, radio-collars, receiver, antenna. Early the second day, Mary, inconsiderate considering the circumstances, tripped and fractured her ankle while struggling along under her big voyageur pack. Michelle and I graciously relieved her of a jacket or two—we did not know her ankle was fractured then—and she hobbled on.

Finally at Mujekiwis Lake we made camp under the pines close enough to the pond-marsh to hear any wolves howl. Nahma 1's radio signal came in from a distance. That night the wolves did howl, seeming to make the water shimmer in the moonlight, stilling the bullfrogs along the shore.

The next day, hot and sunny, Michelle and I left Mary with her oversized ankle at camp and canoed down the lake. Striking through the bush, by good luck we found an old logging road going our way. We reached the pond-marsh and scanned it from a fringe of spruces. No wolves were visible, so we spent the afternoon and evening scouting the area back from the marsh, collecting scats and looking for the bones of kills.

Then suddenly, in the hush of early evening, we were challenged by a wolf—the most distraught wolf we have ever encountered. We were sitting on a log. On a rise above us, no more than fifteen metres away, a wolf shattered the stillness with a sudden burst of deep, throaty barks. Looking up, startled, we saw radio-collared Nahma 1 racing back and forth along the edge of the rise. She was so close and the evening so quiet we could hear her throat rattle as she sucked in air between each series of barks. No attempt at concealment, this wolf was aggressively challenging us.

Hurriedly we stood up. We faced her, talked to her, tried to quiet her down. Our voices often calm wolves when we are collaring them. But she continued racing back and forth and barking. Slowly we backed down the old road. When we were around a bend, we turned and walked away. Nahma 1 stayed where she was, barking less frequently. Finally she stopped.

Why so different from the previous October? We may have genuinely startled her. She may have been almost upon us before detecting us. Upon later inspection we found small pup scats on the rise. The situation was similar to an experience I had in my student days on Baffin Island when three adult wolves barked at me from close range while I was near their pups at a den. It was also reminiscent of a wolf who barked at student Paul Joslin while he stood with his back against a tree. Another wolf at Annie Bay in Algonquin Park once confronted Doug Pimlott, barking at him. Gradually it moved back to rejoin its pups and pack across a clearing. (That barking was recorded on the stereo record *The Language and Music of the Wolves*, narrated by Robert Redford, Columbia Records, 1971.)

These incidents were not attacks, as if we were prey. They were displays of angry, defensive behaviour, of a kind most likely directed toward natural dangers such as bears or threatening non-pack wolves. Wolves, like many other species, usually express ritualized aggression intended to cause the threat to withdraw. Such rituals are less risky than an actual attack and fight.

Michelle and I felt guilty for sneaking around the rendezvous site. Nahma I had a right to be angry. Den sites and the rendezvous sites where wolves move later in the summer deserve respect. We have a rule now for all our crews that nobody enters a rendezvous site to collect scats until the pack has moved on.

Three so-called wolf attacks, as reported in newspapers, have occurred in Algonquin Park during our study. Like none of the foregoing, they all involved wolf-human physical contact. One of these wolves frequented the Pog Lake public campground week after week and often was seen trotting alongside the paved highway. One night it put its jaws around a girl's arm as she sat by a campfire. She received only a scratch from an animal that, if it wanted to, could have broken the arm into splinters with those same jaws in the same length of time.

Another night a little boy was bitten on the side by a wolf

when he left the tent to visit the backhouse. Again, only a minor cut resulted. Nearby that summer, MNR and Algonquin Forest Authority (AFA) employees had unwisely habituated a wolf to approach them and eat doughnuts.

The third incident was different in that a little boy's nose and face were badly bitten. The child, sleeping outside a tent, was dragged a few metres in his sleeping bag. His calls, and the presence of other people, broke off the encounter, but the wolf was reluctant to leave and had to be chased away.

In these incidents, the wolves displayed neither angry challenge, defensive behaviour, nor vocalization such as we had experienced, so the same emotions probably were not involved. In none of these cases were the animals rabid. Nor were the humans regarded as prey, or the wolves would have been far more violent. Preceding all three contacts, the individual wolves had become nuisances to campers in the area. Perhaps the wolves were social outcasts. In all three cases, the wolves appear to have been more curious than aggressive. None exhibited the apprehension that normally prevents actual contact.

Wolves, like dogs, commonly mouth unusual articles out of curiosity, or each other in play. They grab foreign objects. Once, when Jenny was a child, a wolf took her jumper suit from where it was hanging beside our truck and carried it off to its rendezvous site. Maybe the sleeping bag was like this, the object of investigation, and the child in it a surprise.

Whatever the wolves' motives, these encounters represent rare, aberrant behaviour. To a wolf, we are neither prey nor competitor. They do not realize that in the latter case they are so wrong.

Where wolves rarely see humans, as in remote Arctic places,

or experience our lethal forms of aggression, they may exhibit more curiosity than fear. In 1997 on Banks Island in the western Arctic, a white wolf approached our canoe to within a few metres, and was reluctant to leave. On Baffin Island in my student years, sometimes we found a wolf walking along behind us. At the other extreme, a wolf biologist working in Romania tells a story of a wolf that followed him when he left the forest and trotted behind him along a busy city street. Possibly at times European wolves exhibit fearlessness not through lack of exposure to humans, but excessive exposure, as long as they are not being persecuted.

Captive wolves are different, stripped of a wild environment, without any opportunity to disperse, hunt, or roam, all of which are needs encoded in genes. Sometimes with neuroses, always with artificial dependence forced upon them by humans, on occasion they can be unpredictable.

We followed Nahma 1 periodically for two years, learning a little more from each glimpse she gave us into her life. When I pull her records up on the computer, I find 185 entries, each with date, map coordinates, method of location, and a description of events. Most of the entries are from Graham's aerial fixes over two winters: eighty-nine entries for her first winter, twenty-one the next. Only once was she seen from the air, trotting along the edge of a frozen lake with two other wolves. Other times she was hidden in the trees. From tracking her on the ground, we knew her pack consisted of at least six wolves.

From another database, I can pull up on the screen a map of Algonquin Park with lakes and rivers shown in blue and coloured dots representing the locations of specific wolves. The first winter, Nahma 1's territory encompassed 110 square kilometres of prime moose and beaver habitat, with Nahma Lake toward its west side and the Nipissing River forming a southern boundary. Half the Nahma pack's territory fell in especially dense moose range, based upon Graham's analysis of winter data collected over a fifteen-year period by MNR biologist Mike Wilton and others. The second winter, her territory appeared to be smaller, but this is likely the result of fewer telemetry fixes.

The Nahma Lake rendezvous site where we first found her was used only temporarily. Maybe the pack had moved the pups there to be near a kill. In contrast, the site near Mujekiwis Lake, with a system of well-used trails, was used longer and probably included a den that we did not find. The two sites were only nine kilometres apart, a short hike for a trotting wolf.

We collected sixty scats in the Nahma pack's territory, all duly bagged and brought with others to the ecology lab at the University of Waterloo. Each scat was heated in an autoclave to 120°C for twenty minutes, then washed through a sieve. The remaining hair and bones were dried and put in an envelope for later analysis. Colleagues and students working in the west wing of the Environmental Studies Building knew without asking when scat preparation was taking place. When windows were open, they even knew two floors above.

Our analysis procedures involve randomly selecting three hairs from each scat, laying them on pieces of clear acetate, sandwiching the acetate between two microscope slides, and heating it in an oven for five minutes at 80°C. Heating produces a hair impression on the acetate through which light can pass, allowing microscopic examination. As a concession to help researchers identify hairs, evolution long ago decreed that each species of mammal possesses a different pattern of tiny scales on the outside of its hair. By analyzing the hair, we can figure out what the wolves have been eating.

For the Nahma pack, moose and beaver were represented about equally in the summer. Deer didn't show up much, as expected because of their scarcity. Beaver dropped in winter, when they spend most of their time in their lodges.

Wolf deaths figure prominently in our research; too many amber eyes into which we looked did not look back. On March 5, 1989, Graham phoned me at the university to say that when he dialled the wolf's frequency that morning from the airplane, the signal had come in at twice its normal pulse rate. Circuitry in the radio transmitter responds by altering the pulse rate when the collar has been motionless for eight hours. Nahma 1's signal was on mortality mode.

I rearranged my lecture schedule, and we drove north to the town of Sundridge, stretched along the shore of Bernard Lake seventeen kilometres west of Algonquin Park. Graham flew over from the town of Whitney to the east. In a restaurant he pinpointed the location of the signal on a topographic map. The wolf was in a narrow valley about two kilometres east of a lake known to local fishermen as Carmichael. Nothing was unusual about the topography. She was, however, outside her territory, farther west by ten kilometres than she had ever been, even beyond the boundary of the park.

Jenny and I crammed in with Graham, the pilot, our snowshoes, and some survival gear, and we taxied out beyond the ice fishermen's huts. Sun slanted in through the windshield as the engine revved for take-off. With the temperature a few degrees above freezing, wet snow lengthened our take-off run, and the pilot shouted in my ear that he hoped the snow wasn't too wet on tiny Carmichael Lake or we might be there until spring.

Nothing distinguishes the park from land next to it on the west side, at least from the air. Snowy lakes and bogs of all shapes and sizes, hardwood hills spreading like choppy swells on a grey sea, dark conifers stencilling the low places, rivers tracing out the valley bottoms. Only when you get to the ground do you notice the more heavily cutover forests and a scattering of cottages around the lakes.

We circled over Carmichael Lake, sloped down, and landed. Jenny and I climbed out. Graham and the pilot taxied off to complete a circuit of other radio-collared packs to the east. The plane gained just sufficient altitude on its run down the lake to clear the spruces at the far end.

Before we landed, Nahma 1's rapid signal was coming in clearly through the earphones. Down on the lake, however, we could not hear it. We walked to shore, snow clinging to our snowshoes, pushed through the alders, and came upon an old snowmobile trail heading east, our way, which made walking easier.

After about seven hundred metres, a faint signal registered on the receiver. Encouraged, we followed the trail, which ended at a derelict cabin on the edge of a clearing. Past that the valley narrowed, and we followed a small stream, gurgling with muted voice.

Crossbills were in the air, tossing melodious notes into the wind. A raven or two cruised the treetops, and an all-white snowshoe hare hopped out from beneath a snowy spruce branch and posed for pictures, white on white. Two sets of fresh wolf tracks ran our way. Clouds had obscured the sun, and the thought crossed my mind that if it started to rain, the pilot might not risk a landing back on Carmichael Lake at our designated time, two hours later.

The signal strength increased. Then, abruptly as we walked over a small rise, its direction changed, indicating that we had just passed the collar. The signal led us out of the conifers to the base of a hardwood hill. By turning around and pointing the antenna toward the snow, we located the spot to dig.

The snow was unbroken except for the wolf tracks a few metres away. The wolves had not paused, unaware or uninterested in what lay below. We began excavating an area about one and one-half metres wide with our shovel, taking turns at the heavy work.

The collar lay about forty-five centimetres beneath the surface—but no wolf was in it. Its bolts were still fastened. The leather strap and acrylic casing around the radio parts had been heavily chewed. A small piece of frozen flesh stuck to it, and a spot of blood was frozen to the acrylic—nothing more. We dug farther, carefully excavating an encrusted layer shaped like a wolf's body. A few guard hairs were frozen in, but no carcass.

For the next hour we excavated a huge area right down to last year's fast-frozen ferns and bunchberry leaves without uncovering any more clues. The body could have been nearby without our knowing it.

Time was running out, so we packed up and snowshoed back along our tracks to Carmichael Lake, passing the snowshoe hare again and the derelict cabin. The plane came in low to the west end and taxied to us. We climbed in and held our breath as the pilot took us back out. This time, by keeping the skis in their former tracks, he gained more speed, and we cleared the trees with ease.

We were left having to draw a most probable, instead of a definite, conclusion. Nahma 1 had been faithful to a defined territory until mid-December of that second winter. Then she went missing despite repeated flights over her whole territory. On January 3, Graham found her in an area where he had not been searching, south of the Nipissing River and well south of her territory. She disappeared again on three subsequent flights, neither on territory nor to the south. Sometime after early January, she had moved west to the place where she died.

She was a mature adult by then, three and one-half years old. While old for a wolf to disperse in search of a mate, she could have been doing that. Or, she could have been on an extraterritorial foray with other members of her pack. Alone or with others, however, she had been trespassing on land occupied by another pack. The evidence suggested that she had met a violent end. Humans could not have killed her or the collar would have been unbolted. Black bears, which at times kill wolves, were in hibernation. The verdict? Most likely she had been killed and dismembered by the resident pack. One wolf carried the collar off, lay down in the snow, chewed at it, then got up and left.

Nahma 1 and her pack illustrated something about wolf attitudes toward us, and especially their forbearance. They also showed us that harsh rules exist in wolf societies. In years to come, however, Nahma 1's death at the jaws of other wolves began to stand out as unusual. Based on the observations of other researchers, and the large amount of trespass we later recorded, we expected to find more wolf-wolf killing. That lack of killing eventually led our research in a different direction.

We left the Nahma area after that season, except for annual spring scat collections and moose-browse surveys. The old railway bed has had more years of reabsorption into forest, and so has the old logging road near Mujekiwis Lake. Maybe by now beaver have rebuilt their dam and flooded the Mujekiwis rendezvous site again. A new generation of wolves living there doesn't know us, and if any wolves are still alive from back then, they have forgotten. That is the way it should be.

DES KENNEDY
Slugs: Nature's Slimy Recyclers

DES KENNEDY is a gardening guru and resident of
Denman Island in the Strait of Georgia. He has written
several books on gardening, including *Crazy About Gardening:
Reflections on the Sweet Seductions of a Garden* and
An Ecology of Enchantment: A Year in a Country Garden.
"Slugs: Nature's Slimy Recyclers" is from *Living Things
We Love to Hate: Facts, Fantasies and Fallacies.*

SLUGS. THE VERY NAME excites images of things loathsome and
repugnant. Arguably the most despised creatures in creation,
they are cold-blooded, slippery, slow, and, most awfully, slimy.
They slither about our gardens under cover of darkness, tearing
ragged holes in the salad greens, gnawing filthy chambers in
potatoes, their excrement defiling the curds of cauliflowers. We
call things sluggish, meaning slow and unresponsive. "You slug!"
we taunt our enemies. "You slimeball!"

When I first glimpsed British Columbia's legendary "banana
slug," I was freshly arrived on the West Coast from Toronto, and
nothing in the East had prepared me for this obscenity. The slug
looked to be about thirty centimetres long—a sickly, jaundiced
yellow, splotched with black. It oozed vast quantities of slime,

leaving a silver ribbon where it passed. Its tentacled head swung slowly from side to side, absurdly menacing. An involuntary shiver rippled down my central nervous system, as my stomach churned. I had met the nation's biggest slug but little understood how much it had to teach me.

When I eventually settled on the coast and became something of a gardener, my relationship with slugs both intensified and took a decided turn for the worse. Whole spinach plants would disappear overnight. The succulent leaves of hostas would be cut to dirty ribbons. Slime trails would wind suicidally along the thorny arms of rose bushes, their leaves now mutilated. Tulip tips would be snipped like cigars. When marauding slugs finally invaded the greenhouse and set upon my precious eggplants, I declared war.

It was a just war, I told myself, a holy war. I spoke the implacable language of the cold warrior: self-defence and deterrence. After every rain I prowled our garden pathways armed with a stick sharpened to a deadly point. I'd spot a slug, poise the murderous weapon above its mantle, then fiercely drive it down. Often I'd spear two or three dozen big banana slugs in a single expedition. I began to take pride in my kill ratios. I started to boast. Ernest Hemingway among the slugs.

Then I began to realize that these were forest slugs; I saw them in the dark conifer woods all about. Undoubtedly they've been here since the last ice age, part of the forest ecology, so who am I to slaughter them for my own purposes? Glancing through a magazine one day, I was alarmed to discover that the banana slug is not much of a garden pest at all. The real damage is worked by a half-dozen other species, all smaller and less easily detected. Whatever smaller slugs I'd seen—like those little white ones in our spinach salads—I'd taken to be babies of the big ones. Colossally ignorant, I'd been impaling benign natives, blaming them for the predations of distant relatives. And, in the ultimate irony, the real culprits were all introduced here by Europeans in the first place!

Chastened, slightly shaken, I set about educating myself. The literature on slugs is not vast, nor do experts on them abound. Gardening books often contain a section on slugs as pests, their tone typified by one description of them as "a thoroughly nasty bit of business." The most comprehensive work I found was titled *Terrestrial Slugs*, by British scientists N. W. Runham and P. J. Hunter, which details the biology, physiology, and ecology of terrestrial slugs in readable English. Various research papers and doctoral theses helped fill out the picture, though several academics told me that much work remains to be done on these strange creatures.

What we do know already is fascinating. Slugs—essentially snails without shells—belong to a large animal phylum called Mollusca, which includes oysters, clams, and other shellfish. A large group of slugs, including the sea slugs, are members of a class of molluscs called Gastropoda—a huge and varied category numbering many thousands of species. Narrowing further, terrestrial slugs are lumped into seven main families, but there's much confusion about precise species distribution and identification, due to remarkable variations in colour and size within species.

Uncertainty also clouds the land slug's evolution. Lacking hard body parts, the slug has left no fossil record of its evolutionary path. Once upon a time, all Mollusca inhabited the shallow littoral zones of the sea. But despite their primitive appearance, molluscs are a tremendously adventurous and adaptable group.

Over the millennia they've discovered an extraordinary range of environments in which to live. Terrestrial slugs are believed to be descended from sea slugs, which gradually worked their way into fresh water and then onto land. The slug's gradual shucking-off of its snail-like shell is another adaptation that enables it to survive in environments such as highly acidic peat bogs, where snails are not successful. And, lacking a shell, the slug is far more streamlined and able to squeeze into small cracks and crevices for shelter.

Slugs like best a cool, moist environment; frigid winters and roasting summers are not their style. So it comes as no surprise that the mild and moist Pacific Northwest is some of the best slug habitat found anywhere. There are about a dozen major species of slugs found here, some of them natives, others European immigrants; many of them are found elsewhere across the continent.

Ariolimax Columbianus, the giant banana slug whose appearance so assaulted my eastern sensibilities, is a native of West Coast temperate rain forests. It can grow up to thirty centimetres long, and comes in a range of colours—from pale yellow to brown to glistening black. Many are mottled with black spots. Measuring less than five centimetres, the light brown field slug, *Ariolimax laevis*, is common right across the country. Another slightly larger native, the greyish brown *Ariolimax reticulatum*, is also widely distributed and is particularly abundant in the Maritimes.

While these and other native species may cause gardeners and farmers some trouble, their predations are nothing compared with the ravages wreaked by a number of imported garden slugs which have multiplied rapidly in the New World. Perhaps the most hated of all is *Arion ater*, a European immigrant known as the black slug, though it also comes in brown, red, green, and yellow. It attains a maximum length of about eighteen centimetres and has a ravenous appetite, consuming many times its own weight in food every night. Believed to have been introduced in the 1940s, it is now a prevalent species throughout the Pacific Northwest and causes substantial damage, particularly to strawberry and lettuce crops.

The grey garden slug, *Deroceras reticulatum*, is a smaller, but very common, field and garden pest. The midget milky slug, *Deroceras agrestis*, is another nuisance, which gets its name from its particularly sticky, opaque white slime. Also widespread is *Limax maximus*, known as the spotted garden slug or, more grandly, the great slug of Europe. Grey, with a marbled pattern of black spots, it grows up to eighteen centimetres long.

If any slug can be said to live in the fast lane, it is *L. maximus*. It can travel four times as rapidly as the lumbering banana slug. It's also very aggressive and will kill and eat other slugs, even turning to cannibalism of its own species in captivity. Most notably, it performs spectacular courtship and mating rituals, which we shall get to in a moment.

Other slug oddities include *Hemphillia*. Found under rotting logs, this group of small native slugs twitch violently when disturbed. Then there's *Testacella haliotidea*, an imported species that eschews vegetarianism in favour of earthworms. Another slug, *Milax gigates*, specializes in greenhouses, with a particular fondness for marigolds, geraniums, and snapdragons. And there are entirely subterranean species, such as *Arion hortensis* and *A. circumscriptus*.

Like other molluscs, a slug's body has two components: a visceral mass which houses most of the internal organs, and a combined head and foot. It has no skeletal parts, though some slugs retain a remnant shell in an internal shell sac. The muscular system is surprisingly complex. The foot sole ripples with a thick network of muscles that move the creature along on a series of wave-like contractions. Another set of muscles in the body wall controls postural movements, while a set of internal muscles allows the slug to retract or extend its tentacles and genitals.

Where its ancestors once bore a shell, the slug has a noticeable hump on its back, called the mantle. Below or behind the mantle are three apertures, always on the animal's right side: a breathing hole called the pneumostome, through which air is pumped to a simple lung; the anus, usually farther back; and an undetectable genital opening.

Twin sets of tentacles extend from the head, the longer (optic) pair having a small black eye at each tip. Researchers consider it unlikely that the eye can perceive detailed images, but rather that it is highly sensitive to changes in light intensity. The smaller anterior tentacles assist the animal in smelling, and perhaps tasting, food. The simple mouth at the front of the head contains a sharp rasping strap, called the radula. It is used to tear food into small pieces which are then passed back through a cavity, to be digested.

Nothing so much typifies a slug as its slime, and nowhere is the creature more wrongheadedly reviled than in its slime output. Slugs aren't just slimy—they're connoisseurs of slime. They secrete and employ different kinds of mucus for use in locomotion, self-defence, temperature regulation, and mating. A substance of remarkable viscosity and tenacity, mucus is composed of proteins and complex hydrocarbons.

Just behind the slug's mouth, its pedal gland secretes a particularly thick, sticky mucus. To propel itself forward, the front part of the pedal gland touches the surface to stick the mucus, then as the animal crawls over it the mucus is extended. The slug literally glides along, even over sharp and abrasive surfaces, on a smooth carpet of its own making. A second, more watery mucus is secreted by unicellular glands, and moved by cilia to the edge of the foot. Researchers believe the watery mucus may serve as a lubricant between the foot surface and the stickier pedal mucus.

Slugs are mostly composed of water, and their slime is designed to absorb water, helping prevent dehydration. That's why, if you get slime on your hands, you can't wash it off. The slime just absorbs water and gets even slimier. Instead just rub your hands together; the slime sticks to itself and rolls up into a ball the same way glue does.

Some species, when attacked by beetles or other enemies, suddenly exude large amounts of a thick, defensive slime; and certain slugs have been observed following slime trails to find their way back to shelter. The versatile mucus also plays a significant role in sluggish lovemaking.

Slugs are hermaphrodites, possessing both male and female sex organs. This is thought to be another adaptation to ensure reproductive success, since an individual can fertilize its own eggs. But copulation and mutual fertilization are common. The courting ritual may include lunging, biting, mantle-flapping, and tail-wagging, and sometimes involves one slug assuming a dominant or aggressive role.

The most dramatic mating rituals are those of *Limax max-*

imus, and I found them splendidly detailed in a 1987 University of British Columbia thesis by Ph.D. candidate David Rollo on the behavioural ecology of terrestrial slugs. In observing eight species of slugs kept in specially designed cages, Rollo frequently saw a slug locate its prospective mate by following a slime trail. With *Limax maximus*, he notes, courtship is initiated when one slug bites another. The victim flees, and the aggressor pursues, apparently tasting the slime trail for clues. The courtship chase might cover several metres, and climaxes with the slugs climbing to the top of a plant or other raised area.

There they circle around one another, touching with their tentacles, drawing ever closer and eating each other's mucus. This might last half an hour, punctuated with occasional bites. Finally, in limaceous climax, they intertwine completely and together fall into space, releasing a string of mucus attached to the support. Then, hanging suspended together like acrobats, they evert their sex organs and engage in a mutual exchange of sperm.

After this wild exhibition, Rollo continues, the lovers sometimes separate peaceably, but often intercourse is followed by aggression. One or both slugs begin biting and, understandably, the sex organs are quickly withdrawn. Usually one mate ascends the mucus string while the other consumes it or drops to the ground. But Rollo observed that aggression continued in some cases, and in extreme circumstances, the victim had its penis chewed off. In *A Natural History of Sex*, Adrian Forsyth speculates about this behaviour.

> *Ariolimax* often attempt and achieve appophalation: that is, one manages to gnaw off the penis of the other. The castrated slug cannot regrow his penis and is now obligated to be a female

and forced to offer eggs. . . . It may be that the castrator can raise his reproductive success by increasing locally the density of females. No evidence of this exists but as it is known that slugs are sedentary and territorial, the idea has scope.

Slugs characteristically lay their eggs at a specific time in their yearly cycle—generally spring or fall—but they also have the ability to withhold egg-laying if conditions aren't right. Often, some time elapses between fertilization and the laying of eggs. Some species actually construct a primitive nest, while others are content to simply deposit their eggs in sheltered crevices where they'll be protected from temperature extremes.

Biologist Alan Carter, who has studied the banana slug, says it lays only about twenty to thirty eggs, but that "it's quite a spectacular thing, because they look like little chicken eggs— they're calcerous and hard, which may be an adaptation to living on land." Carter says the big slug's eggs will overwinter in the ground and hatch the following spring. Other species may lay over one thousand eggs in a number of different batches, and often eggs hatch within two or three weeks of being laid.

David Rollo says that most slugs can be classified into three growth phases: a slow-growing infantile stage, followed by a fast-growing juvenile stage and finally a slow-growing adult phase. Alan Carter adds that banana slugs reach sexual maturity after the first year and live four or five years. For many species the life cycle is about half that.

Young slugs disperse from the nest and eventually settle down to something of a "home range." Their settlement density will depend upon available food and, most importantly, shelter. Almost all of them are nocturnal feeders, needing to retreat to shelter before the heat of the day, although certain woodland natives remain active on cloudy, moist days. Runham and Hunter observed that "time-lapse photographic records of the nocturnal excursions of *Ariolimax reticulatus* seemed to show definite tendencies to return to the place of shelter from which they had started." Another study in a Hertfordshire garden reported that "slugs tended to follow a circuitous pattern, bringing the slugs at the end of each excursion into a position near their starting point."

David Rollo's observations led him to conclude that slugs follow general, but not rigid, routines through the day and night. For the most part, he recorded, slugs remained in a resting position during the day, with bodies contracted and tentacles withdrawn. Nighttime activities included crawling, resting, and eating, but in bad weather the amount of time spent crawling and resting diminished. In fact, slug behaviour is regulated by a host of environmental factors, including time of day, surface temperature, light intensity, wind speed, moon phase, atmospheric moisture, and barometric pressure.

As beleaguered gardeners know, slugs have a taste for many kinds of leaves, stems, bulbs, and tubers. They also browse on fungi, lichens, algae, and animal faeces. Equipped with an extremely efficient digestive system, ranging up to 90 percent assimilative capacity, slugs are among nature's most proficient recyclers.

One analysis of the digestive tract and droppings of *Ariolimax reticulatus* found it feeding principally on the leaves of creeping buttercup and stinging nettle. Flesh-loving *Testacella haliotidea* likes to eat earthworms. Runham and Hunter describe how its needlelike teeth "converge and clamp round the body of the worm," like the steel jaws of a spring trap, the hapless worm being dragged in through the mouth in stages and slowly digested—a process which may take several hours.

Slugs can detect food from a distance, typically raising their heads and manipulating both sets of tentacles. They'll locate and move toward a desired food, and if you change the location of the food while they're en route, they'll reorient and set off in the new direction.

Competition for territory and shelter seem to be the main reasons for aggression. Although some species are more aggressive than others, slug battles—which are always seasonal—can be surprisingly fierce. Rollo described a typical confrontation as beginning with a touching, withdrawing, and re-extending of tentacles. Often an attacker will rear and lunge repeatedly; or the aggressor will push its head into the other's body, biting up to one hundred times. Rollo frequently observed aggressive slugs pursuing victims by following slime trails in order to mount another attack. Besides fleeing, victims may engage in tail-wagging, lifting the tail and wagging it vigorously so as to strike the pursuer a blow. Another form of defence is to withdraw tentacles and head under the mantle, flaring its outer edges to create a "vacuum seal" around the head area.

Slug predators include many birds, small mammals, and reptiles. I've often watched a garter snake slipping through our flower beds with a great fat slug firmly impaled on its fangs. Less daintily, domestic ducks will scoop up slugs by the dozen, particularly in the spring. Unfortunately, slime often coats the birds' bills, and their attempts to wash it off in water produce entirely repulsive, sodden, and slimy beards. Turtles, hedgehogs, and skunks are said to relish slugs, while gulls and starlings following a plow will devour slugs brought to the surface. Runham and Hunter found that slugs are often infested with parasites which do not bother the slugs, but which may be passed on to domestic or wild animals.

Home gardeners besieged by slugs can look first to making the environment less amenable. Since slugs need a cool, moist shelter relatively close to food, a lot of problems can be solved by cleaning up debris, particularly old boards or shingles piled in a shady corner. Less irrigation and frequent hoeing dries soil out, making it less hospitable to slugs. Scratchy materials like cinders or crushed eggshells spread around plants will also discourage them. I've read that diatomaceous earth works, but several friends have said it's useless for slugs.

There are any number of slug poisons available—the packages often show menacing slugs and snails that loom like Darth Vader—but most contain either metaldehyde or carbonate compounds, which can be toxic to earthworms, mammals, pets, and children. Instead, a hollowed-out and inverted half-grapefruit rind can be used as an organic trap. Slugs love to eat the white inner rind and can be caught there in the morning. A saucer of stale beer is another old recipe. Half a potato impaled on a stick and pushed underground can be effective in attracting small subterranean slugs, which can then be dispensed with.

A few years ago when the staff of Richmond Nature Park, near Vancouver, were looking around for a creature that was "familiar but misunderstood," they settled upon the slug, and began an annual festival called Slugfest. Held each June at the forty-hectare bog park, Slugfest draws dozens of youngsters eager to enter their pet slugs in contests for the biggest, smallest, loveliest, and slimiest slug. The feature event is a race, with all slugs placed around the perimeter of a half-metre-wide circle. First slug to the centre wins, usually crossing the wire in about two minutes. Later the kids are given a pamphlet on "Care of Your Pet Slug."

The kids may have company soon. After years of being held in contempt, slugs are enjoying a public relations renaissance of sorts. Newspapers report that researchers are studying slug slime for clues to the cure of cystic fibrosis. The communications giant A.T.& T. has featured slugs in an advertising promotion for a new generation of computers. "The slug as savant," trumpets the ad. "Nature has shown us there are powerful computer designs very different from conventional machines." There's an accomplished woodworker in Washington who now makes his living turning out wooden slugs designed to hook over the lip of your wine glass, as though taking a sip. I've also been given a wax slug, a ceramic slug, and a chocolate "Slug Sucker" on a stick! Suddenly, it seems, slugs are chic.

Early one morning I spotted a giant banana slug slithering across our garden path. For me, newly educated, curiosity had entirely replaced contempt. I picked it up.

After a few moments of frightened withdrawal, its head emerged, the slender optic tentacles extending like time-lapse flowers. As it began to sense the world around it, one—then both—of its smaller tentacles touched the surface of my skin delicately. I watched the animal apply its pedal gland to my palm. Attaching a silvery ribbon of mucus to my skin, it slipped forward—a cold, smooth softness on my hand.

As I carried it out of the garden, I thought of my past atrocities, of human blundering, of our capacity to wreak havoc on other creatures without knowing anything about them and without realizing what we're doing. Then I released the slug into its native woods nearby.

BETH POWNING
Home

BETH POWNING makes her home near Sussex, New
Brunswick, where she has lived for more than twenty-five
years. Her most recent book is *Shadow Child: An
Apprenticeship in Love and Loss.* "Home" is taken from *Seeds
of Another Summer: Finding the Spirit of Home in Nature.*

> *The vast wild*
> *the house, alone.*
> *The little house in the wild,*
> *the wild in the house.*
> *Both forgotten.*
>
> *No nature.*
>
> *Both together, one big empty house.*
> — GARY SNYDER

HOME, THIS PLACE where I live, is like a soft leaf on a great tree.

On clear summer mornings, I like to come downstairs, bare-
foot, and stand in the kitchen, stretching, yawning. Through
open windows I watch light shining in the tall timothy grasses
which stir like a restless sea all around the house.

It is my twenty-fifth summer here.

The comfortable, homey chirp of swallows and the snipes' mournful, swooping wing-whistle are the sounds of early morning, familiar as water filling a kettle. Wind swishes softly, endlessly, in the maples. I smell the dry-wood, old farmhouse smell of wood smoke and mice; and daisies, their bitter scent riding a dancing breeze. Sun lies in a warm oblong on the wide pine floor-boards. Hiking boots are tumbled by the wood stove, shedding sand from the beach we walked on yesterday, along the Bay of Fundy, under cliffs layered with the earth's past, and bored by the dark holes of cliff swallows.

I can't imagine ever leaving this place.

I put a loaf of oatmeal bread on the kitchen table, slice down through it. The wooden table is criss-crossed with thin knife scars, like smile lines on a man's cheek. A cat mews at the screen door, just beneath the swallows' nest in the wood shed, and I hear the small thunder of wings as the parent birds swoop through the open shed door to harangue the cat.

Home. Would I ever have the energy to start again, to come drifting into an unknown place like a vagrant seed? I've taken root, and accepted the demands of this world. I'm growing, like my own garden that responds to all the particular elements of this valley; long summer days, cold nights, altitude, wind, the distant presence of the sea. I've become what this valley has made me.

My life, and where I live it, can't be separated, like the trout lily that can't bear separation from the soil. I've become a leaf on a tree. I'm connected to a greater whole.

I take my breakfast outside, sit on the back step and look

down the green, blowing valley. Towels flap on the line. It'll be a good day to make hay. *Clear out the hay mow, remember to take the baby gift over to Laura, pull up the spinach.*

Suddenly, like a hawk on a slipstream, I'm swept away. Looking down the valley, bread and marmalade in hand, my experience of this rough and peaceful place runs through me like a current. Twenty-five years of memories are woven into the rushing of the wind, the shining of the grasses. *My neighbour bawling hymns over the drone and clatter of his tractor as he cuts hay. Children sauntering down the road whacking dusty flower heads with sticks. Meetings in our living room, with fervent and heated discussions on how we would improve many things. Me, weeping, heartbroken, face in hands. Twenty people at a saw-horse and plank table, one Thanksgiving, sitting on upended logs before we had any chairs. Children rampaging like a storm blowing through the house. Bringing my infant son home from the hospital, his head like a soft flower in my hand on just such a shining day.*

The ache of homesickness has become a distant memory; a sorrow buried deep.

The moment passes. How often do we experience sheer happiness? So rarely that it's a feeling I examine, and then recognize, like an old friend met unexpectedly. I wipe jammy fingers on my jeans, smiling, shaking my head slightly.

I walk around the house and go in through the back door. The swallows dart in ahead of me. I wonder if the brown barn spider, with fine, ash-grey hairs on her long legs, will return, this August, angling her web across the door frame so we have to duck when we enter.

We can't shut the back door of our house. Other creatures need it. The wild has come in.

Home is like a leaf on a tree; other people, other homes, are the other leaves. They live beneath the same sky, share the same memories, survive the same storms.

But one leaf is a solitude.

Although I laugh, comfort people, am hugged by those who love me, still, and always, I'm alone. Sometimes I feel as frail as the seeds I drop into my garden furrows. We go through life carrying with us a profound ignorance of our own beginnings, our own ends. I imagine myself curled inside my mother. I imagine my body as bits of mineral, ash, and bone, smoking on the wind.

We're all leaves, growing on a tree so vast we can barely imagine it: a tree as infinite and encompassing as the larger darkness of night.

Our homes surround us, strong and safe as a snail's convoluted shell, or a turtle's dark casing. Home becomes home not only when we've added comforts—soft rugs, tablecloths, paintings, geraniums—but when we've made our lives dense with family and friends, and spun memories like spiders.

The world we inhabit, with its skies, rivers, rocks, trees, storms, stars, also surrounds us, a carapace of another sort, that extends far beyond the walls of our houses. It is the tree we can't see. It's our larger home; a home that supports us, just as the bole of a tree carries sap to its leaves.

We make ourselves aliens in a strange place if we choose not to hear its languages, or to see its messages. The land seems a fearful place to those who live inattentively. This is how it seemed to me when we moved to this farm, and I saw the black press of night beyond the wet glass of our bedroom window on our first night. I heard the language of crickets and birds and thought it had nothing to do with me; I couldn't read the meaning of the new position of the stars over the barn, and didn't understand the exuberant message of the sound of the brook in spate.

But just as I feel at home, now, in my valley, meshed in my memories, so I begin to sense the presence of the great tree, like a reality behind reality. The longer I live here on earth, the more I love the light of sunrise, the silent tumble of snow from motionless branch, mute raven's track in mud, moon-set at dawn over a field of silky grasses, sleeping cows, spiders, thin trickling of the world's water.

Now, after all these years, I'm becoming literate in the other language. My feet know the twist of knobby spruce roots. My hands caress soft moss beds. I've smelled leaf mould on autumn mist, tasted sun-hot blueberries. And occasionally, as I touch, taste, and listen, the boundary between nature and me becomes a threshold: I step across. The wild either slips into me, or comes leaping up, like a silver fish, flashing out of my own dark wildness.

February tenth.

I'm longing for a blizzard. Without storms, winter creeps by dully, undelineated, and I become irritable. Storms are like the wildflowers of winter; they mark the passage of time, restore perspective and scale.

A thin, milky layer of cloud creeps across the sky, and the sun becomes pale, without presence. I smell snow on the air, and hear, on the radio, that a storm is approaching from Quebec.

All day, I wait, anticipating. The temperature drops. The air is very still. At suppertime, my son declares he doesn't need to do his homework, there won't be school.

At bedtime, I take Hooper, our terrier, for her nightly pee. As I slide open the glass door of the sunroom, she pushes past me, and then stops abruptly; she squints her eyes and lifts her nose to the wind. I follow her outside.

It is snowing hard.

The small flakes swirl on a northeast wind and it is very quiet. Out in the darkness, a barely audible whistling begins, a steel whine in the branches of the trees. It's a sound I've heard before. I know it the way a sailor knows the meaning of the wind in the rigging. The dog knows it too; she has her pee under the lilac bush and comes right back.

In the light from the kitchen window, I can see snow swirling around the broken stalks of phlox in the garden; already there's a place where the snow begins to gather, a tiny, sinuous curve defining the massive drift that always forms in the lee of the house.

According to the kitchen thermostat, the temperature has dropped four degrees since supper. I take down the transistor radio from its shelf so we can listen to the school report tomorrow without getting out of bed. I stand in the darkness and think about the barn, the animals, the tractor, all the things and creatures asleep or still in the night while forces build around us, pressure drops, wind rises, cold increases.

Suddenly, the wind buffets the house and there's an icy whisper, a handful of tiny diamonds flung against the black windows.

I go upstairs and undress in the same northwest room where

we spent our first night in this house, when we slept on a damp mattress huddled under rugs. Tonight, the bed is warm, it's a nest that my body knows. I roll into it and pull the quilt high over my shoulders. I listen to the rising, roaming wind, hear the icy tap of snow against the window. I can hear the furnace rumbling in the cellar. I feel myself gathered by the dark wings of sleep and I drift easily, knowing that the storm is rising, glad that no one can stop it.

Sometime in the night we wake, Peter and I, at the same time. We lie silently, listening.

The wind is a full-force gale that rages across the open fields, encountering nothing until it slams into the house. It speaks in many voices, making a hollow liquid moan at corners, shrieking as it streams unimpeded over the roof. A lifted section of steel roofing bangs insistently. The house feels like a ship; it has come alive. The bed trembles.

We go downstairs and slide open the glass door. Instantly the noise is deafening, vast as the boom and crash of surf, a wild sustained howl. Across the darkness, the wind and the snow race and twist like maddened horses.

The next morning, we waken to a muted light. It's like being inside an ice cave. We can't see anything out any of the windows except swirling snow. The maples at the edge of the lawn have become grey brushwork, steel-wool scrapings in the white-out. The wind still pummels the house, still rages down from the northwest.

When we go downstairs we find the cats pressed against the glass door, their whiskers frosted, their mouths open in piteous mews that we can't hear. When I open the door to let them in, the vast roar and twisting whine of the wind is suddenly in our kitchen, and snow blows onto the geraniums.

The radio tells us that a low pressure system is stalled over the Maritimes.

I go outside to tend the animals in the barn. I pull my hood up. The plastic toggle on the drawstring whips in the wind, hits me in the eye. I lean on the wind and watch my feet coming forward, and forward, the only colour in the whiteness. Already, between the house and the barn, there's a drift deeper than my knees.

In the barn, snow sifts through cracks in the north wall. The horse and the pony have snow on their eyelashes, on their coarse manes and in the grooves along their spines. They move restlessly about their stalls; the black mare tosses her nose impatiently. I brush snow off the hay bales, fill their mangers. When I stamp back into the boot-hall, I'm panting, my face is wind-whipped, dripping wet. I lean forward and shake snow out of my hair.

I spend most of the day curled in the corner of the couch, reading, drinking tea. Hours pass with no change in the intensity of the snow or the wind. We go to the windows, report to one another on the drifts which grow wherever the wind is checked. Snow streams steadily off the crests of the drifts, and their knife-edge lips become sharper and thinner, then begin to curl like fortune cookies.

By late afternoon the weather forecasters are predicting the biggest storm in fifty years.

The house hums with current: the refrigerator and the freezer whir, hot air pulses from the ducts, music plays from the stereo. Nonetheless, we search through drawers for candles and stick them into whatever we can find—beer bottles, glass jars. I rummage in the pantry for kerosene lamps and place the box of "strike anywhere" matches on the kitchen table. We fill the tub with water. Just in case.

At seven o'clock we lose power. It is a swift failing. One minute the house is humming, ticking, clocks keeping track of time, electronic seconds pulsing on the VCR, we're spinning through the storm in our space-ship, warm, comfortable, and then the lights shut down, not the way they go when you click them off, but a swoop, a diminishment. A failure. A power failure.

First there is the darkness. It is pitch dark. Then there is the absence of any sound but the wind, and the flicking of snow against the windows. I see the line of red light around the lid of the cook stove, hear the quiet snap of the fire. I pick up the telephone, but it is dead. A piece of white plastic in my hand.

We light the candles. Shadows flicker on the walls as candle flames leap and shrink in the cold drafts. The only heat comes, now, from the kitchen stove, and the rest of the house gets cold, rapidly. It's quiet, *so quiet*—there are no distractions. Only the reflection of candles in the black windows, the snapping of the fire, and the unceasing rage of the storm, the wild howl and moan, the rampaging of the wind.

All of us, mother, father, son, dog, and two cats, come to the kitchen. We come to the room where there is fire. By the stove are two buckets of water and a ladle. Steam wheezes gently from the kettle's spout. We bring a book and pass it around, taking turns reading out loud. Often we stop to listen to the storm.

Nothing compels us to do anything else. Nothing pulls us, fractures us.

We wavered, when the power died, caught in actions half-completed, all our choices gone. In that instant, we were people in amber, caught between times; and now we return to something barely conceivable. People without power.

There's a particularly heavy buffet of wind, and the house shudders on its foundation.

Our senses are shaken awake, to shadows, shelter, measured words. To one another. The storm holds us; we have no control over our situation, and yet we are not diminished but wrapped in the mystery of wind, of shadows, of water in a bucket.

The boundary vanishes. We cross the threshold, and glimpse how we, too, are part of the night's world, the storm's song.

Nothing is so freeing as being snow-bound.

It snows all the next day. Then, just at dusk, the wind dies, the clouds thin. Light comes into the rooms of the house, the humble light of late afternoon, when a sheen of cloud cannot mask the blue sky.

I pull open the wooden door at the end of the entry hall and am met with a neat wall of blue snow, as high as my chest. I take down my grandmother's snow-shoes, work the toes of my boots under the leather thongs, buckle the straps.

I clamber up onto the snow and walk out into the evening.

A star hangs over the ridge. There's not a breath of wind. In the west, the sky is the colour of apricots, dusky orange fading to the pink of a conch shell; and high above the valley, the sky is the softest blue, darkening in the east where the moon is rising.

As if it has been here forever, the snow lies serenely, its separate flakes flashing with the dying light. Drifts curl like frozen combers, pure, wind-shaped.

Nothing moves. The valley lies buried under snow, just the

way the storm left it, and great swells obliterate the road.

It is silent save for the dry shirring of snow on snow, shifting in a tendril of air. No cars, no airplanes, no tractors. Not even the beat of a raven's wings.

My snow-shoes carry me over the drifts. I stride over the buried garden fence and stand on top of the raspberries. I watch the sun setting, feel it flushing my cheeks, see the snow turning rose-red, and blue shadows pooling along the porch.

Someone lights a candle inside the house. I watch its tiny flame move from room to room.

I stand there for a long time, feeling myself blending into the night as the hills darken around me, as stars prick the sky.

No lights shine from our house.

Our small, human home is an element of winter's silence, as indistinguishable from the black sky as a rock, or a tree. It becomes, simply, another creature that lives on the great home of earth; and its bulk folds gradually into the darkness, like a black horse grazing at night.

HEATHER MENZIES
When Roots Grow Back into the Earth

HEATHER MENZIES is a journalist and the author of seven
books, including, most recently, *Whose Brave New World?*
The Information Highway and the New Economy. Her
next book will be about time in the digital world.
"When Roots Grow Back into the Earth" is from *Witness*
to Wilderness: The Clayoquot Sound Anthology.

I've always been skeptical about loving the whole planet Earth.
For me, you can love it best when you love a particular place, and
even then, you can't do it in a moment, but only as you know that
place and are involved in it over a long period of time. So I
dateline this essay very specifically: 1st. Concession, Locheil
Township, Glengarry County, Ontario. Spring 1994.

I'VE READ THAT the women who used to live here went off by
themselves when it was their bleeding time. In sacred menstrual
huts, they sat on the ground, on beds of moss. They rested,
meditated, and visited with each other while their blood seeped
out of their bodies and into the living earth.

I think of this as I walk between the trees I helped to plant as
a girl. Every spring, beginning when I was eight, we planted

trees here, in the thin, hard soils of eastern Ontario, on a run-down little farm my parents had bought in the 1950s, in lieu of a summer cottage. Armed with shovels and buckets, we tramped the land where it slopes up from the river, digging hopeful seedlings into the inhospitable ground.

I worked the ground with my bare hands: scratching among gravel and stones, finding the edge of rocks and prying them out, then foraging around for handfuls of precious soil, sweet black humus with which to cover the roots of the ten-inch nursery trees. The idea was to re-forest the land, which probably should never have been cleared in the first place. The soil had become too poor for farming. "Barren," they called it in the soil-testing lab: leached and eroded from having been used too hard, then left open, and exposed to the elements. The 200-acre farm had been abandoned like so many others around here after the Second World War, when mechanization imposed its implacable choice: get bigger or get out.

The trees came through a government reforestation program. Red pine, white pine, and spruce, they arrived in bundles of twenty-five packed in peat moss in slapped-together wooden boxes made of spruce lathe. Once, the year we planted 13,000 and my mother carried a solution of soda and water in a screw-cap bottle to keep herself from throwing up, there were ten boxes, each five feet long and three feet deep. When the last tree had been taken out and planted, my brother and I made forts with the empty boxes, our hands too tough to catch the splinters.

It's my hands in the ground I remember the most: eight-year-old, nine-year-old, ten-year-old hands. And the ground perpetually cold, with frost still glinting amongst the stones. I'd bang away with my shovel, trying to find a way in for the trees, and hitting rock after rock under last year's withered weeds. The reverberations jarred my head, and I threw the shovel aside.

On one side of me, I sensed my older brother and sister moving steadily ahead. On the other side, my mother kept an eye on my little brother while working her own row of trees. She worked doggedly, stooping but never once getting down on her hands and knees—a girls' school product even there. My father was, as usual, way on ahead, never stopping, never even slowing down. But I knew he'd double back, then help me catch up. He had a shiny, round-mouthed shovel, which he sharpened regularly so it would cut fast and neat.

My hands are stiff with cold, and puffed up pink like sausages. I know this, but I don't really notice as I work in a universe reduced to impenetrable earth riddled with stones and rough-edged gravel. I've pulled or shovelled aside a scruffy brown patch of last year's twitch grass, along with the collapsed seedhead of a burdock plant. The burr barbs are lodged in the skin between my fingers. My fingers are caked in half-dried mud as I rake through the ground, seeking passage for the tree roots. The stones here are a mix of shale and granite, the tag end of the Precambrian Shield littered like bones beneath the surface. I find the edge of the stone I'm up against, and yank to pull it out. Nothing happens. I scratch for a fingerhold deeper underneath, feel the dirt drive farther beneath my nails, the nails separating a little from the skin. Still I push, past gravel and frost crystals hard as diamonds. I get a grip and brace myself, knees apart, on the thawing ground. I pull hard, shoulder and stomach muscles straining. My fingertips burn as they slip from under the unyielding stone. Tears run down my face. The rock's too big. I'll have to dig another hole. Warm salt water drops onto the backs of my hands, moistening where the dirt has dried. My head throbs as I dig again, kneel again, and struggle with the stones.

I plunge my hands into the bucket. Sweet release. The water's cold, yet seems warmer than the ground. And the wetness soothes my fingers. I pull out a tree. A seedling with its spritely main shoot, its tentative side branches, and its prodigious roots.

I hold the tree by the stem, my swollen fingers tingling. I tuck the root filaments carefully into the hole. I curl them around so they all fit in, and push the tips down into the fertile hole. I do this with every tree, an extra boost so they're sure to take root here, and survive. The root tendrils lie there like a hank of my own fly-away tangled hair, kept in place only by my twelve-year-old hand. Still holding, I pile the precious black soil in on top of them. Crumbs of still-fecund living earth for them to cling to, draw nourishment from.

Take, eat. This is my body . . .

I scoop a handful of muddy water out of my pail, pour it off the tips of my fingers, and watch it seep into the ground, down among the root hairs.

I rake last bits of dirt into the hole, then plunk the patches of turf back on top, and press them in place with my hands. One tree planted. One out of thousands and thousands and thousands. And now they blanket the slope, a skein of green in infinite tones and variations, with the wind sighing through them, lightly or heavily, depending on the weather.

Now their trunks are thicker than my body. Their roots are gnarled fingers worrying the edges of the few still-protruding rocks. Whether it's new soil building up or the rocks themselves subsiding, I don't know. But now only the boulders are visible.

The biggest boulder we pulled out of the fields, a fisted hunk of pink-tinged granite, is now a sort of family monument. It's parked along the path between the hayfields in the lowlands close to the river and the higher ground where we planted the trees. My father hired a stone mason to write on the rock, beginning with the phrase: "They cared for this land." He listed all our names, and our birth dates. Then, at the head of the list, he put the name of Duncan "the Night" Macmillan. Some research I'd done in the archives established that he was the first to clear this land. And that's how my father counted things.

The man was nicknamed "the Night" because he was such a fine, hard-working Presbyterian that he worked at night if there was a moon to see by. He cared that much for his family: children of emigrant Scots seeking a better life in the New World. I can imagine him out there day and night, hectoring his workhorses as they strained to pull out the deep, resisting tree roots. I can imagine his relentless labour, and the faith that kept him at it. Until he'd broken the land to the plow and the discipline of crops.

It never occurred to me while planting those trees every spring that it was his diligence I was covering up for. Nor did I consider the compulsion to be productive as anything but admirable. He was hard-working. So were we, pushing ourselves from early morning 'til nearly dark those cool, sometimes cold and wet, spring weekends. I have no memory of what we did after we returned, exhausted, to the farmhouse and the stew Mum simmered at the back of the woodstove. We were weekend pioneers, with little time for contemplation.

When my father died, we buried his ashes at the memorial rock, and I visit it often when I'm walking these woods. The rock is overshadowed now by the trees. A thick branch of a spruce droops down and brushes the top. Lichen and moss creep microscopically across its surface, obscuring my father's chosen words.

I gaze at the bough of spruce, its deep dark green turning black in the shadows beyond. I see the buds where new growth will emerge, fragile as seedlings, in the spring. I see where old needles are sloughing themselves off, cascading across the rock and settling on the ground. I understand these trees, know them as minutely as I know the flesh of my son named after my father and now twelve years old himself.

It's strange I came to love these trees, after all I went through helping to plant, then tend them through their first years of life. Every spring we walked the still rock-strewn land where we'd dug in the seedlings, trying to find them under the collapsed remains of last year's overwhelming weeds. Spotting a toothbrush bristle of green, I'd pull the grasses apart and frisk the tiny branches free of entangling debris. It sometimes took days to find all the buried ones, and not all of them in time.

Then it was the snow itself which posed a threat. The red pines got it the worst, with their bushier boughs and thicker needles. The snow took them down, and by spring, they'd be bent right over, twisted sideways and unable to right themselves. It became our chore as children to scout out these cripples and set them straight, using broken branches from dead elm trees, or hawthorns and other scrub bushes that had infiltrated the long-abandoned fields. It wasn't hard work. In fact, I remember actually enjoying it. At some point too, I crossed over, and continued doing it on my own. For them. For us. I'd encountered the word "pantheism" by then, and I was a pantheist; though still a church-going one.

It was pleasant solitary work, and I used to alternately talk to the trees and sing to them: hymns in the early days, then Beatles tunes about love, love, love.

There's been a little rain, and now the sun is coming out. I walk toward it, up the path through the woods, in the direction we moved with our buckets and shovels over thirty years ago. A mellow, honey-thick glow slants through the trees and onto the path, which is spongy with moss and fallen pine needles. The sun comes through the branches of an overhanging pine, and I stop to contemplate a water droplet hanging, like a diamond, at the tip of one of its needles. I duck in under the branches knowing it's drier there, and sit on a mound of moss-covered ground.

I think of my mother, busy as ever and still battling headaches. I think of my older brother, my younger brother, and my older sister: one's a lawyer, one's a doctor, one's a telecommunications manager. Then there's me, busily writing to meet the next deadline, to have another book in print. A drop of water descends from a branch above me, and lands on the back of my hand. It occurs to me that the whole bunch of us could be out there clear-cutting at Clayoquot. It's that much in our blood, the diligence and hard-working spirit; what Nietzsche called the endless becoming, with no horizon but the perpetual invention of new objectives: the next tree to cut, the next one to plant, the next cause to write about.

The drop of water slides down my hand where I rest it against the ground. But I think it's not the will and the diligence themselves that are so bad. It's their monopoly within us: our hearts, minds, bodies, and souls all dedicated to the dynamo of doing, without respite. No time for rest and contemplation. No time for rooting and taking root. No time for remembrance and reciprocity.

I watch the drop of water, now warmed by my skin, roll steadily down my hand, and slip away into the earth. I feel the moss soft beneath me, feel its moisture seep into my jeans. Around me, shadows drift up like root hairs seeking passage. A breeze whiffles the upper branches, light as surf bubbles caressing a shore. I sit on the moss, enveloped by these trees I helped grow into this ground over so many years. They're in my blood now. I feel them.

When I take the time
to remember myself as part of them,
and remember them
as part of me.

—*The information about Native women's menstrual rites comes from Anne Cameron's* Daughters of Copper Woman *(Press Gang, 1981) and from Beth Richard's article "Blood of the Moon," in* Herizons *(Vol. 7, No. 4).*

DAVID CARPENTER

The Place Where the *X* Is

DAVID CARPENTER lives in Saskatoon, Saskatchewan.
His ode to a good fishing hole, "The Place where the *X* Is"
appears in *Courting Saskatchewan: A Celebration of Winter
Feasts, Summer Loves and Rising Brookies*. Carpenter has
written four works of fiction (*God's Bedfellows, Jewels, Jokes
for the Apocalypse*, and *Banjo Lessons*) and two nonfiction
books, *Writing Home: Selected Essays* and *Fishing in the West*.

THERE'S A STRETCH of the year when time goes by too fast to be
marked. If I could guess, I'd say that it starts about the end of
April, when we dig the garden, and begins to slow down in July,
when the backyard is in full bloom.

On the first sunny day in May the light is so intense I feel like
a mole in a tanning salon.

The leap from April into May is saturnalian.

It's almost time to head up north to Little Bear Lake and
Narrow Hills Park. It's just about time, friends, one and all, to go
fly-fishing.

All through March and April I have purchased everything I
might need for the fly-fishing season. New fly lines, wet and dry.

New leaders for my fly lines, new tippets for my leaders, new flies for my tippets, wet and dry. I've practically memorized every trout stats column in my latest "Fish Facts," bought my fishing licence, booked off a week, lined up my fishing buddies, phoned the Mogensons (who run Little Bear Lake Lodge) about a dozen times. Perhaps even more than a dozen times.

"How's the, ah, ice situation, Alice?"

"Frozen tight as a drum, Dave."

"How're things looking up there, Ken?"

"Little early yet, Dave."

"How's the, ah, ice situation, Alice?"

"Not much to report, Dave."

"How goes the battle, Ken?"

"Try ringin us next week, Dave."

"How's the, ah, ice situation, Alice?"

"Oh, Dave, we had us a real blizzard yesterday. You might just ring us up a little closer to opening day."

"Things still frozen up there, Ken?"

"Well, Dave, we've had a small bit of melting around the cabin, but the lakes are all froze up yet."

"Oh, Alice, by the way, how's—"

"Pretty much the same, Dave."

"Say, Ken, while I'm talking to you up there, what's the—"

"We'll call you, Dave. Okay?"

"How's—"

"Froze up."

"Still—"

"Yup."

But something happens. It always does. The sun performs its patient work on the deep drifts of snow that lie heavy in the northern woods and the pale blue carapaces that cover every northern lake until the second week of May. And fishing comes to those who wait.

I have only a few fishing buddies who approach my certifiable state of obsession. Warren Cariou is the most obsessed and the most athletic, the Wayne Gretzky of Saskatchewan fly-fishing. He has the fine co-ordination of a Swiss watch. He is focussed and he's deadly.

Bill Robertson is the very embodiment of determination. He will stop short of nothing to get the trout in the net. This includes death-defying dives in scrotumtightening waters that would discourage even otters, beavers, and muskrats.

Bob Calder is more of a Clint Eastwood character. He wears dark glasses, an ancient black flotation jacket, and a wide-brimmed Tilley hat, and he casts for trout through the mystical smoke of a Ritmeester cigar, which he uses for camouflage as well as to fend off mosquitoes. He hauls the trout in, releases them, and moves on like smoke into the muskeg. You can almost hear that theme music from *The Good, the Bad and the Ugly*, the refrain that sounds like a calling loon.

Doug Elsasser is a compact, sturdy guy who looks like Bruce Springsteen. Rumour has it that he gathers leeches and uses them for bait, but who am I to judge the moral worth of a man who can carry a big canoe on his shoulders and slap mosquitoes *at the same time?* You don't impugn the worth of the man who carries the canoe.

Kever is a combination of Meryl Streep in *River Wild* and Annie Oakley. She goes it alone with the belly boat, drifting to her own music among the trout like a synchronized swimmer until the trout begin to feed beneath her inner tube. She picks them off one by one. Some of her casts take fish less than a canoe's length away from her flippers.

We eat well in May.

More than half of Saskatchewan is northern forest and Precambrian rock. This combination makes for thousands of northern lakes full of fish, many so far back in the bush that they haven't even been named or seen a floatplane. Up around Little Bear and all through Narrow Hills Park there are clusters of blue and green ponds so clear you can see to the bottom a hundred yards from shore. The water is clear as a Jasper lake and packed with nutrients. Freshwater shrimp, boatmen, caddis nymphs, midges, stickleback minnows, dragonfly nymphs, ciscoes, mosquito larvae, water beetles, leeches, snails, frogs, mayfly nymphs. The trout grow fast and taste even better than wild chinooks and coho. The trout meat is moister and sweeter. The idea is to catch enough for the next day's breakfast or for supper and let the rest go.

You clean the little ones, dip them in egg and flour, line their bellies with fresh dill and lime, and fry them in butter. Add a dash of pepper.

The big ones are nice for baking or barbecuing. I love to stuff the biggest brookies and brown trout in the spring and the even bigger rainbows in the fall. That way I avoid messing with spawning fish, since most rainbows are spring spawners, most brown trout spawn in September, and most brook trout spawn in October and November.

My stuffing for large trout is from an old family recipe. It's made of sautéed onions, celery, and wild mushrooms, with dried bread crumbs, pepper, and fresh basil. Make more than you need to stuff the cavity of the big trout and pack the extra stuffing just outside the cavity. No need for skewers to close the cavity; just wrap the stuffed trout and the overflow stuffing in one or two sheets of foil and stick it on the barbecue or into the oven. Barbecue about ten minutes for each side or bake for up to an hour at 350°F. The trout bakes in its own abundant fat and juice. It's done when you can sink a paring knife or a skewer easily into the side of the fish, through the thickest flesh, right down to the backbone.

Two years ago, Calder caught a rainbow that fed six people. Last year, Cariou caught a brown that fed everyone in camp. Last year I caught a brook trout that was twenty-five inches long. I couldn't wrap its body in one piece of foil, so I had to double up. A few years ago, Kever caught an eight-pound rainbow that towed her belly boat. We have all lost trout so mighty that we still mumble into our pillows about broken lines and boat-high leaps. Most of the time, however, we are lucky to catch a few good trout and are content to release most of our day's catch. Again, because of spawning, we tend to release more rainbows in the spring and more browns and brooks in the fall.

I talk about these three species as if you knew them as intimately as I. A few introductions are in order. The most exciting fighters are the rainbows. Not only do they grow larger than the other two species, but they are olympic runners and jumpers. They feel like chinook or coho salmon, except their runs are generally shorter and their mighty leaps more frequent. Never look for subtlety in a rainbow. Look for spectacle.

The brown trout is by far the hardest to catch. Not only is the brown a powerful swimmer, but it knows every snag in the stream. It is wily and subtle. Browns are not native to this part of the world; they are native Europeans. They used to thrive in the small clear streams of northern Europe and the British Isles. They must have learned their cautious, nocturnal habits from these clear streams where a trout in the open is vulnerable to birds, otters, and anglers. They've brought this wiliness over here. Only the fly-fisher has a realistic hope of catching one or two.

The brook trout is perhaps my favourite. It is the smallest of the three. Landing a two-pounder is a real occasion. A real good brookie is more often about fourteen inches long and weighs less than a pound and a half. Brookies are wonderful to eat and wonderful to catch. But their greatest appeal is surely their extraordinary beauty. They vary a great deal, but the brookies we catch up north usually have olive-green backs with a distinct pattern of wormlike markings called vermiculations. Their sides are sometimes golden, sometimes pale green, with bright pink spots surrounded with bluish halos. When the spawning is about to begin, the flanks of the male brookies take on a brilliant orange hue. Their fins are red, edged with black and creamy slashes.

Perhaps some day our brookies should go on a stamp. Canada has the finest brook trout fishing in the world.

My friends and I have evolved a method of locating hot spots that depends a lot on teamwork. There are about thirty good lakes and several good streams in the vicinity of Narrow Hills Park. Almost never do these waters all yield good trout at the same time. The feeding activity can vary from lake to lake, depending on what the temperature of the water is, how much food is available, whether some fish are spawning, or how well the fish have survived the long winter. On our first day out, we tend to split up, fish for a while in a likely spot or two, and then pool our information at the end of the day.

Sometimes it might take us two full days of trial-and-error fishing until we hit the right spot. In the fall of 1992, we were in an unusual bind. We had invited a CBC crew from the radio program *Ideas* to do a piece on our fishing trips. It was unusually cold, we were all freezing half to death, and after two days of advance scouting we hadn't caught a single fish. What made this state of affairs doubly bad was that the recording crew was insisting that we do our interviews while catching fish!

Just before the CBC crew was to arrive, Kever took a walk down by the shores of Sealey Lake. She found an elderly woman there scanning the waters for her husband, who was trying his luck at the far end in a motorboat. Kever confessed to the woman that we hadn't caught a single fish and that we needed to show the CBC crew *some* signs of life. The woman looked at Kever for a moment and said, "Why not try over there?" She was pointing northeast at a small bay surrounded by bush. "Come on," she said. "I'll show you." She took Kever along a path over a rocky ridge and through some dense berry bushes. It looked like an ideal spot to encounter a bear. But when they arrived once more at the shoreline, Kever spotted a rising trout. Then another. They were dimpling the water only about twenty feet from shore.

"My husband caught a six-pound rainbow right here last May," said the woman. "And on that same day in May, I caught a four-pound brook trout."

Kever thanked the woman profusely for this information. She returned with her rod and cast into the boiling water. Immediately she had a strike and pulled in a nice foot-long brook trout. She killed the fish, put it into the creel, and brought it back to camp.

Maybe I'm overdramatizing things here, but as I remember it, this was the very moment that the CBC crew arrived in their van. Producer Wayne Schmalz called out from the driver's seat, "How's the fishing?"

Kever held up her brook trout and tried to look casual. "Not bad," she said.

This turned out to be a prophetic remark. From that moment on, fishing was great.

On one particularly challenging trip in May, a more recent one, we had exhausted ourselves on lakes in which the water was still too cold to promote much insect activity. The fish were there but they were dormant. We had a meeting. We compared all of our findings and "Fish Facts" stats and brought out the maps. There was one lake no one seemed to fish, but reports from the provincial fisheries guys were pretty positive. An abundance of good-sized rainbows and brookies. The lake was hard to get to, it involved some hiking, and going there would mean some pretty heavy lifting of equipment.

But we had Elsasser and a reasonably light seventeen-foot Grumman canoe. This canoe would seat three of us, a paddler and two anglers. We also had a belly boat for our fourth angler. The idea was that we would all get to trade off with each other. So we all had a pretty heavy load to carry into the bush that morning.

The weather had been brutally cold, but on this particular morning, the sun came up into a windless blue sky.

I am going to call this hike-in lake by its unofficial name. It is The Lake That Cannot Be Named. You have probably guessed why.

We carried rods, lunches in a large cooler, fishing vests and boxes, life jackets, paddles, a belly boat, creel, waders, frog fins, and rain gear and followed Elsasser into the woods. To be more precise, we followed our big aluminum canoe into the woods. It seemed to float through the trees like a well-fed shark and did not stop once until it came to the lake it was meant to glide in.

This lake is not much more than a large pond, probably less than a hundred acres. Our arrival was announced by the call of a loon at the near end, and it was answered by her mate at the far end. On all sides the lake was sheltered by high-rising cliffs and gentle slopes. If a wind came up, there would be no danger of squalls. The shallows were pale green, the deeper water emerald, and the deepest holes sapphire. One by one we clambered down to the little beach where Doug had placed the canoe. The water off the far shore was dimpled with rising trout.

We began at once to tie on flies. When you have puffed your way along a trail that leads to the fly-fisher's version of Treasure Island and finally reached the place where the X is, you discover that the simple job of tying on a fly is fraught with difficulties. The idea is to turn away from the lake and try to think of anything but trout. Think of potatoes or the label on a tin of Ovaltine, think of people you owe money to, or try to recall the exact wording for the French version of "O Canada." Anything to get your mind off the feeding frenzy of several thousand plump silver torpedos about to make your day.

Judging from the language unleashed behind me at leaders and hooks and snags, I would have to say, with embarrassment, that my friends have failed to master this simple meditation.

Kever's fly rod was finally ready. On the end of her line she had a fly that imitates a large black leech. She pulled on her set of neoprene waders. Then she sat down on a log and pulled on a huge set of frog fins. For added security and buoyancy, she put on her life jacket, and then she stepped into her belly boat. This is a fancy inner tube equipped with many pockets for equipment and lunch and a harness affair that she stepped through. Then, holding onto her big tube, she moved on flippers backwards into the water.

Ungainly and waddling on shore, she was positively balletic on water. Away she went, flippers churning the silt, her body suspended in cool water, her fly rod aloft, elbows leaning at ease on the belly boat. Periodically she checked her progress by turning around to zero in on where the trout were rising. She had to do this because in a belly boat you can only move forward by going backwards.

Finally the three guys were ready. I paddled us out onto the lake and headed for the deeper water. They began the day by trolling backswimmers and muddler minnows. The former is a wet fly with two arms that imitate the "oars" of a water beetle sometimes called a boatman. The latter is a fly originally tied by Ontarians to catch brook trout in the fabled Nipigon River. Trolling flies is a good way of testing the waters. You simply point your rod tip in the direction of your submerged fly, keep the tip down, and wait for something to hit that is strong enough to pull your arm off.

It didn't take long.

"I've got one," said Calder in a whisper.

I'm not sure why he whispered. It sounded as though he were trying not to publicize his good luck to all the anglers—who might have been hiding by the dozens in the bushes, scanning our progress with binoculars and electronic devices. But we were all alone on that small lake.

Calder's rainbow grabbed his fly and took off for the middle of the lake. His reel was buzzing like a chain saw, and then the line went limp.

"Damn."

He slumped over in the canoe and was about to reach for a cigar when his fish leapt right beside us a good three feet out of the water. It was a very big rainbow.

I was heard to give the following sage advice. "Gone not on your lift it! Lift it! He's fish on your! Calder! No! Yes! Bob! In! Reel hold your up! Tip! Rod! A fish!"

Kever looked over from her belly boat perhaps to see if I were suffering from a stroke or dyslexia. She too was landing a fish.

Elsasser kept his cool, reeled in his line, and grabbed the landing net.

Calder's rainbow took a second long run, and once again the reel buzzed. Then his fish repeated his little trick of turning around and coming back at the boat like Moby Dick about to ram the *Pequod.* Calder reeled in as fast as he could, but not fast enough. Again, the rainbow sailed out into the sky and re-entered with a histrionic splash. And off he went, gone. Escaped.

Well, no, just free on a slack line, and this time Calder was wise to his fish. He reeled in and felt the surge of another mighty run.

Kever's fish was a brookie, a deep fighter by the looks of things. She played it, led it into the net, released it, and before Calder had managed to tire his big rainbow, she had a second fish on.

Looking a bit wrung out, Calder finally led his fish into the net and handed it over to Elsasser, and Elsasser brained it with his priest. When the rainbow was safely in the bottom of the boat, Calder finally lost his composure. He offered up the angler's equivalent of a loud hosanna: "Yeeeeeeeeeeehaaaw!"

The loons looked up from their lovemaking.

We paddled past Kever, and Calder held his fish up. It had obviously finished its spawning. This rainbow was as silver as silver and had a faint purple stripe down both sides. It was almost twenty-one inches long. Kever responded by raising up her second brookie of the day, a plump fifteen-inch beauty. (This brook trout was to feed all four of us that night.) I took our canoe through a narrow gap and into the smaller half of the lake, the northern half, so well shaded that the water is a very deep emerald, the air cool and piny. Here the surface was virtually without a riffle and sent back unbroken reflections of the high cliffs and shaggy spruce. Near shore in deep water next to some steep mossy boulders, a rise on or near to the surface. Another rise. A bevy of rises. We were all afloat on a lyric dream of emerald and rising trout.

"Got one."

It was Elsasser's turn now, another big rainbow. This one was loath to jump and streaked for the centre of our bay. It seemed even stronger in its runs than Calder's mighty fish of half an hour ago.

Kever paddled behind us and into the bay. She began to cast. Calder brought in his line, but before he could lift his fly from the water, his fly rod plunged down for the bottom like a diviner's willow.

"My God, I've got another big one!"

By now, no one was whispering. Chaos was about to take over. I paddled hard for the centre of the bay. I needed to keep us all in deep water so that the fish couldn't dive down into the snags and snap our lines.

"Kever!" I cried. "We need you over here to help with the landing!"

"Okay."

Kever wound in her line. She hadn't recovered twenty feet when she was fast to a burly diver of her own. She looked my way, shrugged.

"Sorry," she said.

Calder's rainbow dove under Elsasser's line and soared out of the water. A chunky three-pounder. It swam back the way it came and the lines crossed. At last Elsasser's fish, a much bigger, darker rainbow, breached beside the boat, drawing a host of exclamations and gasps.

Kever's fish was a brookie. It seemed to be curious about the melee near our canoe. It plowed over in our direction.

"No!" I cried.

"I can't stop it!" yelled Kever.

"Well, do something!"

Kever lifted her rod tip, palmed her reel, and put on all the pressure she could risk, and at last her brookie came back toward her belly boat. It began to sulk in the deep water below her and would not move.

"Thank God," said Calder.

"Close one," said Doug.

Then his rainbow took off once more and broke the surface on the run. It seemed to get bigger with each new leap. It had become so badly tangled with Calder's line that Calder must have felt as though he were landing two rainbows.

"Something has to give," he said grimly.

It did.

Doug Elsasser's line snapped, and he was left with a memory of the biggest rainbow he had ever seen. Open-mouthed and mumbling, he wound in his line. Now hookless, it came free from Calder's fly line, and Bob brought in his three-pound rainbow. He smiled over at Kever as she held up her brook trout, the fat twin of her second brookie. If ever an opera is written about fly-fishing, there would have to be that inevitable exchange between anglers over the rise and fall of Fortune's Wheel. (The magic wheel, in angler's jargon, is the fishing reel.) Such an aria would give voice to Calder's triumph and Kever's exultation and Elsasser's whispered imprecations at an unkind fate. I've gotta see Placido Domingo in Elsasser's role. He's got that tragic range.

It doesn't happen very often, but on that day we simply lost count. We lost some big fish, we regained our composure, caught and released our limit, and emerged from the lake and the trail by late afternoon. We were exhausted, but what an amazing day. The hiking in, the shore lunch, the fishing—it all went by so fast we could only gush in wonderment all the way back to the camp.

The day I've been writing about was so entirely perfect it deserves to be set aside as a national holiday. May 22, 1993. The next day the fishing was just as good, the weather even warmer. The water beetles gathered beneath the cooler shadows of the fallen trees, and even the frogs moved languidly around the edges of the pond. Something was in the air.

We drove back to Saskatoon on May 24, and the whole week's accumulated heat seemed to warm everything up, even the depths of parkland soil so long frozen during five months of winter. The heat seemed to rise in great waves off the pastures, newly seeded fields, and aspen groves. In the city, legions of songbirds gathered beneath the cool gloom of the trees. When we left Saskatoon, the buds were on the trees in a sweet profusion. Now they were in full leaf. Several days before the end of May, summer had arrived.

TERRY GLAVIN
Hundreds of Little Jonahs

TERRY GLAVIN is an award-winning author and journalist who lives on Mayne Island in the Strait of Georgia. Glavin's books include *Nemiah: The Unconquered Country*, *This Ragged Place: Travels across the Landscape* (nominated for a Governor General's award in 1997), *A Ghost in the Water*, and *The Last Great Sea: A Voyage through the Human and Natural History of the North Pacific Ocean*. "Hundreds of Little Jonahs" is from *Dead Reckoning: Confronting the Crisis in Pacific Fisheries*.

There is simply nothing in Creation that does not matter.
Our tradition instructs us that this is so, and it is proved to be so,
every day, by our experience. We cannot be improved—in fact
we cannot help but be damaged—by useless or greedy
or merely ignorant destruction of anything.
— WENDELL BERRY, "The Obligation of Care"

WHEN I WAS A BOY, Byrne Creek arose in little rivulets from a wooded ravine, and that ravine is still there in 1996, spared the fate that has befallen so many of the Lower Mainland's urban streams. Byrne Creek was badly weakened, but the water course survived pavement, condominiums, and industrial landfill partly by luck, partly through Burnaby municipal council's forward-thinking policy of protecting ravines, and partly through the generosity of the local service clubs who saw to it that Ron McLean Park, between Rumble and Marine Drive, would be set aside for coming generations of kids.

Byrne Creek's headwaters now lie mainly underneath Burnaby's supermarkets, suburban streets, and apartment buildings. Powerhouse Creek flows underneath Kingsway, just west of its intersection at Edmonds, and joins Byrne Creek somewhere in the storm drains underneath the Edmonds SkyTrain station. On these streets, Byrne Creek's cascade can be heard only during the autumn rains, by standing quietly on street corners and listening above the drain grates. Underground, Byrne Creek flows southwest and emerges alive in its ancient canyon, within the remnant forest of Ron McLean Park. Continuing downhill, the creek picks up some more water just below Marine Drive, where John Matthews Creek trickles down its own ravine between Royal Oak and Gilley Avenues. In the industrial area between Marine Drive and Marine Way, Byrne Creek takes in more water, this time from Froggers' Creek, which flows down Burnaby's south slope through another ravine, this one cutting through the suburbs between Royal Oak and Nelson, and then passes between the Chinese Evangelical Church and the Iglesia Ni Cristo onto the flats.

On the flats of the Big Bend, it is different again. The boulders give way to streambed rocks just below the ravines, but once on the flats, the rocks give way to gravel, and Byrne Creek takes in some more water from Gray Creek, which trickles out of the ravine between Nelson and Sussex Avenues. From that point the gravel has given way to sand, and the creek flows slowly southwest, through blackberry and sedge and cattails, toward the dyke. In the 1800s, Byrne Creek used to flow east toward the Fraser, through John Woolard's farm, and back then it was called Woolard's Brook. In 1893, Peter Byrne dug a new, straight channel to allow the creek to run due south to the river, and the Gilley Brothers' logging company cut the timber on the south slope, hauling the logs by oxen to Byrne Creek, to float the timber south to the river and then up the Fraser to the New Westminster sawmills. But by the 1990s, Byrne Creek flows southwest, and it empties through flood-control gates into the North Arm of the Fraser River, where it disperses within the waters of thousands more streams from throughout the Fraser basin and continues its life as it began, a small, barely noticeable part of something much bigger. The muddy, roiling North Arm curls gracefully around the Big Bend, taking in Glen-Lyon Creek, Kaymar Creek, Boundary Creek, and what little is left of all the other creeks along Vancouver's south slope. The last is Musqueam Creek, and then there is the Strait of Georgia, where the great river itself becomes a small, barely noticeable part of something much bigger.

But salmon notice these things, and sea-run cutthroat trout notice these things, and whatever mystery accounts for it, the olfactory glands, or the molecular memory, or some other intelligence, the fish come up out of the sea after it, and whatever it is that they notice in all of this, they follow it up from the sea into the rivers. However dispersed within the Fraser River one of these tiny creeks might be, they find it, and they trace the underwater course of it, and if they swim too far up the big river they will turn around and find it again, and they will jump right out of the river if that's what they have to do to get to it. They will keep on going, on and on until they are above the sedge and the cattails, and they will head for the gravel, up near the boulders where they began, and they will fight to their death to get there, and they will fight against the very mountains themselves to return to the place they were born. This is the miracle of the salmon we all marvel about. More of a miracle is that they come home to us at all after everything we have done to them. But they do. That's the important part.

They come to Railroad Creek, where a remnant population of coho and chum that somehow survived the Canadian National Railway's excesses continued to return from the sea to spawn, down through the years. Railroad Creek empties into the Fraser River at Dewdney, just east of Mission. At about the time of Hell's Gate, railway crews built up earthworks all along the marshy lowlands behind the river's north bank, not unlike a long, low dam, below the base of the mountains. Crews laid the tracks on top of it all, to keep the line above flood water, putting in a bridge here and there to let the creeks through, punching through a culvert where they had to, but otherwise ignoring the hydrology of the place. Over the years, between the tracks and the mountains, loggers cut down the trees and farmers cleared the land. Countless little creeks were lost, and they were the types of creek chum and coho particularly like—the kind that arise from cold, upwelling springwater at the base of hills and mountains, the kind that flow quickly across gravel-bottom streambeds and empty into a big river nearby, nice and close to the sea. Down through the years, there wasn't much left of the little stream that came to be called Railroad Creek. But there were some chum and coho that spawned there still.

On a winter day in the late 1970s, a spawning pair of coho ventured a few metres past the gravel where they had emerged as eggs. They swam through a culvert that had been constructed through the embankment underneath the railroad tracks. They travelled a short distance up the ditch and found cold, bright water trickling in from a farmer's cow field. Battered and weary, the two coho jumped up and out of the creek, in the direction of the falling water, and landed in the soggy field. Together, they followed the flow of the ankle-deep water to the place where it was welling up through the grass. There, they began to dig with their tails. They unearthed the spawning gravel of their ancestors, at the old source of the creek, and there they spawned and died.

Their offspring returned in great numbers. They returned to Railroad Creek and kept going. They swam through the culvert, up the ditch, and into the field, through the grass to the place they were born and began to dig some more. They were followed by chum salmon, the offspring of fish born in Railroad Creek alongside the pioneering cohos' parents.

And so it went. On a cold January afternoon in 1988, biologists Matt Foy and Dave Marshall stood at the edge of a textbook-perfect spawning area, a gravel-covered expanse filled with bubbling, clear, bright springwater, in the middle of a farmer's field. Above the spawning beds, cedar posts hung in mid-air from lines of barbed wire. What had once been a fence wasn't really a fence any more, because the ground had been excavated out from beneath it, bulldozed downstream by the shredded and mangled tails of scores of chum and coho salmon. "I know," Marshall said. "It's hard to believe." A lone male chum salmon, bruised and ragged, swam in the shallows among carcasses of fish that had fought to regain the spawning grounds their ancestors had lost so many decades before. One of the dead fish hung, like vengeance itself, from a strand of barbed wire. "They punched through a cow field, through that little ditch," Foy said. "The fish themselves actually constructed their own spawning grounds, and every year the run is expanding."

Marshall and Foy are among dozens of fisheries biologists and technicians, many of whom work for the Salmonid Enhancement Program, and many of them senior SEP managers as well, who had little faith left, by the 1980s, in elaborate construction plans for cement hatchery complexes. Watch the fish, these biologists proposed instead. See what they want. Help them get it.

The salmon come to Worth Creek, not far from Railroad Creek, another place where it was obvious to Foy and Marshall what the fish wanted. There were spawners in Worth Creek. SEP technicians bulldozed a cut from the creek to its old source of springwater and emptied truckloads of gravel into the cut. It worked. In 1984, salmon were spawning in it. SEP crews left two dump-truck loads of gravel at the head of the cut and returned in 1987 to make the spawning beds bigger, but the coho and the chum had beaten them to it. The gravel pile was gone. The fish had dug away at the base of it and spread the gravel out neatly, beneath the water, moving it out and downstream. They dug their nests and spawned in it.

A short drive upriver at the mouth of Maria Slough, the long, hot summers and the logged-off mountains cause the slough to get silty and dry up in spots. When the rains come and autumn turns to winter, the coho and chum come back to Hicks Creek, which empties into the slough. The fish clear out the muck every year, opening up the beds again. "It looks like some outfit's gravel operation," Foy said. "Every winter, the coho move in there and dig it away."

Sometimes, it's as though SEP is getting help from the fish, instead of the other way around.

After building a series of costly artificial spawning channels above the Chehalis River, SEP engineers encountered an unforeseen problem. The channels were silting up badly every year, and the whole thing had started to look like a bad idea. Lots of money needed to be spent every year on bulldozers and backhoes to clear deep drifts of sand off the gravel beds. But as the years passed, it became obvious much of the machine engineering was unnecessary. SEP managers cleared out the upper ends of the channel, letting the sand settle downstream. The fish cleared out the rest. "When it settles out, you get it in piles three to four feet deep," said biologist Bruce Shepherd. "The fish move it out themselves. They just dig it out and move it downstream."

In the furthest reaches of the Fraser basin, in the Stuart River system, there are sections of the Tachie River and the Middle River that don't look like any salmon could ever spawn there. As Shepherd described it, "It's muck as deep as you can poke a stick," and the rivers are slow-moving, meandering through flatlands. But over the years, chinook and sockeye salmon have constructed their own spawning platforms that run from one bank to the other, at right angles to the current, with gravel forming the upstream side and mud and sand forming the downstream side, raising the water velocity in the bargain.

So while we have been taught to marvel at the wonder of salmon the great navigator, salmon are also engineers, and they are colonizers, and it took them less than 10,000 years to colonize or recolonize just about every river, stream, creek, and ditch between the coast and the Rocky Mountains, much of which remained covered under sheets of ice miles thick, for several centuries after the close of the last great ice age.

It is true that coho were extirpated from Byrne Creek when I was a boy, and there was no evidence of any sea-run cutthroat trout in Byrne Creek by the time I was in my teens. But in the autumn of 1995, I was walking along a trail in Byrne Creek's ravine, just above Marine Drive. It was Sunday morning and the sunlight fell through the cedar and the fir trees, and there was movement in the creek, in a pool below a boulder. I had a fleeting glimpse of something. It was too hard to see. There were shadows, and whatever it was, it was just a tiny thing, in a quiet reach of the creek, in a tangle of roots, below some over-hanging ferns.

"There. Look at that, there. Do you see it?"

Ken Glover, who is seventy-four, and played in these woods and along this creek when he was a boy, was pointing at the water below the boulder. He stepped carefully in his gumboots along the bank, and knelt down. Tony Pletcher, sixty-three, who graduated from my old high school a quarter-century before I did, was upstream a few paces, in gumboots, peering into the shallow water just above the boulder. Bert Richardson, sixty-seven, who has been tracking the fate of Byrne Creek for the past three decades, was wading just downstream. He stopped, and stood still.

Everything was quiet, just the faint hum of traffic coming through the trees. And there it was. A dark flash, the colour of gun metal, not much bigger than a rifle bullet. A tiny fish darted in a quick triangle pattern, then vanished. Then another, and another.

Cutthroat. Probably yearlings.

Glover, Pletcher, and Richardson never gave up on Byrne

Creek. Over the years, their friends at the Vancouver Angling and Game Association tried to be understanding about their stubbornness, but few were convinced that Byrne Creek was anything more than a lost cause. The meetings of the association's Byrne Creek subcommittee were never exactly standing-room-only affairs.

Over the years, Glover, Pletcher, and Richardson have worked with Salmonid Enhancement Program staff, lobbied municipal council, begged and borrowed from the Department of Fisheries and Oceans and the B.C. Environment Ministry, and organized teams of schoolchildren from Suncrest, Nelson, Clinton, and Stride Avenue schools into bucket brigades every year, releasing coho fry trucked from Kanaka Creek a few miles up the Fraser to the parking lot at Ron McLean Park, where the kids carry the baby fish down into the ravine to watch them swim away.

The coho transplanting began in 1979. There have been returns of jacks, precocious young males who couldn't spawn with a female if they wanted to. And there has been the occasional sighting of adult fish, and it might be that a male and female have paired off, but it's hard to say. Whenever a heavy rain follows a long dry spell, the accumulated toxins in the storm drains produce a lethal "first flush." It is the same all over the Lower Mainland, and what it produces is dead fish. The day we walked Byrne Creek, Chris Savage happened by, walking his dog. Two weeks before, he had seen a dead cutthroat fingerling, followed the foamy water upstream to a cul-de-sac, followed the water halfway down the block. It was just a man innocently washing his car in his driveway, killing fish.

So there are setbacks, but there are victories. Mundy's Towing helped the Byrne Creek volunteers pull tons of truck parts, whole cars, a deep freeze, several refrigerators, several couches, beds and mattresses and dozens of shopping carts out of the creek. Tighter provincial laws and tougher Fisheries Act enforcement have restrained some of the excesses of urban development in the watershed and around the flats. But there remains the question of whether a pair of coho returning to Byrne Creek would survive long enough to spawn, with the water quality as unstable as it is. And there is also the question of whether the baby coho would survive, since insect life has not returned to the creek all that much. But that is life, and you don't give up, Pletcher said. You identify the problems. You work hard to fix the problems.

There are untried remedies, and there are old, tried and true remedies, and there are remedies 'round the world. Maybe there is some scientist somewhere, Pletcher said, working on a methodology that would assist in the restoration of mayflies and crane flies and whatnot—sort of an insect enhancement program. There are experiments that have proven that natural vegetation can be used as a filtration system for toxins, and a simple system of catchment basins might be enough to eliminate the first flush problem. A remedy as low-tech as bags of charcoal dumped in the creek at certain strategic points might serve as a filtering system to maintain water quality, sort of an interim measure until non-toxic detergents are the rule rather than the exception.

"Gumboots," Glover said, walking the trail through the ravine. "More gumboots, fewer computers and word processors, and more gumboots."

"Fish weirs," said Pletcher, himself a biologist. "The Indians should go back to them. Everybody should try using them."

It is these little things that make a difference, in the long run. It is individuals, and small groups of people, working on local initiatives, that end up making a difference. It is not just the fishing industry that has caused the salmon to decline so precipitously. David Salmond Mitchell, the fisheries officer who argued against the dismantling of aboriginal fishing technologies at the turn of the century, understood this only too well. It wasn't just the big things, like Hell's Gate, Mitchell said. It was the little things. It was the hunters who made it their practice to shoot so many eagles and ospreys out of the skies above Shuswap Lake that the salmon-eating coarse fish they preyed upon, like freshwater ling, ran rampant throughout the lakes of the central interior. In the winters that followed the Hell's Gate disaster, Mitchell ventured out into the blizzards, out onto the frozen surface of Shuswap Lake, cut holes through the ice, and speared as many lingcod as he could, day in and day out, week in and week out. He enlisted armies of schoolchildren to help him, hauling up the lingcod, cutting open their stomachs and freeing salmon fry, "hundreds of little Jonahs," and Mitchell's contributions to the rebuilding of the great Adams River sockeye runs are incalculable. Maybe he didn't make all that much difference. Or maybe he made all the difference in the world.

Back on Byrne Creek, Ken Glover was taking a rest for a moment in the cool of the ravine. "These things take a long time," Glover said.

The bottom of the ravine was dark, choked with underbrush and alder among the trunks of towering cedar and fir and cottonwood. Byrne Creek riffled quietly at Ken's feet. Every now and then, a dark flash, a tiny fish, darted out and back into the shadows. This is the spot that Glover and the others have been gently herding schoolkids to, year after year. Just upstream from here, the previous winter, Glover had trapped three six-inch, pan-sized cutthroat, just to see if there were any there, and let them go. "When I was a kid, we used to herd the fish back and forth in the creek," Glover said. "What did we know?"

Across the creek, there was a small opening in the side of the sandstone ravine wall, shrouded by broad-leafed maple. I looked closer, and it was as if there was a stone wall back in there, half-covered in the undergrowth. I crossed the creek on the boulders and the stones. It was an old outfall pipe, set in a cement bunker with iron grates covering its dark entrance. Some kid had spray-painted "Hell Hole" above the mouth of the tunnel. It was pitch black inside, as though it went down into the middle of the Earth. I knew this ravine once like it was my own backyard. I didn't remember this.

I crossed back over the creek on the stones, watching the water for movement, and every now and then I caught a little fish out of the corner of my eye—or my mind's eye, anyway.

"It used to come from Dominion Glass," Glover said. "That's what really killed off the creek back then, I think."

And it all started to make more sense. When I looked across the creek, I could see that below the cement wall with Hell Hole gaping out of it there was no underbrush, just exposed stones from the torrents of the years. The drain tunnel led backwards, underground, to the place where the mammoth Dominion Glass factory used to be. I worked there when I was twenty, as far down on the union seniority list as it got. I worked deep within the dark tombs of the place, on the night shift, in winter, shovelling melted, molten glass and huge lumps of silica and caustic fixatives and colouring additives that dropped in great red-hot lumps from the furnaces and the machinery upstairs.

There were no face masks or oxygen tanks or health and safety inspections involved. There were no elaborate settling ponds in the tombs. And it would rain, and eventually all that stuff would sizzle and melt and muddy the pipes, and it would all end up pouring out of Hell Hole. And then the factory shut down, the dump was closed, the condominiums came, and the office towers went up.

So it is not good enough to say it was the government, the greedy fishermen, the seiners and the gillnetters and the trollers and the trawlers and the Indians and the poachers, or the seals, or the multinational fishing companies, or the forest companies or the greenhouse effect. I killed Byrne Creek. Who didn't?

It was the jam factory at McPherson and Beresford where I used to beg pop bottles from the women on their lunch break, in the summer, when John Matthews Creek ran red from the berry pulp. It is the man in his driveway on Ewart Avenue washing his car in the fall. It is the antifreeze for his windshield in the winter. It is the bark mulch in the spring around the flowers in your backyard. It is the politician you voted for, the trees you cut down, the grass cuttings you dumped down the hill, and the chlorine you put in your pool.

It is as big as Hells Gate, and it is as small as Hell Hole, and the world gets smaller as you grow older and you learn that things take time, like Ken Glover says. And then you learn that we don't have much time left any more, that we have had all the time in the world.

The world may well be a big place, but it's just as small as Byrne Creek.

PIERRE BÉLAND

Book of the Dead

PIERRE BÉLAND is a writer and scientist from Montreal
who has dedicated much of his life to efforts to save belugas.
He has written for many magazines, including *Nature,*
Scientific American, and *Whalewatcher.* "Book of the Dead"
is from *Beluga: A Farewell to Whales.*

LINING UP MY CAR on the pier at Rivière-du-Loup on the south
shore of the St. Lawrence, I realize how much I love to board a
ferry. Particularly this one, with its childhood memories of a
large white ship cruising away on the river. As a young boy wading at low tide among the seaweed-covered rocks, I was halted in
my search for clam worms by the sight of the ferryboat. I would
watch it become a tiny craft before it disappeared in midstream
behind the long green streak of Hare Island, which hides the
coastline on the other side. I had never been on the water, never
been on the ship, never seen its berth across the river. I could
only imagine that the boat would take its passengers for a tour
around the island and find an idyllic beach on which to land
everyone for a picnic, as families did in one of my picture books.

I am on standby in my old green Volvo, enjoying the bustle
that surrounds a docking ship. The Sunday fishermen move

over with their lines dangling to make room for the landing. The leads to the mooring cables explode from the ship like broken coil springs, startling the gulls that are always hawking for some scrap of food. The drivers about to disembark are anxious, their car engines running, their heads perked up behind steering wheels, as if they might be able to leave before the boat even docks. On the pier, in the meantime, the drivers waiting on the dock look equally worried, contemplating how they will squeeze down the steep ramp into the ship, which sits so low on the tidal estuary.

My car is the last to board, behind a huge trailer truck that rattles the openwork steel ramp. The ship sinks noticeably and rises up again after the truck is finally aboard, leaving me temporarily halted at a steep angle. When signalled to move forward, I show my free pass to Officer Belley. I know him well, and as usual he invites me to the wheelhouse for the crossing. Driving into the bowels of the ship, I get a last glimpse of the fishermen holding onto their rods on the wharf. They stare at each passenger entering the ship as if they were double agents entrusted with the compiling of statistics on the profitability of the ferry. They count me, too, at each sailing, but they don't seem to remember that I was one of them many years ago.

What brings me here nowadays is not the fish lurking under the greenish-brown surface but the bigger animals who feed on them. Mammals like us, blind in murky waters, but possessing their own efficient means of catching fish. Porpoises, we called them when I was a kid on the wharf, still unaware of their true identity. Like us, the whales would move back to their favourite spot to resume fishing as soon as the ferry left. The boat's propeller would stir the mud, bringing food up through the water column for fish to feed on. And for mammals to catch the fish. Kids and whales. From my favourite fishing spot on the wharf, a clam worm wiggling on the hook at the end of my line, I watched the whales' gleaming crescents on the water, and heard their blows mixing with our laughter. I often wondered if they could make out against the sky our dark silhouettes and dazzling haloes. I wondered if they could hear our calls every time we caught a fish.

I park on the car deck among the other sardines, who can barely open their cans to get out. Most are families on vacation, the children excited to be on a real ship at sea, their parents somewhat anxious to get to the other side. Presently, they seem unable to make up their minds about whether to take a sweater and other things along, stressed as they are by the sign that reads DO NOT STAY IN CAR FOR THE CROSSING. I wait until the main herd has reached the upper deck, then climb up and try to find a nice hidden spot where I can scan the river in peace. I am eager to see if there are whales in the vicinity, and my search for them must be a private affair: I may see an animal that I know by name when the other passengers would see only one more beluga whale.

A few minutes after the ship has left the dock, a small group of whales surfaces in the distance, heading upstream on the tide along Hare Island. No one else has seen them, for all that is noticeable are flashes of sunlight that come and go in the distance. I know that such sparkles on a windless day can only be whales. Some time later, we get closer to the whales, and a number of passengers spot them. Some kids who may have heard about them on TV call out excitedly, pulling at the sleeves of their parents, who, unable to make out anything, say there cannot be whales so close to land. Still others, with the look of people who are getting what they paid for, respond contentedly that this is what the travel guidebook said. And then there are those who watch in silence and with respect, conscious of witnessing animals in their own environment, doing their job honestly, and deserving not to be disturbed.

The belugas roll smoothly with an unhurried determination, as always instilling in me a measure of serenity. Unlike the slender dolphins, they do not speed or jump as they come out for air. They look more like small, plump whales than porpoises. They do not swim close to each other yet move together as a single pod of adults, whiter than the surf on a wave in the wind, opaque as creamy milk. They are so bright against the dark water that you would swear you could see them miles away, even beyond the curvature of the earth. At close range, their bodies show no colour patterns, bands, or streaks, although they usually bear scratches of undetermined origin. One animal has nicks across the barely noticeable ridge that runs along the middle of its back, where the dorsal fin stands in other species. The lack of a fin makes it difficult for the untrained eye to follow the progression of a beluga's body when it arches over the surface of the water. From a distance, the animal seems to emerge and sink without moving ahead, as if a crescent of the moon had been pushed up from underwater for exactly three seconds and pulled back in.

I do not recognize a known animal but notice a young boy and girl looking at me intently. Feeling discovered, I climb to the officers' quarters on the top deck. As soon as I walk into the wheelhouse, careful not to trip over the high sill, Captain Harvey asks me about the whales: *How is your work going this year?* But I have my own questions for the crew. Have they seen many young this season? The exchange of data on the whales is our greeting ritual. I give some details about our latest findings while perusing the wheelhouse, always amazed at how spotless and well ordered it is. I am careful not to let my fingers touch the polished brass lining the windows and the navigation instruments. I pick up a pair of binoculars to look at the river toward the southwest, where we are headed.

The ferry makes six crossings a day from April to the end of the Christmas holidays, each time spending an hour and a half in the heart of the beluga range in the St. Lawrence. Technically, the domain of the whales is an estuary—an area where fresh water from a river mixes with salt water from the sea. The map, however, labels this body of water the St. Lawrence "River," and that is what people here usually call it. But unlike a river, the St. Lawrence flows downstream only half the time, its main current reversed every six hours by the tide. Twice a day, millions of tons of light-brown water are flushed downstream, exposing the outer fringe of the riverbed. Sailboats that enter the marina at Rivière-du-Loup at high tide will be sitting in the mud as much as eighteen feet lower six hours later. Then, in one slow breath, green salt waters flood the shore again, bringing in seaweed, marine fish, and seabirds, along with assorted seals and whales. Gazing upstream or downstream, your eyes can see only water as far as the horizon. It sparkles, it is cold, and it has drowned many ships and killed even more mariners. That is why those who live by the lower St. Lawrence also call it the sea.

At Rivière-du-Loup, the St. Lawrence is twelve miles wide; across it are mountains, at the foot of which the water is four hundred feet deep. The St. Lawrence boasts a fjord, which lurks

under the fog to the northeast like the fjords on the coast of
Norway in the North Atlantic. Ancient saline waters reside permanently in these troughs, reminders of when the St. Lawrence
truly was an arm of the sea and the beluga, an arctic species,
came into this area. Around twenty thousand years ago, much of
Canada and the northern United States was covered in glaciers,
and arctic whales and seals fed at the ice edge in the Atlantic off
the exposed continental shelf. Then, as the climate started to
warm up, the Laurentian ice sheet melted away and the sea level
rose over the continent, which had sunk considerably under the
immense weight of ice. In the northeast, marine waters pene-
trated into and beyond the Gulf of St. Lawrence, filling a huge
area west almost to the Great Lakes and southwest to New York
and Vermont. Finback, humpback, and bowhead whales; narwhals and harbour porpoises; harp, bearded, and hooded seals
came into this inland sea. Belugas roamed in huge herds, and
their skeletons account for most of the whale remains found in
the sediments deposited at the bottom of this Champlain Sea
9,300 to 12,400 years ago. In ecological terms, this was the Arctic
of the day.

In time, relieved from its burden of ice, the land rose, the
basin dried up, and the St. Lawrence River took form in its
midst. Its lower course, where the Rivière-du-Loup ferry now
crosses, remains an ever-changing realm between the continent
and the ocean. It is in this estuary that the North Atlantic, hundreds of miles away to the east, and the Great Lakes, hundreds
of miles inland, meet every day. As fresh water rushes out to sea
at the surface, a cold wedge of saline water flows inward beneath
it, all the way from the Gulf of St. Lawrence and the ocean. This
frigid layer, replenished by cooling during the harsh winter,

surges to the surface where submarine walls of rock stop its course, or when the wind blows from the land. Here, although the climate warmed up long ago and narwhals, bowhead whales, and walrus have departed, belugas have remained, along with a few arctic fish and crustaceans that thrive in this arctic oasis far from the polar region.

It does not look like an oasis at all in winter. By Christmas, the river is already covered in pack ice. Floes drift from shore to shore, up and down the river, slaves to wind and tide, and pile up in huge stacks all along the coast and around the rim of every island. When the wind is from the northwest and masses of frozen arctic air swoop down the mountains, the deep water in the troughs at their foot surges to the surface, where it smokes like a smouldering fire. This weather signals the season of the harp seals, who come in to breed on the floes and to feed on capelin made sluggish by the freezing water. For a few weeks, the seals take over the estuary. The beluga have deserted it for the gulf, where they share open waters with the hardiest of sea ducks. By then, the ferry has stopped running until the spring to avoid being crushed by floes in the middle of the night.

I am happy to chat with the crew, who have become dear to me over the years, but I have something else in mind. I want to know if the watch officer has spotted the whales that I saw minutes ago from my restricted view on the deck below. Pretending to amble around and somewhat ashamed of my deviousness, I walk to the chart table. On it, next to the ship's logbook, lies another book, the whale logbook. It is a binder that I have prepared for the crew, with hundreds of identical pages, each one a reduced photocopy of the nautical chart showing the ship's course between the shores and around the tip of Hare Island. One page per crossing, on which the officers have agreed to mark down their whale sightings. The book is opened at today's crossing. There they are: six whales going upstream by the island, five minutes ago.

From March to December, the whale logbook is where live beluga sightings are recorded every day. The voluntary work of the crew is important because the ferryboat's route is inhabited by a large number of females with young. What happens here is critical to the future of the St. Lawrence beluga whale population. Several more seasons of dedicated work will be required before any pattern in the whales' movements can be recognized and any change in their numbers detected. Every day, the crew is on the lookout, hoping to make more entries in their book than they did the previous year.

My own book is much smaller, and I would rather not add anything to it. It is a record of dead beluga whales, with 180 entries since the fall of 1982. The St. Lawrence belugas are a small resident population of about five hundred animals, isolated from other belugas, who live in the Arctic. Fifteen dead animals per year is therefore a sizeable statistic—and I may be recording only a fraction of the deaths, certainly few of those that occur during winter. Beluga whales can live thirty years and more, but healthy females in their prime give birth to a single calf only once every three years. This means that replacement is slow under the best of conditions. Even slight disturbances can check the growth of a small population. The present St. Lawrence belugas are the remnant of a population of several thousands who were heavily exploited for almost three hundred years. When they were given legal protection in 1979, only about five hundred whales remained. Since then, the population has failed to recover. My Book of the Dead tells why: the whales are dying of pollution.

Even as I write it, I realize how strong this last statement is—"Far too strong for a scientist," many of my colleagues would say. I would not have dared say such a thing a few years ago. Maybe I have grown bolder as my experience and interest in these animals have matured. But in fact I am simply echoing the conclusion that most observers of our work have come to. It is very plain.

By the time a St. Lawrence beluga whale reaches age sixteen, its body's burden of mercury has already exceeded the load considered to be necessary to cause developmental and neurological effects in humans. This load increases as long as the whale lives in that river, which means until its death. Take organohalogens, for another example. These are a family of man-made chemicals that includes insecticides like DDT, dieldrin, and mirex, as well as industrial chemicals like polychlorobiphenyls (PCBs). Because of the hazardous nature of these compounds, ships on the St. Lawrence carrying waste with more than fifty milligrams of PCBs per kilogram (or fifty parts per million) require a special transit permit. An average male beluga roaming these same waters already has that concentration of PCBs in his blubber by age nine—without the permit—and that level will double by the time he is twenty-two. Adult females are more fortunate: their blubber PCB levels will not reach fifty ppm before age thirty-four—an age very few belugas ever reach. But the lower level in females is not actually a good sign. It is only by unloading their contaminants onto their calves through nursing that females reduce their level of intoxication.

The ferry is now coasting close to Hare Island, that imagined haven of my childhood. I scan its shore to locate the site where I finally landed recently on my first visit to the island. Even after all these years, the place still held an aura of mystery when I first approached it in a small research boat with two colleagues. It looked like a beautiful, unspoiled garden and would have been romantic, had I gone there for a picnic and not to answer a call about a dead beluga whale. We spent some time searching for the whale among the driftwood, dead reeds, and assorted plastic refuse littering the pebbles at the edge of the forest. After much effort, we found a tiny carcass. It was a newborn calf, and already several like him had been recorded in my Book of the Dead. They had died of intoxication or because their mothers had passed away, unable to survive the stress of giving birth.

The other pages in my book are mostly records of adults who suffered the effects of long-term exposure to chemicals, as opposed to acute poisoning. There have been no mass mortalities in the St. Lawrence, only unspectacular deaths of single individuals drifting to the shore, as if the population were undergoing slow attrition. We would not even know about the belugas' plight if we had not taken these carcasses every year to the necropsy room at the veterinary school of the University of Montréal, far upriver, driving for hours through the night on the highway, hauling strange horizontal ghosts like gigantic alien sausages.

It all started in September 1982, when a veterinarian from Agriculture Canada dropped in to my laboratory on the university campus in Rimouski. He told me about his summer sailing trips on the St. Lawrence and in Saguenay fjord, where he had often observed white whales come to investigate his boat. He thought that studying these animals would be a welcome change from his regular and tiring travels all across the Gaspé Peninsula, treating cows and sheep. He wondered whether the federal government research centre that I was heading at the time had an interest in the whales. I had to tell him that we were a fisheries ecology research centre, already involved in several research projects, none of which had anything to do with belugas. In retrospect, I may have even added that whales ate fish and that our job was to understand how fish were being produced in the river, not how they were being consumed. Over the next few weeks, this gentleman came to see me a few more times, always enquiring about beluga whales and invariably leaving his name and phone number. I came to find his visits rather annoying. I have long since forgotten his phone number, but I remember his name very well: Daniel Martineau.

Soon afterward, Dr. David Sergeant, who had been researching belugas in the Arctic and the St. Lawrence, was invited on campus to give a talk on his work. I phoned Dr. Martineau, happy at last to have something to offer him. On the appointed day, we were holed up with other members of academia in a university classroom, both listening to David's talk. He was about halfway through his slides when my secretary peeked into the room and silently handed me a note: a dead beluga had just been found washed on shore a few kilometres away. It was the first such notice we had ever received, and it was undoubtedly due to the presence of Dr. Sergeant among us. As soon as the talk was over, Daniel and I rushed up to David with the note, and within minutes, all three of us were driving toward the lighthouse at Pointe-au-Père, where I saw my very first beluga whale in its entirety.

I had had some exposure to belugas when I was a child drifting through the summer holidays at a small village by the name
of Rivière-Ouelle. Sometimes I went for walks with my mother
on the beach along the St. Lawrence when she managed to slip
away from her household chores. We waded over the flat at low
tide in the small haze that rose from the cold mud exposed to the
sun, and I stopped here and there to overturn a stone with a
stick, careful not to let my shoes dangling from my hands fall in
the soft mud. I remember vividly how my mother would call to
me, excitedly pointing at some inconspicuous specks out there
on the majestic river. *Do you see them? Do you see them?* I would
turn toward her instead of to the river, my feet sinking into the
dark brown goo that left grey patches where it had dried on my
calves.

My mother had always looked at the world the way she did
on her first Christmas morning: everything to her was magic,
beautiful, new. Her love for the river and for everything that
lived in or by it burst out each time she walked on its shore.
I had become blasé about her constant wonderments, but being
a respectful child, I would take a look at the oceanlike expanse
of water. Sometimes I saw the small white crescents on the water
in the distance—not so different from the countless whitecaps
borne in the wind that seemed to inhabit that moving kingdom
perpetually. More often than not, I was not sure that I saw anything in particular. Those white flashes could just as well have
been pieces of ice that had survived through the spring and that
accounted for the water's being so cold all the time. *Yes, I see
them*, I would answer, feeling uneasy about lying. *They are
migrating upstream today*, my mother would say. *How numerous*

they are! Like waves on the sea! Look at those white whales! Look at those belugas! I would look at her, thinking of the innumerable everyday things that she kept pointing out to me, whales being only one of them.

I eventually got to know these animals better, since they seemed to feed on the same fish that I tried to catch from the pier. But even then, I was never quite convinced that these white porpoises in the brownish water by the wharf were real whales. After all, the St. Lawrence was but a river, and all I ever saw were rounded white shapes without heads or tails. Now, a quarter of a century later, I stood on the beach next to a real beluga whale. I did not have to lie anymore: here it was, dead at my feet, rather smallish for a whale, stark white against the collage of blue mussel shells and brown seaweed on which it had so obtrusively landed. Having spent my childhood thinking that whales did not belong in the waters of a river, I now surmised that they belonged even less on its shore.

Daniel was immediately all around the body, measuring it, examining it, and discussing it with David. It looked very fresh and so perfectly smooth, with only a few rough patches inlaid with gravel where gulls had picked at the skin as the corpse drifted toward the shore. When I approached for a closer inspection, Daniel uttered fateful words: *Let's have a look inside.* I was flabbergasted. How does one look inside a whale? *Let's open it,* repeated Daniel. And with these words, he launched us on one of the most successful and challenging research projects any of us had ever been involved in. In the dozen years since that fateful day, we have examined scores of beluga carcasses along that same river. The shores of the St. Lawrence are dotted with sites that we have trodden to pick up dead whales. Strangely, every new death is still a wonder to me. Like my mother, I cannot get used to this everyday thing of life.

It was ironic that Daniel's interest in the whales, sparked by his observations of live animals in the river, had taken him away from his sailboat and back on the road and around the estuary and along the gulf shores, this time looking for dead animals. It was a very demanding project, and each new season saw him with a different helper, usually a summer student. Eventually, I took over the beachcombing part of the study and enlisted Richard Plante to help me. Fresh out of school, Richard had trained to become a fisherman but had discovered that he preferred to make fishing nets. My lab had commissioned him to make plankton nets and other gear for collecting various sea animals for scientific studies. One day, he walked in with a custom-made net for loading the dead bodies of marine mammals into our truck. Richard had tremendous energy and dedication. Together, we have retrieved dozens of carcasses of several species of whales and seals from the shores of the St. Lawrence.

It was exhilarating. At a single phone call we were off in a minute for a long trip. We spent many hours of hard work on the beach in all kinds of weather, which left us with the satisfaction of a physically demanding job well done. We savoured the camaraderie and the splendour of daybreak on the water, when all was silent and we were on the road with a whale. But there was also sorrow. Driving along the sparsely inhabited shore, where long, dark stretches were broken by small villages with high-steepled churches, old trees alongside ancestral houses, and small wooden boats pulled up on shore, I passed through the country of my childhood. This was the land where I had been raised and where I had only dreamed of being able to visit every bay and cove. The dream had come true, except that I had become not an explorer but some kind of mortician.

Every call had to be answered. For some reason, the whales tended to die before sunrise or on weekends when I had some family outing. In the evening one December 31st, the phone rang at home and I could hardly understand the voice on the other end over the noise of the party going on at my place. I gathered that the speaker had been climbing some ice falls by the river in the morning and he had seen a white, rounded shape sticking out of the ice on the beach. He thought it might be a beluga. I told Richard and another friend, Paul Robichaud, who were among the crowd dancing and drinking to celebrate the end of another year. The following morning, the three of us set out walking on the shelf ice by the river, dragging our gear and my daughter Martine, who was seven years old. It was New Year's Day, thirty degrees below. The wind was a bitter north-wester, the snow hard as wood, the ice like steel. We walked a mile and a half over the beach to the ice falls. The whale was there, creamy white, just a patch of its flank emerging from the snow and ice. We whacked at its ice casing with axes like miners in a quarry, until Martine went nearly numb with cold and we realized that all of us might die there too.

After finding my first dead whale in 1982, I could not help but think of its kin still out there in the river. Driving the long road from Rimouski to Montréal on business trips, I wondered where the whales were at that moment. I began taking the ferry to see what the whales did in June and July. But the season on the river is shorter for humans than for whales and by September the yachts and sailboats have been pulled up on shore. After the fishing nets have been retrieved and piled up in their sheds, after the navigation buoys have been taken out of the river and even the ferry has stopped passing the icebound island, where do the belugas roam? I spent hours scanning the river from a number of vantage points where I made regular stops.

I seldom saw belugas from the shore. There were none of the herds that my mother had once pointed out to me. The whales seemed to have stopped migrating upstream lately. Or downstream. I was afraid that they had begun to migrate into history. But I could not get a proper idea of what was happening at sea. Therefore in addition to our work on dead whales, we launched a series of projects to look at live whales and to understand how they lived. We ran surveys from the air and by boat, and were able to determine how many belugas there were and where they were. We photo-identified many animals and learned something about their social structure and movements. In particular, we discovered that females arrived at the area plied by the ferry in April, stayed through summer to give birth and to feed their young, and then left in October. We found out that there did not seem to be as many young belugas in this population as in those that lived farther north.

The tide is ebbing now, and the brackish water from upstream bulges higher against the bow of the ferry. It is greenish-brown and opaque, uninviting—aspects that are usually and wrongly associated with pollution. The water is rich with plankton and particles of organic matter that scatter sunlight, not with silt contaminated with the toxic chemicals found in the whales. The poisons are concealed within larger packages, mostly in fish, especially some species that migrate from far away. I arrived at this conclusion after adding the amounts of chemicals measured in the tissues of many whales and finding that local fish could account for only a small percentage of the total. Where the remainder came from puzzled me until I saw a newspaper article about eels caught along the river. They had been banned from the German market because of their high levels of the insecticide mirex, a chemical prominent in belugas, and one that had a single source near Lake Ontario.

Eels enter the rivers and lakes of the St. Lawrence and Great Lakes basin as larvae from the Atlantic Ocean. They remain in the rivers and lakes until they become adult. Each fall, mature eels swim back down the rivers and lakes into the St. Lawrence on their way to the ocean where they were born, to spawn in the Sargasso Sea south of Bermuda. Those that migrate out of Lake Ontario carry mirex and other chemicals that have accumulated in their bodies as the eels fed in the lake. For just a few weeks in October, beluga whales catch migrating eels as they pass through the estuary on their way to the sea. This brief feeding period is sufficient to account for almost half of all the chemicals present in the belugas' blubber. Most of these toxic chemicals have long been banned in North America, but they still circulate through the ecosystems where they were once used or dumped. The Great Lakes and the land that drains into them are the main North American reservoirs for such chemicals. Lake sediments, invertebrates, fish, and birds all hoard toxic chemicals, some of which drift down continuously into the St. Lawrence from Lake Ontario. Every year, more pollutants are added via long-range atmospheric transport from countries that use these pesticides and chemicals, such as Mexico, and even faraway India, China, and Siberia.

From his post on the Rivière-du-Loup ferry, helmsman Girard is a keen observer of life on the St. Lawrence. He knows that the water flowing by his ship comes mostly from the Great Lakes and from the rivers that drain the farmlands and industrial areas of Québec. Like other members of the crew, he is alarmed. He tells me that these days, many fishermen no longer dare to eat some of the fish they catch. But the whales still do, he says, looking at me. *How could they know that the fish are chemically tainted? Even if they could tell that the fish are no good, what else would they eat?* The crustaceans, worms, and organic particles stirred up from the mud by the ferry are contaminated, too. Belugas do not have access to sterilized and toxic-free canned food from the store, although the helmsman is quite sure that the whales often do find empty cans down at the bottom of the river . . .

We are now two-thirds of the way to the north shore, and the dock at St. Simeon begins to show behind the western tip of Hare Island. The village is perched on the slopes of the mountains, and through my binoculars I can see that the ferry will not be returning empty. The ferryboat veers sharply to starboard around the buoy marking the passage to the other side. This is an area of strong eddies and rip currents that marks the border between the two main channels of the river. There are reefs on either side of the buoy where cormorants and ducks fish during the long summer days and where belugas come in the spring and fall to feed on herring spawn stuck to the rocks and seaweed on the bottom.

All summer, this is a favourite hangout for female belugas and their young. They have long since grown accustomed to the ferry and dive right under it as we churn through the tidal eddies beyond the edge of the shoal. I walk to the other side of the wheelhouse to see where they will surface and find that I am being observed by the two children who were watching me earlier on the lower deck. They, too, have drifted up here and are climbing and peeking over the NO ADMITTANCE sign on the handrail for a better look inside the cabin. Their smiles catch me, and I walk out on the bridge toward them. They know who I am and have come to say that they are brother and sister from Montréal. Their school has adopted one of our photo-identified beluga whales. I remember their school, where I was invited to celebrate their sponsoring of a whale the children named Omega. Pupils from every school in the district had participated in raising money for the whales, selling T-shirts with a custom design. On that day, I had walked through their exhibit of drawings and paintings, listened to songs and poems, and watched a play, all on the subject of belugas. Now the boy and girl want to know if Omega has been spotted this season, and I promise to check with our team working on the water every day out of Tadoussac. They run back to the passenger deck, and as I watch them disappear down the gangway, I know that they hold one of the keys to the future of the whales.

Suddenly the phone rings in the wheelhouse; *It's for you,* says the captain, handing me the receiver. Who on earth would phone me here. I pretend to wonder . . . but I know. The marine operator has a call for me from the *Bleuvet.* A bad omen: this is the name of our research vessel working on beluga photo identification somewhere downstream. This is exactly where I was headed to spend a few days observing live belugas in the wild. Over the phone, I recognize the voice of Daniel Lefebvre, our captain, calling on his VHF. Normally I am tense during these one-way conversations, in which one must wait for the end of the other's message before speaking. But at the moment I am in no mood to say anything. I don't even have to listen: I know what he is going to tell me. He has just found a dead whale in the river, and he is towing it to shore. I will be there in less than an hour. And back on the road to the necropsy room in less than two, with the senseless guilt that comes from driving with a dead whale behind me. I hope it is not Omega.

DON GAYTON

Landscape Mathematics

DON GAYTON, who earns a living as a range ecologist,
is one of Canada's most acclaimed nature writers.
After spending fifteen years in Saskatchewan, Gayton and
his family now live in Nelson, B.C. Gayton's most
recent book is the award-winning *Landscapes of the
Interior: Re-Explorations of Nature and the Human Spirit*.
"Landscape Mathematics" is from *The Wheatgrass
Mechanism: Science and Imagination in the
Western Canadian Landscape*.

EARLY MORNING LIGHT slowly flooded across a plateau, illuminating first wheatgrass, then sagebrush, then lichen-stained rock. This sunrise was a private showing, held for an eighteen-year-old on a Greyhound walkabout. Ninety-nine dollars for all the prairie the west had to offer. I had gotten off that bus at a late night stop in some distant community (it could have been Eastend, Rifle, Merritt, or Omak) and walked to the edge of town. The few blocks of uncomplicated houses, streetlights, and cottonwoods ended abruptly at a three-wire fence and dark, unfathomed space. I crossed over into the blackness, shuffling slowly, and lay down on my bedroll. This was new country, reached at night, and I had no sense of what was around me. But the air was warm and still, and I was glad to be free of the bus for a few hours.

Morning was a revelation. Silence and a cleansing odour of sage enveloped me. A moving curtain of first daylight fired each landscape element in turn with clean, level light. The frayed and blackened trunks of sage were softened by foliage of grey velvet. Coarse mineral soil reflected motes of glassy pink. Rigid seed stalks of nameless grasses strained upward, away from their curving profusions of basal leaves. I turned around to see five spectral antelope, held in the brief and naked moment between curiosity and flight. In the path of advancing sunlight, a distant windmill and watering trough spoke of some lean and minimalist human use of the land. Beyond that lay an enormous mountain-bounded chunk of western space. This was a charmed circle, of parched and improbable beauty.

I plunged deeply into that heart-rending landscape. Back on the bus I wrote letters about it to imaginary women, describing the place as if it were my home, and asking them to join me there. Plains and prairie landscapes, and the small communities they supported, became my passion on that trip, almost a compulsion. I felt the immigrant's urgency at each new place, wanting to embrace the land, to couple upon it, to quickly learn the meaning of its antelope and its burrowing owls, and to understand how livings were made from the brittle bunchgrasses.

Landscape, vision, synaptic firing, memory; the powerful walkabout sequence went on and on. Too long, in the end, when it spilled over the borders of the West to become mere travel, but the memory of grass and sagebrush prairie endured. Years later I redeemed the promise to come back to the region of those persistent images, and settled in to learn from the slow, equinoctial rhythms of an Okanagan cattle ranch.

The headquarters of the Double L lay in a dry glacial valley, surrounded by Ponderosa pine, bluebunch wheatgrass, and rock. This time I was no tourist on the landscape; now I could poke and prod it, explore along its seams, and come back to it again and again. The irrigated hayfields became my laboratories for plant response, the pastures my observation plots for grazing and recovery, the bluebunch rangeland my magnificent herbarium. I developed a kind of grass kinship, along with a lasting allergy to brome pollen. The Double L offered me the chance to participate in a working anachronism; hired man on an eighty-year-old cow-calf outfit that had changed little over the years. This was a job having much to do with landscape, allowing me to fill in some of my prairie images with detail and response. I began to understand the careful and conservative process of making a sustainable grassland living. But all along I knew there was another class of landscape detail, beyond that required for work and wages. After four seasons on the Double L, I finally shifted my focus to the fifth floor of a university library.

Beginning Plant Ecology graduate students were not expected to devote massive blocks of time to library reading, having many other things to attend to, but I became possessed. Journals such as *Planta*, *Botanical Gazette*, and the *Journal of Range Management* became close companions, and I began to wait impatiently for library staff to shelve the latest issues. Other journals appeared as I summerfallowed through the stacks: *Compost Science*, the *Journal of Irreproducible Results*, and *Aquatic Biology*, among others. All this unsung agony and triumph was found in the labyrinthine shelves of the "Q-to-QK" section.

The pact made with that morning landscape years before had led me to this library, by way of the Double L. Here I found bizarre, almost ritualized views of the same grass and sagebrush: digitized landscapes, creative analogues of function, razor-thin splinters of experience, multiple treatments, and sacred controls. I found all the mystery of a dark Nostradamian heresy, hard by a scientific rigour that verged on the autistic. This was Middle Earth.

I struggled at first with the mere names of my chosen land-scape, "prairie," "range," "plain," and "steppe," finding them more evocative than definitive. "Grassland," which evoked little but didn't attempt much either, seemed a useful, functional term. Maps drawn by dogged men like J. E. Weaver showed me how this North American grassland could be divided into pro-vinces. The Northern Great Plains province takes in a vast swath of western Canada, the Dakotas, and eastern Montana, plus a part of Colorado and Nebraska. Continuing southward into Texas and northeastern Mexico are the Southern Plains grass-lands. The valleys of the Rockies and other ranges of the west coast hold the dry and narrow Pacific Northwest Grasslands; to the south of them, in Nevada and Utah, are the Great Basin Desert Grasslands. Each of these provinces is subdivided into a patchwork quilt of subtypes based on the dominant vegetation.

Our northern prairies are relatively young landscapes, devel-oping after the last late Pleistocene glaciers retreated and the southern forests collapsed in the face of increasing drought. The grassy vegetation that colonized this vast new niche did not evolve in place. Instead, forest understorey grasses slowly speci-ated outward from the eastern and northern fringes on to the new land, honing new mechanisms of survival as they spread.

Native grasslands also form the matrix of what western identity we have, since they are only found west of a line drawn through Manitoba and down along the Mississippi River to the Gulf. The grasslands have produced a style of dress, a traditional literature and an emerging one, a sense of political alienation, and a sense of individual independence. Somewhere, in the dense overlay of political boundaries and administrative divisions, lies a thin and shadowy republic of prairie.

Climatologists can define prairie as simply a level, unprotected region where evaporation through the growing season slightly exceeds incoming rainfall. On our prairies, that differential is created by the powerful rain shadow effect of British Columbia's mountains. They force the great inbound masses of moisture-laden Pacific air upward, extracting their moisture in the process. By the time these air masses drop exhausted down the eastern foothills, they are bone dry. The exposure and dryness during the growing season discourages trees and favours shrubs and grasses that have tough, minimalist aboveground structures, and massive root systems.

Fire is another creator of grasslands, killing woody trees and shrubs that have aboveground growing points and sparing grasses, which regrow from ground level. Man has always been a creature of grasslands and savannah, and his presence in North America is probably intimately linked to fires and the maintenance of grasslands. If fire did not start naturally, then humans probably set periodic fires, for reasons that are interesting to speculate on.

At some point early in this century man's commitment to the use of fire reversed itself, and modern fire suppression has led to massive forest ingrowth into traditional grasslands, notably along the Rocky Mountain Trench. Our society will eventually have to come to terms with the rejuvenating power of fire in the landscape. Since fire comes inevitably to forest/grassland interfaces, occasional small fires, intentionally set, may be preferable to storing fuel indefinitely for the inevitable large wildfire.

Most days I worked at the same large corner table on the fifth floor of the library. The table was also used by a very elegant older woman who was doing a doctoral thesis on the Irish playwright J. M. Synge. We shared an enthusiasm for primary sources, and occasionally we used each other as cross-disciplinary sounding boards. If I could give her a clear and enthusiastic summary of my day's reading, or vice versa, that was a good sign.

Through the narrow windows of the library I could see a fair-sized chunk of the Canadian prairies, and that view was a good reminder of the place-context of my studies. This was no fecund, temperate birthplace of plant research, like England's Rothamstead, Holland's Wageningen, or Maryland's Beltsville: this was a cold near-desert of short, violent summers and murderous winters. Captain John Palliser once declared most of it not suitable for habitation by Europeans.

I found out early on in my studies that many of the sophisticated plant mechanisms and symbioses described in the research journals did not operate here. What I found instead were multiple systems of endurance and individual survival. Western wheatgrass, for example, produces tiny wax plates on its leaf surfaces to help seal off water loss. The leaf is deeply ribbed, like a piece of corrugated cardboard, and its stomata are nested in the recesses between ribs. Under drought stress, the leaf edges will curl upward to form a long narrow tube, still allowing the leaf to function but reducing drought exposure. Most of the stomata of western wheatgrass leaves are on the upper side, so the leaf can continue atmospheric transactions within the protected space of the tube. The plant reproduces by extending rhizomes outward in the relative protection of the soil, rather than risking seed production aboveground in the ever present summer sun.

To imagine endless seasons passing over a stand of western wheatgrass, and the slow accretion of these mechanisms into genetic identity, is to glimpse a very fundamental prairie timeline.

Most of the grasses and forbs on this dry prairie flower early, I discovered. They shoehorn their life cycle into the generally cooler, wetter months of April, May, and June. The rest of the season is devoted to the slow building up of food reserves for the winter, until frost draws a curtain on the growth period in late September or October. Then the prairie juggernaut—winter—arrives, bringing wind, precious little snow, and paralyzing temperatures.

Botanist Jan Looman puzzled over the distribution of the so-called warm-season grasses, the C4 species that make up the tallgrass prairie. Why were they only found on the very eastern edge of the prairies, when summers on the western side were just as warm, if not warmer? Looman studied the problem and proposed the following answer: warm-season dropseed and bluestem grasses flower in late June and July, at least a month later than the cool-season wheatgrasses and stipas, and they must have sufficient midsummer moisture to complete their life cycle. He found that by mapping spring/summer precipitation ratios across the prairies, he could predict the location of warm-season grasses wherever summer rainfall was greater than spring rainfall. Looman's theory fit over the biogeographical reality quite well: those regions that historically supported tallgrass vegetation had summer precipitation at least equal to, if not greater than, spring precipitation.

Winter is the next hurdle. January on the prairie will usually deliver at least a few days that approach minus 40, but oddly enough, the critical period for the survival of a prairie plant is not those arctic mornings, but early spring. April is a month when winter and summer can splice deeply into one another, with devastating results for plants as they green up. Regina weather in the spring of 1981 was a typical example. Daytime highs for the first twelve days of April of that year were well above freezing at 7, 12, even as high as 17 degrees Celsius. Lows were modest, averaging around minus 3. Then, on the 13th, a cold front moved in, and the daytime high reached only 1 degree Celsius. That night the mercury dropped to minus 13. The next day was clear and calm, allowing the temperature to soar to 24 degrees. The night of the 15th the temperature dropped again to minus 6.

For many cultivated plants that had survived the previous winter, April 1981 was the last straw. Yet the great bulk of native grasses do survive the roughest of prairie winters and springs, a remarkable feat of thermal stress engineering.

A slight excess of evaporation over precipitation creates grassland. A greater excess, as in the case of British Columbia's Okanagan valley, results in a desert grassland. There, plant surface areas contract even more and diameters increase, as in the sagebrush, bitterbrush, and cactus. Roots of the scrubby Ponderosa pine explore deeply into gravel and rock outcroppings. Opportunist species like the annual cheatgrasses race through brief life cycles in the few precious days of wet spring.

Climatology is a fascinating prism for viewing and defining landscape and ecotype. The concept of water balance is clear and intuitive. But more personal, more synaptic visions of Canadian prairie abound that are equally elegant. Here is one the library produced, from the Irish adventurer William Butler, writing in the 1870s:

> But [this] ocean is one of grass, and the shores are the crests of mountain ranges, and the dark pine forests of the sub-Arctic regions. The great ocean itself does not present more infinite variety than does this prairie-ocean of which we speak. In winter, a dazzling surface of the purest snow; in early summer, a vast expanse of grass and pale pink roses; in autumn too often a wild sea of raging fire. No ocean of water in the world can vie with its gorgeous sunsets; no solitude can equal the loneliness of night-shadowed prairie . . .

The North American prairie has been ravaged. Between plowing and overgrazing, it is perhaps the most extensively altered biome on the planet, and we know very little of its original ecology and function. Thus the historical observations by Butler and others—who saw this land in an essentially virgin state—become tremendously important to contemporary students of this landscape and its resources. "We don't know what we're doing because we don't know what we've undone," is Wendell Berry's commentary on prairie agriculture.

A new discipline must be forged—historical ecology—that will reconstruct the evolution of western North American landscape from the Late Pleistocene to about 1950. Outrageously diverse sources would be consulted in building this discipline:

pollen rain in lake sediments, radiocarbon bone analysis, glacial air-bubble sampling, aboriginal legends, and explorers' journals. This would not be the recovery of an existing history, but the synthesis of a new one.

I have daydreamed of commanding William Butler off his horse, down onto his knees amid the dusty grass and roses, to tell me exactly what he sees. Lovely poetry, Bill, but now I want you to give me details about species composition, percent cover, buffalo grazing patterns, rates of litterfall, fire frequency, and soil microbial populations. As a matter of fact, sit down, Bill, this may take a while.

For a long time I was transfixed at that fifth floor library table, using the window at my elbow as a reference point, and reading prairie. Plant physiology and plant ecology gradually emerged as my specialties, my favoured prisms of view. The memory of that distant morning landscape did not become a faded photograph from another time; it simply shifted from simple experience to part of my identity.

When I look back on that walkabout I realize that love is hopelessly entangled in our landscape equations. We see new country as a conjugal garden, or occasionally as a boundless plain for cowboy solitude and misogyny. We have a recurring need to commit ourselves, and the western landscape is always available. What a spectacular host for that commitment.

The entanglement of the factors of landscape and love has given us a culture of the West, an urgency, and a closeness to the earth. But somewhere in one of the parent equations is another factor for tearing down and remaking landscape. This factor, by which we hope to provide for those loved ones and prove something to them, is the virus that is slowly destroying the whole mathematics.

There is a famous photograph by Ansel Adams called "Moonrise over Hernandez, New Mexico" that shows a tiny community of adobe houses and ancient cottonwoods, set in a vast layered landscape of dry riverbed and desert, with the Sangre de Cristo mountain range in the distance. A print of that photograph hangs on the wall of my study. I think Hernandez may represent, in spite of its rural stasis and Hispanic contradiction, one of the finest sustainable relations between man and land that North America has yet produced. The Hernandez human community expressed great passion and empathy for its landscape and revised it very little, probably paying a price in its lack of material progress. Adams, who worked in natural landscapes almost exclusively, must have felt there was something special about this village, something very harmonious about its landscape equation, in order to include it in his portfolio.

Hernandez is not a dream: it actually exists, produced as a conscious choice by its inhabitants, the same way Calgary and Trail are produced. I hope we can someday rewrite our own landscape mathematics to include some small fraction of the Hernandez factor.

JAMIE BASTEDO
The ABCs of Bug Protection

JAMIE BASTEDO is a resident of Yellowknife in the
Northwest Territories, where he works as a writer, a naturalist,
an environmental consultant, and the host of CBC Radio's
Northern Nature program. He wrote *Shield Country:*
Life and Times of the Oldest Piece of the Planet.
"The ABCs of Bug Protection" is from *Reaching North:*
A Celebration of the Subarctic.

Insects form the hair shirt of the north country.
— TED NAGLE, *The Prospector North of Sixty*

BITING INSECTS give the north woods a bad name. Awaiting
you there, amidst the black spruce and Labrador tea, is a distinc-
tively Canadian torture. An evil scourge. A terrible pestilence.
Flying hypodermic needles. In some cases even the scientific
names ascribed to these bugs by normally impartial taxonomists
reflect the prejudices born of too many bites in the bush. Among
the many northern species of mosquitoes are *Aedes excrucians*,
which speaks for itself, *Aedes fitchii*, which calls to mind both
fidgeting and itching, and *Aedes inornata* (meaning "ugly or
unseemly"), which is about as far as a taxonomist can go before
labelling this species as downright repulsive.

The verdict is still out on which is worse: blackflies or mosquitoes. Prospector Ted Nagle, remembering his 1904 trip along the south shore of Great Slave Lake, cast his vote for mosquitoes.

> For sheer discomfort it is difficult to imagine anything worse than blackflies. They slipped beneath our clothing and set our skin afire. But worst of all were the mosquitoes. The number of northern mosquitoes that appear after a hatch is unimaginably huge. We often wake up mornings to find a velvety grey ring around the campfire. Hundreds of thousands of mosquitoes had settled on the warm ground just far enough from the fire to feel safe. They rose in a cloud to fasten on anyone of us who approached them unawares.

Before squashing them Nagle sometimes took a morbid pause to closely examine their anatomy. "There were two different kinds of mosquitoes. The smaller grey ones were much like those known in the south. But there were also large yellow mosquitoes, at least half an inch long. The big yellow mosquitoes had augers on their noses that could drill through clothing."

For renowned naturalist Ernest Thompson Seton, who explored Canada's western subarctic in the early 1900s, it was blackflies, hands down, that gave him the greatest grief. "The blackflies attack us like some awful pestilence walking in darkness, crawling in and forcing themselves under our clothing, stinging and poisoning as they go."

The journals of early visitors to this region are replete with loathsome accounts of blackfly invasions. Here's another from a 1930s prospector working in the Mackenzie River Valley. After listening to the "driving rain" of flies on his tent all night, he finally braved a dash outside to make breakfast. "In a few moments, the bacon in the frying pan was mottled with hundreds of black dots—flies that had perished. In the coffeepot floated a layer that covered the whole surface."

Besides molesting humans, insect assaults on domestic animals also checker historical records from the north woods. One account from northern Alberta describes cattle keeling over dead within fifteen minutes of a blackfly attack—from some sort of mysterious shock effect, not from loss of blood. While journeying through the same region in 1915, explorer and anthropologist Vilhjálmur Stefánsson wrote of farm animals driven mad by bugs. In one journal he claimed that young calves and piglets were known to have died as a result of multiple attacks by bulldog flies and mosquitoes. In forest clearings and crude fields he observed huge smudge fires built not for farmers but for their cattle, which occasionally would slip out from the protective cover of smoke to risk a few mouthfuls of grass.

For some contemporary northerners, many of whom are recent transplants, the Bug Problem sucks all the pleasure out of their brief subarctic summers. In a desperate plea for some sort of civil defence action, one unnerved city dweller from Yellowknife shared his plight with the local newspaper editor.

As you are well aware, the mosquito population is taking over our fair town. The number of critters has reached the point where it is becoming virtually impossible to spend time outdoors without risk to ongoing blood supply. Ambulating twenty feet from one's vehicle to residence is a race for human survival. Mowing the lawn, weeding gardens, taking the dog for a walk, strolling on our well-conceived nature pathways have lost appeal due to the voracious airborne pests.

Are these simply the accounts of northern travellers and residents who have been struck blind with entomophobia, a morbid fear of insects? Or are all such horror stories true? Dr. Harold Lutz, a forestry professor from Yale University who "endured" several summers of field work in Alaska back in the 1950s puts his faith in the stories. "The credibility of some of the accounts relating to the severity of the torture inflicted by mosquitoes is sometimes questioned," he asserts, "but only by those whose experience does not include at least one summer in the northern forests."

Come what may to the North, nothing short of another ice age will rid us of biting insects no matter how insufferable they may be. So what do we do in the meantime? Try these simple offerings: my ABCs of self-defence against bugs.

A is for Attitude. Let's face it, fighting for all-out victory against the vast northern battalions of bugs is a lost cause. Their combined biomass exceeds, by an order of magnitude, that of the million caribou that roam freely across northern Canada. Biting insects are the dominant life-form North of Sixty and in human terms always will be. Extermination is out of the question. But fighting our own bigotry against them is a battle we *can* win. The road to peaceful coexistence with our insect brothers and sisters begins with tolerance, which, said some sage, is a sapling that grows only when rooted in the soil of understanding.

Bloodthirsty? Of course they're bloodthirsty. Wouldn't you be if this was the food for which your exquisite mouth and digestive tract were so designed to process? Malicious, spiteful, purposefully needling? Such designs could not enter their little brains, such as they are. The motives of biting insects are as pure as any creature, be it grizzly or grasshopper, innocently absorbed in the act of nourishing a rapidly growing family. For instance, in some species of mosquitoes the female can carry out all her life functions, even nourish her developing eggs, getting by on plant nectar alone. But blood is richer than nectar, particularly in proteins, and can increase egg production a hundredfold. There. In the service of motherhood, are you ready to make peace?

No? Well, then consider their colossal ecological importance. Biting insects collectively pump astronomical amounts of energy into countless northern food chains. As aquatic larvae they provide food for many species of fish and ducks. Insect-eating birds such as swallows, flycatchers, and warblers absolutely depend on them. For instance, a lone tree swallow on the wing can gulp down as many as twenty-five hundred flying insects during a good day over the marsh. These insects also help satisfy the voracious appetites of dragonflies and damselflies, which in turn become food for many kinds of birds and the occasional frog. And in the process of foraging for nectar, they serve as the main pollinators for innumerable northern plants, including most berry bushes, a favoured source of food for many animals, both four- and two-legged.

"Biting flies are a strong indicator of healthy environments," says my former biostatistics professor and bug counter, Dr. Steve Smith at the University of Waterloo. Biting flies are his entomological passion. His life would be much impoverished without them. And so would ours, he argues.

> Their absence would mean that something serious has happened to an area of wetlands and streams. Sure, we bitch all the time about mosquitoes. But the reality is, if you said "Would you live in an area without them?" I'd say no because then I wouldn't have the frogs in springtime . . . and I wouldn't have the birds associated with wetlands, and I wouldn't have the flora associated with wetlands.

Where Smith lives, in southern Ontario, wetlands exist as isolated islands surrounded by a sea of urban and rural development. In the wild and well-watered northland, moist breeding pockets for biting insects abut every hummock and hill. Here they thrive in numbers that only physicists can understand. Try to imagine, for instance, close to one hundred million squirming, wriggling mosquito larvae per hectare of breeding habitat. The ecological upshot is that such numbers represent a healthy starting quota for the multitude of organisms that absolutely depend on these bugs for survival.

The next time you are besieged by bugs, keep their motives and munificence in mind. A positive attitude toward your attackers may serve as a last line of mental self-defence when all else fails.

B is for Behaviour. Not theirs, ours. Exactly where and how and when you go through the north woods can make a big difference to the condition of your skin (and your nerves) upon your return to camp. One early surveyor did just about everything wrong in this respect and suffered accordingly. He described northern bugs as a plague that followed him every summer everywhere he went. This particular surveyor happened to spend most of his summers hacking rectilinear seismic lines through that jumbled patchwork of wetlands known as muskeg. This boggy soggy landscape is dimpled with countless small ponds and puddles. Some might call it a waterscape. So in a sense he asked for the bugs when he took the job. Or rather his superiors sentenced him to them when they drew those straight lines on the map. A prisoner of predetermined compass bearings, he had to pass unswervingly by terrain features that would have delivered him well out of the reach of probing insect mouths, places shunned by bugs and embraced by savvy northern travellers. That poor surveyor had to walk right past places of refuge rendered bug-free thanks to the wind.

As passive riders on the wind, mosquitoes are known to have blown across distances approaching one hundred kilometres. But wind has a debilitating effect on both the coordination and appetite of most biting insects. The stronger, the better. Fifteen kilometres per hour seems to be the magic threshold at which flying insects are knocked off their little feet. So get out of the wet woods and find a high windswept outcrop or open shoreline for your traverse or campsite. Should the bugs persist there is no surer escape from them than pushing off the land and paddling to a breezy platform of water. The moral in short is to take the high trail or windward shore to reduce blood loss.

As an alternative there is always your tent if the wind has died completely and your forbearance for bugs has evaporated. Claustrophobic in there? Instead you can simply smudge them away by throwing a rotten punky log or a few green spruce boughs onto the fire. Smoke is anathema to most insects, but so is it to most campers. The trick of carefree smudging is to place yourself close enough to the smoke to smell it but not inhale it. Even amidst a maelstrom of mosquitoes, you can with practice quickly regain your composure and redirect your attention to matters of importance, like savouring your tea, watching the sun set, or exchanging bear-attack stories.

In the thick of an insect infestation a smudge fire provides a practical alternative to going temporarily insane, according to geologist Charles Camsell. "They rose up in clouds with every step I took," he wrote in 1920, while surveying the Mackenzie Valley.

> I had no protection from these pests . . . and from time to time as I got tired I also became almost panicky. When I felt myself beginning to run I immediately pulled up and made a small fire so that I could get some relief in the smoke. I could easily imagine a man going off his head if he should have to endure such torture for any length of time.

Exactly *when* you choose to do your tripping—or for that matter mowing the lawn—is your business. But in bug country a proper sense of timing can help keep your blood pressure low and blood volume high. Most mosquitoes are crepuscular feeders, preferring to binge on your blood at dawn and dusk. You are safest in your sleeping bag or around the fire during these times. But get this: blackflies have an altogether different meal shift. They are generally diurnal—daytime feeders—seeking blood most intensely in the early morning and late afternoon. Should you decide to take no other precautions against bugs, this leaves you just a few hours during the hottest part of the day to hike or paddle like hell.

It's late June, peak of the bug season. You are on foot traversing a large spruce bog several kilometres from camp. You are wearing shorts, a T-shirt, and a tired pair of peat-stained runners. All you have in your daypack are binoculars, a granola bar, a ball cap, and last April's ski wax (it happens, I know). You are caught in the subarctic wilderness without wind, a canoe, a well-sealed tent, some matches, or a watch. The whining random pulse of insect wings is rising fast. So is your dread. You can run, but you can't hide. You can, however, opt for one last surefire defence: find a lake or river or slough and jump in. They won't find you underwater.

C is for clothing. Light and tight is all you need to know. Light, since most biting insects are cued to home in on dark colours reminiscent of the tawny browns and blacks of their fur-covered natural hosts. And tight, since many biters, particularly blackflies, like to creep down collars, through loose sleeves, and up dangling pant legs to find dark cosy feeding troughs (they make their own). After swallowing the last of your urban pride, button up your collar, batten down your cuffs, ram your pant legs into some thick woollen socks. Immunize yourself against attack in true northern style.

Those putting their faith in less homegrown technologies can put down a large handful of tens and buy a bug jacket. There are two main kinds. My favourite is a fine-meshed "dopeless" bug jacket equipped with elasticized ruffles from top to bottom. The ruffles serve to elevate the surface of the jacket away from your vulnerable skin. As well, they give this model the look and feel of some kind of bizarre bodice that Queen Victoria might have worn after hours. Trail chic. The other kind of jacket, *sans* ruffles, is sold with several ounces of high-proof bug repellent, which you are supposed to dump all over the jacket before putting it on. Hopefully you like the acrid smell of bug dope, because whatever clothes you slip this jacket over will be gassing off in your closet weeks after you return to civilization.

Though I am dead against them, it would not be fair to omit some mention of the infamous bug hat. Perhaps I have negative associations with its use. I reserve it for emergency situations, putting it on only when the bugs are so thick I can't breathe. Furled for storage deep in your pack, the industry standard looks like a squashed bowler hat made from insipid green nylon. Unfurled, a thick sun-glinting screen drops from its rim, revealing at the bottom an elastic choking device meant for your neck. With one of these things on, you can't see straight, you can't eat or drink anything, you can't carry on intelligent conversations (even with yourself), for who could take you seriously? What is worse, when a few errant bugs manage to squirm their way past your constricting neck band, as they inevitably do, you can't for the life of you get them out. There you are, eyeball to compound eyeball with the pestiferous pip-squeaks you are trying to evade. When caught in such a pickle, I can't help thinking of the head-mounted torture device described in George Orwell's *Nineteen Eighty-Four*. Do you remember that scene? The story's hero, Winston Smith, is trapped in Room 101. "The thing that is in Room 101 is the worst thing in the world," explains his interrogator as he prepares to clamp the device over Smith's unwilling head. "It was an oblong wire cage with a handle on top for carrying it by. Fixed to the front of it was something that looked like a fencing mask . . . [Smith] could see that the cage was divided lengthwise into two compartments, and that there was some kind of creature in each. They were rats." Which is worse: a dozen caged blackflies chewing on your neck or a couple of hungry rats? I'm not sure. The bug hat. Don't leave home without one. But pray you never need to use it.

D is for dope, bug dope. My favourite: citronella oil, a natural insect repellent extracted from a sweet, lemon-scented grass of the same name that grows in Southeast Asia. Though its effects are short-lived, it does work, and the big cosmetic companies like Avon know it. Hence the burgeoning new line of alternative no-risk bug repellents. Alternative to what? In a word: DEET. In many words: Di-ethyl-m-toluamide. This wonder chemical was developed in the 1940s by uniformed entomologists working in secret laboratories owned and operated by the U.S. military. To a mosquito or blackfly zooming toward you on its final approach, the smell of DEET in effect jams its radar by seriously meddling with its natural impulses to land and bite. "Eureka!" said its discoverers. "A high-potency, easily fabricated, long-lasting bug repellent." Among this chemical's many wonders is what it does to your polyester pants, camera case, and the varnish on your paddle. It eats them. Another wonder is that anybody of sound mind might actually apply this stuff, full-strength, to their bodies, let alone to those of their children.

It stands to reason that a chemical developed just down the hall from a laboratory developing nerve gas might make you nervous. For most users DEET causes tingling, a mild irritation, and occasional desquamation (the erosion of uppermost skin layers). Apparently small sacrifices compared to the blight of bugs. But look deeper. Almost 20 percent of the DEET you apply to your skin is flowing freely through your bloodstream within one hour. And on what organ does it go to work? Your brain, of course. High concentrations of DEET (over 30 percent), when applied as directed on the spray can label, may result in varying degrees of toxic encephalopathy, a poisoned brain. According to the *American Medical Sciences Bulletin*, symptoms vary from headache, restlessness, and unexplained crying spells to "rapid pressured speech, gait disturbances, and delusions of grandeur," the latter of which may explain at least some of the stories told by dope-smearing fishermen. Extreme symptoms include acute manic psychosis, writhing convulsions, and "stupor progressing to coma or death." The *Bulletin* suggests that "great caution should be exercised in using DEET on children. Only the products containing the lower concentrations (usually 15 percent) should be used." Even at these levels the *Bulletin* concludes that "application should be sparing." Everything in moderation, as my father used to say. Myself, when I need a dope fix, I'll reach for sweet citronella.

Across southern Canada, doping whole towns is a popular panacea to the Bug Problem. Popular at least with city councillors who would like to be seen as rectifying the apparent injustice of sharing precious urban space with a few million bugs. Starting around 1920 they used to spray waste motor oil and kerosene to coat the water surface of mosquito-infested ponds and ditches. Yuck. The idea was to suffocate the little suckers before they hatched. By the 1940s whole cities were routinely blanketed by powerful new chemical pesticides that fried the nervous systems of adult mosquitoes along with many other unintended organisms. Not environmentally kosher these days. The current rage is to spray synthetic bug hormones and so-called bacteriological insecticides all over the place and hope for the best: fewer bugs and more votes. Because of the profusion of widely varying natural factors that normally dictate mosquito numbers—the rate of spring melt, amount of standing water, abundance of insect predators, direction and strength of winds, to name a few—no town in history has ever been able to conclusively say whether or not their spraying campaigns really worked. What *is* certain is that whenever proposals for spraying campaigns creep into the headlines each spring, some colourful debate soon follows.

Proponents of the new so-called environmentally friendly insecticides promise "effective relief from the insect swarms." Crusaders for a pure environment, on the other hand, promote personal self-sufficiency in warding off bugs while calling for an all-out ban on spraying. This debate routinely reaches a fever pitch in Winnipeg, which is ironically home of the Canada Biting Fly Institute. "The whole city is sprayed with poison by ground and air crews," wrote one longtime opponent. "Some mosquitoes and all their predators are killed; infant birth defects and allergies increase; the chemical companies show a wonderfully healthy profit; and all bodies of water soon become perfect, predator-free mosquito incubators so that even more chemical poison can be sold to the suffering and gullible taxpayers the next year."

Undaunted by such uncertain track records and possible hazards, the city of Yellowknife in the mid-1980s decided to follow suit and launch its own campaign of wholesale slaughter of mosquitoes. A familiar controversy soon buzzed its way onto the front pages of the local newspaper. "Please, I beg of you," pleaded one Yellowknife resident in favour of the plan, "fog, spray—do *something*—to deplete the mosquito population. It has become intolerable." In the same issue, the paper's editor countered this position: "One bad bug season cannot justify the spraying of chemicals all over the place, year in and year out. We might as well ask politicians to do something about the cold temperatures during winter." The editor went on to remind his readers that no matter how effective an urban spray program may be, you can't take it with you. "Remember also that the most enjoyable part of summer in the North is not a weekend on the deserted city streets. It is out in the bush and on the water. You cannot take a publicly funded abatement program to the lake." The pro-spraying lobby won. But after a few springs of spraying yielded nothing but inconclusive results and large bills to the taxpayers (one estimate came to fifty cents per dead bug), the city decided to sell off its spraying arsenal and scrap the whole program. The wiser among city councillors now knew that spraying insecticide to kill bugs in the subarctic is like trying to subdue a volcano with a garden hose.

In India there is a small sect of Jain monks who always mask their mouths and carry with them a dainty white broom. When walking about, they use the broom to sweep the ground in front of them to avoid inadvertently crushing underfoot any of God's tiniest creatures. The mask prevents accidental swallowings of the same. In the western world, Yellowknife resident Chris O'Brien comes as near to anyone in equalling this level of respect for all life, including biting insects. During his twenties this man spent many happy hours clutching the wheel of a Formula III race car hurtling down road courses in Britain and Canada at speeds over two hundred kilometres an hour. Now a car-less naturalist in his early fifties, O'Brien has anchored himself firmly and enthusiastically to the subarctic, bugs and all.

Clear, searching eyes, silver midparted hair, and a fulsome beard give O'Brien an outwardly monkish appearance. His voice is low and mellow, like that of a late night FM announcer, and he speaks with a self-effacing authority that makes you listen. When I asked him to declare whether or not he kills mosquitoes, he responded, with unfeigned sincerity, "Why should I?" He told me that under no circumstances does he willfully squish them. "There's really no point since even if you try to kill every one that lands on you, others are still going to find you and bite you. Besides, there's nothing to fear from being bit by a few mosquitoes unless you're in malaria country. I simply brush them aside. The big ones like bulldog flies—the ones that *really* hurt —I give them a good whack with the back of my hand as a kind of warning shot. I'm telling them to bug off and look for a moose instead. It usually works." O'Brien admitted that such forms of persuasion may fail when the bugs thicken the air. In this case he dons his dopeless bug jacket, then dabs a bit of 7 percent DEET cream on his neck and hands. "None of this 95 percent nonsense for me. The stuff's bloody toxic at those concentrations."

There is nothing on earth that now brings O'Brien more joy than settling into a lakeside bush camp of his choice and spending the entire subarctic spring and summer observing in Thoreau-like fashion the ever-changing face of nature. Standard equipment amidst his humble camping gear is what he calls a bug sucker. It consists of a rigid tube with a clear wide-bore compartment attached to one end. Most people use this device to siphon up gunk from the bottom of their home aquarium. O'Brien uses it to live-trap mosquitoes. "The fellow at the pet store helped me put it together. The only modification is some fine netting at the tube end so I don't inhale the bugs." Before retiring for the night, he applies his bug sucker to the canvas walls of his tent, gently sucking any deviant mosquitoes and blackflies into the screened holding compartment, then releasing them *en masse* back into the wilds where they belong.

O'Brien's benign equanimity toward bloodlusting insects is the product of disciplined patience, logistical preparedness, and a heartfelt belief that everything in nature has its place. "They belong here as much as you do," he told me bluntly. "There are simple ways of getting around them." O'Brien bucks more orthodox views that would welcome mass extinctions of northern bugs. He does this by demonstrating quietly but convincingly that a state of peaceful coexistence with them is not only desirable but attainable. Before we get there, those of us with harder hearts or more stubborn prejudices can take solace in the words of a Yellowknife woman who was stopped on the street one buggy June day by a local newspaper reporter and asked, "What do you think of the mosquitoes?" In her thoughtful reply she likened them to "the five o'clock rush hour and warm beer"—things we ultimately can learn to live with given the right frame of mind.

KEVIN VAN TIGHEM

Recognition

KEVIN VAN TIGHEM is a naturalist and writer
who lives in Waterton Lakes National Park, where
he works for Parks Canada. Van Tighem is the
author of eight books and a four-time winner of the
Outdoor Writers of Canada Environmental
Writing Award. "Recognition" is from a collection
of Van Tighem's essays called *Coming West:
A Natural History of Home.*

I SET MY CANOE into the silt-grey waters of the Athabasca River
one evening and slipped quietly away into the gloom.

It was barely May, too early in the year for birdsong. The only
sounds were the muted chuckle of the river and the occasional
distant hiss and whine of passing traffic on the Yellowhead Highway. Elk watched my canoe drift past. Higher, on the open
slopes of Mount Colin, a herd of bighorn sheep picked their
way up a shadowed meadow. They knew where they were going.
I did not.

They were at home. I was just passing by.

I had thought about doing my field work on foot with a
flashlight, but common sense suggested I look for alternatives.

Grizzlies haunt the river flats in early spring, avoiding the lingering snowpack of the high country while they forage on sweet vetch roots and winterkill. The thought of meeting a grizzly nose-to-nose in the dark was sufficient to make me look for other ways of counting owls.

Owls were only a few of about 250 species of vertebrate animals I was supposed to inventory for Parks Canada. Soil scientists and botanists had already mapped this part of Jasper, tracing lines around discrete ecosystems and landforms. Now it was my turn to document how many mammals, birds, reptiles, and amphibians were at home in each ecosite, as we called the map units.

Owls are hard to find except in early spring when they give their distinctive territorial calls. I had no choice but to seek them at night, which is why I was now tunnelling silently into the gloom. My canoe tipped and tilted beneath me, responding to the icy boils and back eddies of a river that, a few miles upstream, was glacier ice. I looked into the silt-shadowed water and shivered, contemplating the consequences of an unexpected encounter with a sweeper.

A boreal owl tootled briefly as I slipped past a large stand of old-growth white spruce. From time to time I heard the familiar hooting of a great horned owl or the monotonous high-pitched whistles of a saw-whet. Once something went crashing out of shallow water and vanished into forest gloom.

The moon rose beyond Roche Miette. It silvered the landscape, casting trees into relief and spilling a path of silver across the river's rippled surface. Navigating was easier now. The lower Athabasca River in Jasper National Park is fast-flowing but gentle. I was not too worried about swamping. Still, it was good to be able to watch out for sweepers or gravel bars in the cold glow of the moon.

The mountains silhouetted on either side stretched off to the northwest and the southeast, separated by high valleys trending in the same direction. I had seen these mountains once out the window of a commercial jet. From that elevation they looked like giant waves that had suddenly hardened in place—long lines of limestone breakers forever waiting to crash down on west-central Alberta's boreal plains.

From canoe-level I could see the way in which each range ended abruptly at the edge of the Athabasca River. Glaciers long ago shaved off and steepened the mountain ends. A few thousand years ago the glaciers melted back to where they wait, now, cupped among the highest peaks, poised to advance down-valley when the climate cools again.

Those shrunken glaciers fed the river on which I now floated. The valley's glacial origin was obvious to me; even the mighty Athabasca River is too small to have carved the broad valley through which it flows. It was a river of ice, not water, that carved this valley.

Another owl tootled, high on the forested benchlands above the river. I back paddled, ferrying away from a spruce sweeper and bouncing down a shallow riffle. A pair of geese began to clamour. Their long necks bobbed up and down as they paced me down the far side of a midstream island. They were still complaining when the canoe carried me around a bend.

A sudden confusion of channels glistened in the moonlight. The river widened here, slowing as it approached Jasper Lake.

A freshening breeze—spilling down the broad valley from the high country to the west—nudged the canoe gently out of the main channel. I had to paddle hard to get back into the current. The channel turned. The breeze pushed me toward the bank.

The channels widened and coalesced as the current bore me out onto the shallow waters of Jasper Lake. Twice I ran aground on silt, pushed off, drifted a few yards, and ran aground again. The water was wave-rippled, silt-laden, and secret. It offered no clues where the deep channel had gone.

Jasper Lake is only a lake for part of each year. When the glaciers melted back, they left the valleys of the Athabasca and its tributaries filled with loose gravel, silt, clay, and other debris. The Snake Indian River joins the Athabasca from the northwest at the same point where the Rocky River enters from the southeast. Both rivers swept countless tons of raw sediment out of their new valleys each year for centuries, depositing it where they lost power upon entering the main Athabasca Valley. Over the years, both rivers built alluvial fans that spread across the valley and joined, blocking the Athabasca and damming up Jasper Lake.

The Athabasca also carries a heavy load of sediment. Pooled behind the natural dam, the Athabasca has deposited ten-centuries-worth of silt and sand in Jasper Lake. What began as a lake is now a deep deposit of fine glacial flour. Only in summer, when the Columbia Icefield and other headwater glaciers melt most feverishly, does water cover the silt flats and Jasper Lake again become worthy of the name.

Tonight was a bad night to paddle Jasper Lake. The spring runoff had begun to cover the silt flats but the resulting lake was only a few inches deep at best. Bit by bit, by trial and error, I found the deep-water channel, drifted further into the lake, and ran aground again. Even when I was sure of where the channel lay, the stiffening breeze confounded me by blowing the canoe off course. Repeatedly I found the channel, only to lose it and run aground.

Finally, in frustration, I decided to wade across the moonlit lake to shore, cache my canoe beside the highway, and hitchhike home. I stepped out of the canoe, grabbed the bow rope, and began to walk. Semi-trailer truck rigs burrowed through the darkness along the south edge of the lake. I was just contemplating the shock that one of those truck drivers would experience if he or she happened to look my way and see a man walking across the surface of a lake, pulling a canoe, when I had a shock of my own: I found the missing channel.

Soaked, furious, and frustrated, I gripped the side of the canoe and drifted until my feet found the silty bottom again. I clambered back into the canoe and began to paddle down the channel. The wind took control and again blew me aground in shallow water.

Exasperated and discouraged, I sat shivering in the darkness, watching wind ripples chasing down the long silver reflection of the moon. Listening to the stillness, I became aware of a strange, high-pitched hiss like vibrating power lines. There were no power lines, however. Alone in mid-lake, I listened carefully. The sound seemed to come from the canoe.

Leaning over, I watched the grip and scurry of water flowing along the sides of the canoe. All at once it dawned on me that what I was hearing was the saltating hiss of millions of tiny silt particles. Silt was sliding against the aluminum as the river bore it out into the lake. Glaciers had ground this flourlike silt from mountain rock. The melted waters of those same glaciers carried it in suspension down-valley to my canoe, and Jasper Lake.

As I contemplated my discovery, a low moan rose out of the darkness far across the lake, swelling into a long, resonating howl. It faded, died, and was gone, leaving only a faint hissing, the tug of wind on wet clothing, and a silver line of moonlight spilling across a dark lake.

Later that night I finally made it to shore, stashed my canoe, and went home to a hot bath and a dry bed. When I awoke the next day, the Athabasca Valley was transformed.

I had thought I knew the Athabasca River: its valley-bottom forests, steep-walled mountains, and wolves. I had visited the headwater glaciers. I understood the story of how they had once extended east onto the central Alberta plains. But that night in the middle of Jasper Lake was the first time I came to see that they were not separate things: all were one.

The wind that blew my canoe aground had only recently kissed the surface of glaciers that were the source of the water on which I floated. The same west wind, year after year, had pulled moisture in off the Pacific Ocean, lifted it high into the Rockies, and shed it as snow—the snow that fed those glaciers.

Depleted of moisture, warmed by the sudden descent to low elevations, those same winds funnelled down the Athabasca Valley—which those same glaciers had carved in times gone by—and swept winter snows away. In doing so, the west wind helped create a rich habitat mosaic for elk, sheep, deer, and other animals upon which the wolf I had heard relied for food.

Silt ground by glacier ice from those high mountains, washed downstream by glacier meltwater, had filled Jasper Lake. Each winter, when the glaciers froze rock-hard, the lake level fell. Those same west winds swept up the silt, depositing it in dunes where those same wolves denned.

Wind and ice, river and mountain, wolf and water: all were part of the same whole. All were linked by cause and effect, time and consequence. All were threads in the same landscape tapestry.

For days I gazed around me, wide-eyed, seeing my home landscape as if for the first time. My midnight awakening had opened me to discovery. Over the months and years that followed, my intimacy with this place deepened and accreted as I followed the threads of my discovery into new understandings.

Years earlier, a friend had a similar experience. Dale Zieroth and I worked as park naturalists in Kootenay National Park. He was a poet by choice and a historian by training. Each summer Dale chose a subject about which he knew little, and forced himself to learn all that he could about it. Then he sought within his imagination a way to bring it to life in the interpretive programs he delivered in campground theatres.

One year he decided to focus on glacial geomorphology—how glaciers change landscapes. He knew next to nothing about it. Every day he cloistered himself in the park library, poring over geography books. He poured himself into a crash course on aretes, eskers, moraines, hanging valleys, and all the various landscape features that result when ice, rock, and water spend a long time in each other's company. Each evening he drove home, bemused, from the park office in Radium Hot Springs to his house on a hillside near Invermere.

By mid-May he was irritable and distracted. He had filled himself with facts, but nothing had gelled. He knew the details, but he could not find a story.

Then one day he flew into the office, ecstatic.

"What happened?" I asked.

"I've got it!"

"What?"

"An esker connection," he cried, grinning with relief. "I've made an esker connection."

The previous evening, driving down Highway 93 in the golden light of a May evening, Dale had found himself slowing as usual where the pavement traced an elegant S-bend along the benches above Stoddart Creek.

"All at once," he said, "I realized that the S-bend was there because they built the highway right along the top of an esker. I've driven that S-bend almost every day for years. I'd never even wondered about it before. And then I looked around and I saw that the benches were kame terraces. Then I saw other eskers and drumlins in the valley bottom, and hanging valleys along the edge of the Columbia Valley . . ."

Deer were feeding on the sunburnt side of a kame terrace. A raven drifted above the esker, looking for road kills. Dale came home that night through a landscape he had never seen before. The irony confounded him: he and his wife had built a house, raised a child, and spent years delighting in the surroundings they had chosen for home. Yet they had never seen the eskers.

Most animals are acutely aware of landscape. Humans, for the most part, can choose to ignore it.

We do not need to seek out sunbathed south-facing slopes on cold days in fall; we merely turn up the thermostat. We do not retreat to the shelter of old-growth forests or seek a familiar rock overhang when the rain falls; we go indoors. Engineers design our roads for speed so that we can waste as little time as possible when we travel between artificial places of our own creation. Highways negate landscape. The engineers who build them fill valleys and carve down hills so that drivers need not notice the natural ups and downs. All the curves are smooth. Mileage signs tell us how much longer until we escape the landscape and get home.

Ranchers, loggers, and others who make their living outdoors are necessarily more aware of landscape than most of those who huddle in cities and towns. Hunters—true hunters who leave their vehicles behind and venture quietly into the wild—seek to become creatures of landscape much in the same way as their prey.

All, however, return at night to heated homes, flick on the lights, settle before the television, eat something from the fridge. All are part of a culture that assumes going home must entail turning one's back on the living landscape.

There used to be people who viewed things differently. Keith Brady, a park warden, showed me one of their camps in Waterton Lakes National Park one day. It was at a place called Indian Springs.

The campsite filled a grassy bay where rolling fescue grassland swept up against an aspen-covered sidehill. A small spring issued from the ground and chuckled away into the prairie.

"That spring doesn't freeze in winter," Keith said. "They would have had water all year round."

A nearby ridge gave the people who dwelt here shelter from wind, too. Trees grew tall along the ridge and around a nearby wetland. Shelter from wind, in a landscape where winter winds commonly gust to hurricane intensity and last for days on end, is a vital matter to every living creature.

Firewood was abundant on the hill above. The long-gone

people whose campsite we had found would only have had to drag it downhill.

We sat our horses, studying the landscape. Chief Mountain, one of the most important mountains in the Blackfoot Nation's mythology, stood forth from the rest of the Rockies several miles to the east. Closer, a complex of eskers, moraines, and hollows stretched along the edge of the Waterton River Valley. Wind-whipped grassland covered the knolls and ridges. A few bison fed on the crest of one hillock. They were part of a captive herd; a century ago there would have been wild bison in the same place. The Waterton valley's howling winds ensure that this eskerine complex remains snow-free—except lee slopes and hollows—through most winters.

The native hunters who camped at Indian Springs hunted the bison by herding them down the long draws between eskers and forcing them into deep snowdrifts where they could slaughter the big animals. The people camped at the one place in the landscape where they were consistently assured of open water, shelter, firewood, and proximity to good hunting. There was no need to go home after hunting. They were already there—like the bison, the aspens, the wind, and the eskers.

Modern North America's landscapes are now our homes too. We just tend not to think of them that way. Instead we drift, unanchored, into a future that frightens most of us, feeling vaguely incomplete, but unable to define that which is missing. We profess concern about "the environment," but it is an objectively defined environment—not a subjective home—about which we express an abstract concern. Our concern, in any case, is limited to those brief periods when other matters, concerning the world-within-a-world we have created, do not distract us.

We can always "go home" and shut the door when it all gets too much for us.

Gail and I lived briefly in a bedroom community south of Calgary. We chose Okotoks because the Calgary we had both grown up in was long gone. We hoped a small foothills town might offer some kind of link to the things of the past we value most. Reality soon disillusioned us.

All that first summer I watched over the back fence as a developer eradicated one square mile of foothill landscape. As the summer progressed, heavy equipment rebuilt it into a generic suburb that might have been anywhere in the western world: a placeless colony for domesticated humans. The northwest-southeast glacial scours vanished; branching, interlinked roadways replaced them. Bulldozers and earth-movers recontoured and dammed the coulee to make little ponds and terraces. The swales that once spilled spring runoff into the coulee vanished overnight. The new landscape had a new hydrology, buried in sewer pipes. Exotic shrubs and lawns of tame bluegrass replaced the native fescue, wheatgrass, silverberry, and pasture sage. The very scent of the place changed: silver willow musk, wild rose, and curing hay gave way to 2,4-D, dust, and engine exhaust.

By the time the first snow fell, another piece of Alberta landscape had become mere real estate. Looking around at the street where we lived, I realized that only a decade or so ago it, too, had been foothills prairie. Yet Gail and I, our neighbours, and those hopeful young families moving into the new subdivision next door proudly declared ourselves Albertans. We professed to be at home here, amid all the For Sale signs.

By the time we left, Okotoks had become a place of horrified realization: the flip side of Dale's esker connection. It had forced me to see, beneath the common and accepted urban cityscapes and pastoral farmscapes among which I grew up, the fading shadows of what could, and should, have been home. I felt as if I had watched helplessly as vandals defaced my home—and then, as one turned, seen that he wore my face.

When we moved to Okotoks Gail and I were closer than we had been in years to the houses where we grew up and the places we had known in youth. We soon realized we were more homesick than we had ever been. We had tried to go home. We just had not known what that meant.

We moved again, coming home to Waterton, far from the scrapers, cats, and landscaping companies. Still, they are not far behind. The dust cloud of haste and unconcern will continue to rise from the near horizon until we western Canadians succeed in redefining home and establishing a more reflective and honourable relationship with the places of which fate grants us the chance to be a part. Like the vandals in my vision, those scrapers, cats, and contractors wear our faces. Our eyes stare blankly from those faces, failing to focus as they sweep the living landscape. Interest flickers only when they see familiar things—bank machines, televisions, asphalt, other products of artifice and desire.

What we recognize depends upon what we can see. What we see depends upon how our senses have been trained: who we are. Who we are depends, usually, on the kind of home we grew up in.

I still return to my family home at Christmas and Thanksgiving. I visit my mother in the house that has been a part of my life since the age of four. There is a crucifix on the dining room wall; I remember holy cards tucked behind it after my first Communion and palm leaves drying behind it each spring. I know which stairs squeak, what the furnace sounds like late at night, which walls are patched, and why. Everything about that house is familiar, rich with association, memory, and significance. The faces around the table are people I know and love. We have laughed together, suffered together, learned to give each other space and to take pleasure in the times when we reunite.

That house and those people are home. They matter deeply to me. I could not stand to be cut off from them. I could never bring myself to do harm to any of them. They are all inextricably bound up in how I have come to know my self.

So, too, I now know, are the Athabasca River Valley, the eskers and kames south of Radium, the wind-whipped aspen forests of Waterton, and the wild places and living landscapes I've come to know—however imperfectly—and grown to love through years of exploration, contemplation, and growing concern about their well-being.

It is time to come home. It is past time. It is time for each of us to rediscover the living landscapes of the wounded West and recognize them as the home places that make us who we are— no less than our families, the houses in which we live, and the ways in which we earn our livings. It is time to seek our own esker connections—moments of epiphany that transfigure our surroundings and transform us. No matter how hard we race toward the horizon, it recedes ahead of us. Perhaps home is not beyond the horizon after all. Coming home may be a simple matter of learning to see more clearly where we are already.

MARK HUME
with Harvey Thommasen

December: Moon When the Sun Rests

MARK HUME is an award-winning journalist and writer with a deep passion for rivers and fish. Hume, a resident of Vancouver, is the author of *The Run of the River* and *Adam's River: The Mystery of the Adams River Sockeye.* "December: Moon When the Sun Rests" is taken from *River of the Angry Moon: Seasons on the Bella Coola*, written in collaboration with Harvey Thommasen, who provided information about the natural history of the region.

A HEAVY, WET SNOW has fallen during the night, spreading a humped white blanket across the estuary. Here and there clumps of tired blonde grass push through. A flock of mallards bursts from a tidal channel, scattering snow crystals in the air like pollen. Far out on the flats a drift of trumpeter swans stirs and shifts as an eagle circles overhead. Along the river, as the morning warms, clumps of snow drop from the tree branches, vanishing as they become water. The snow eats the sound of the river as it passes over its stone bed; it eats the sound of the forest.

Driving up the highway, travelling east from Bella Coola,

I set out on the last fishing trip of the year. Somehow I know that today I will find a steelhead that is buried somewhere in the river, its heart beating like a drum. In the back of the truck I can hear the tip of my fly rod tapping against the window as it picks up the vibrations of the road. It seems to be chattering with anticipation. Every fishing trip starts with a sense of optimism, but sometimes there is a deeper level of certainty, a predator's instinct that comes from a vision of a steelhead rising through layers of green water to take your fly. I have seen steelhead stand on their heads to pluck one of my flies from the bottom, and I have seen them tilt up to take a floating dry fly with an audible snap of their jaws. I have seen them rise, head, dorsal, tail, and I have seen deep, slow glints of silver, far away, as they twisted sideways in the current. I have taken them unseen too, by intuition, striking for no apparent reason, but finding a fish there.

The dream I have now, however, is of a fish and a rise form that I have never seen. The steelhead materializes over a bed of mossy stones; it rises on a steady diagonal line to intercept my fly, which glows like an orange spark. The river that divides and joins us seems to be made of sheets of tinted glass, which rotate slowly. When the fish takes the fly, the dream ends. I know that to finish the dream I must find the steelhead, and I know that the steelhead is somewhere in the Bella Coola River, waiting for me, as it has been all year.

Few people fish the river in December (Siimt) any more. There used to be a small but strong run of steelhead in the twelfth month, a continuation of the November run, but that stock, like all the others, has dwindled to a point where it is not really worth going out. Still, some do fish and one, I know, found steelhead this week. A Nuxalk spin fisherman told me, in the quiet way that anglers will sometimes share the most precious information, that he'd just taken a fresh steelhead in a pool known as the Classic.

"Nice fish," he said. "Big. Silver as chrome." He held his rough hands far apart. And when he put his hands down the steelhead was gone.

I knew he'd killed the fish, exercising his Native right, and that was troubling. But I appreciated the information, which needn't have been shared and which didn't appear to be in general circulation, at least not yet. It jarred me out of my lethargy, and on a cold day with clouds as grey as salmon backs hanging over the mountains, I set out. In search of a wild steelhead.

Passing up through the farming district, I saw houses steepled in snow, smoke rising warmly from their chimneys. Trucks and cars were safely parked in driveways, covered with a ten-centimetre-thick blanket of fresh snow. The crops were long in and for most people there was no reason to go out. They were content to wait, knowing that sooner or later rain would come to wash the roads clear.

A highways crew had been through, plowing the main highway. Here and there I slowed to avoid hitting flocks of purple finches that were feeding on road salt. They rose up before me and settled back once I had passed. In thickets along the ditches I saw the flash of evening grosbeaks and common redpolls as they feasted on the tiny seeds inside birch cones. Occasionally, in the depth of winter, there will be an eruption of birds in the valley, as cold weather or poor feeding conditions on the Chilcotin Plateau push flocks down to the coast. Sometimes a weather front will move snowy owls down from the north, and they will sit along the field margins, startlingly visible in the dark green trees. Sometimes you can see them, white birds gliding over white fields in search of invisible mice, voles, and shrews that are busy tunnelling under the snow cover. Owls hear rather than see the small mammals and dive, like ospreys into water, to take their prey. Sometimes you will see the long brush strokes their great wings have left in the snow.

The Classic Pool is more than forty-eight kilometres from Bella Coola, and it is nearly noon by the time I turn off the highway onto the Talchako forest road. There is no reason to fish early in December; it is better to wait for the day to warm a little and, one hopes, give the steelhead a reason to stir. The gravel road is layered in ice and deeply rutted. I shift to low four-wheel drive and slither along, the undercarriage of my truck scraping on the snow ridge between the deep tire tracks. I cross the Bella Coola River, running smooth and dark, turn east again and after several kilometres find a spot to park. There is no trail visible, but I know if I work my way through a clump of small firs, aiming for a grove of old growth in the distance, I will find a route through a slough to the river.

I slip down the steep bank next to the logging road and push through the wet undergrowth, knocking clumps of snow off the branches. My breath is steamy and heavy with moisture. Except for the crunching of my boots, the forest is silent. Then, just a rod length away, a ruffed grouse leaps into the air, its wings drumming hard against its breast, snow flying. It soars and tilts off through the trees, leaving an exit hole in the snowbank where it had spent the night. Grouse, ptarmigan, and even redpolls routinely bury themselves in snow, flying right into a drift, where they settle for the night—waiting to startle unwary travellers.

Tracks of snowshoe hares lace through the thickets, and twisting among them are delicate ribbons of deer mice footprints. Snowshoe hares sustain many predators, including wolves, foxes, cougars, lynx, hawks, and owls. In a single winter up to 40 percent of the hare population is eaten by its hunters. Hares are prolific breeders, but their population rises and falls in a six- to twelve-year cycle. At one time lynx were blamed for declines in snowshoe hare numbers, but studies have shown that the availability of food is a more important factor. Too many hares will overgraze their habitat, leading to starvation and a crash in the population. Not surprisingly, when snowshoe hare populations drop, lynx numbers decline soon afterwards. Over time the vegetation recovers, the hare population builds, and there is food again for the predators. It may be that ancient humans were once caught up in a similar rhythm, but now when a game or fish population declines, the number of people just keeps on increasing.

The deep snow is hard going, and it's a relief when I finally get down to flat ground and into the grove of old-growth trees. The snow is not so heavy under the dark canopy, and the well-worn trails cut by deer show I'm not the only one to find the walking much easier. A movement catches my eye, and I see a herd of about ten mule deer, frozen in the shadows. Their reddish-brown coats of summer have been replaced by thick, grey winter fur. One of the bucks has a single antler on its head and, compared with the does around him, is quite thin. When I stop, they all bound away, vanishing with surprising ease. The deer have penned here for the winter to feed on twigs blown down from the tops of the Douglas-firs and on the yellow lichens that fall from upper branches. It is hard to believe that lichens can support deer, but research has found the beardlike plant is vital to their survival. The lichen only flourishes on old-growth trees.

There's the soft outline of a path through the woods now, one first made by animals but since expanded by anglers, and it takes me upstream through another forty-five metres of old-growth cedar and spruce. At the base of one tree is a spattering of blood and a pile of ruffed grouse feathers. I look up to see a marten dart for cover, dragging its limp prey with it.

Beyond the old growth I pass again into a logged area, where the snow is thick and I have to scramble over debris. Then I walk through a stately grove of black cottonwood and cross a frozen bog, where the ground is lumpy and slippery. A beaver lodge, steeped in snow, with a wisp of warm air streaming up from inside, sits in the middle of a frozen pond. The farmer is home from the field.

I tread carefully on the ice, testing to see if it will crack, and then half-skate, half-walk to the far side. Finally, I push through a thicket of hemlock and break out onto the banks of the Bella Coola River. The walk has taken only about thirty minutes, but it seemed much longer. I unzip the neck of my jacket to let cool air pour in. The sky has begun to open up, and sunlight is shining through a large break in the clouds for the first time in days. I can see a smattering of blue. The air is a few degrees warmer than the river, and there's mist rising off the water; it swirls up in spirals and seems to catch in the thick branches of red cedars.

A gentle current flows into the head of the Classic Pool, re-fracting light over a shallow, sand-and-gravel bottom, giving the water a golden colour. Along the far bank the water turns dark green as it grows deeper. The boughs of overhanging trees, some still trimmed with snow, reflect on the surface. It is so quiet I hear the gentle surfacing of a fish near the head of the pool and turn to see the back and tail of a coho going down, its air bladder refilled. The last of the coho are spawning now, and the salmon are dark and exhausted. I wouldn't fish for them.

There aren't any tracks in the fresh snow, but at the top of the run the pure blanket of whiteness is marred by a smudge. I push back the cover with my boot. This is where the steelhead was killed. All that remains is the stain of frozen blood. There are eagle prints around it and the strokes left by pinion feathers. Lumpy, under last night's snowfall, are the angler's tracks.

The winter steelhead are the last adult fish of the year to return to the Bella Coola River. They hold in the deeper, slow-moving pools of the upper river until spring runoff raises the Atnarko; then they move again, to spawning grounds far upstream.

Winter steelhead are said to be the most challenging of all of British Columbia's freshwater game fish to hook on the fly. The Bella Coola winter steelhead are no exception. To be successful, you need not only skill but the right water conditions, and you need to know exactly where the fish lie. You also need a little luck. More often than not it is too cold, it is raining too hard, the water is too high, or it is too muddy. When it gets too cold, a sheet of ice forms along the river's edge and islands of slush drift in the current. It's dangerous to walk along the shore, and the floating ice makes it impossible to control a fly line.

Today conditions are perfect. Snow lines the bank, but there's no ice shelf and I can easily wade into the river. I sense the steelhead are lying in the deep water along the far bank, in the shadow of the forest.

When steelhead find a lie they hold hour after hour, day after day, barely moving. It must be strange for such powerful, active fish to become almost comatose. But their main function now is to conserve energy, while their eggs or sperm ripen. They won't spawn until next March.

The cold water slows their metabolism, making it less likely they'll go for a fly. Bait fishers, who drift balls of sticky salmon eggs along the bottom, even have trouble at times and know they'll have to put their lure within thirty centimetres or so of a steelhead before it will take. A fly must be within centimetres, and even then it may be ignored.

The water is so clear I can see pebbles on the bottom three metres away. I tie on a long, slender leader. I choose a small egg fly, barely big enough to cover a fingernail. It will look like a single coho egg, drifting in the current, and I hope a steelhead will take it in the tip of its mouth.

Edging out into the current, my boots feeling their way over the smooth, cold stones, I start to cast gently across the river. I fish the fly at a dead drift, retrieve it quietly and cast again. Every few casts I take three steps down and repeat the process. I work the fly far out. In what seems like moments, an hour passes. I have become as mesmerized as the steelhead themselves, and time has become as fluid as the river. I cast and breathe and step down. The forest surrounds me as the waters of the Bella Coola surround the fish.

An invisible rectangle exists in space and time, encompassing the river and the stones and history. I have been searching for it in a dark forest, along an endless shoreline. Without knowing, I step inside. I am at one corner and the great, sleeping salmon is at the other. The line drifts between the opposing points.

I do not see the steelhead rise, but on this day I do not have to. I have seen it in my dream, so when it comes, I know. Suddenly in the middle of a cast that is exactly like a thousand before it, I sense the fish is on. I drive the rod up—and it bends hard. I feel a head shaking, deep in the river; it is powerful and slow, as if the steelhead is awakening under the weight of a glacier. I catch my breath, I hear my heart drumming like a grouse, I see the red blood on the snow, I know that somewhere river mist curls from the mouth of a running wolf and that great white swans are leaning forward to plunge their heads into the rich mud of the estuary. I know that the coho are moving gently together, shifting the stones, and I can hear salmon eggs falling. I know that the river glints like sunlight on the wings of a dipper and that night folds itself over the valley like the soft brown wings of a sedge. I hear the Nuxalk drummers, but their song falls like snow into the river and becomes silent. Everything is water.

Then the fish runs. It goes up along the far bank, the line hissing as it cuts through the reflection of the trees; then it dives under the swirling current at the head of the pool and runs, fast as a frightened deer, back down my side of the river. I strip line frantically, throwing loops up into the snow. The fish goes all the way to the tail of the pool, and the line I have regained shoots out through my hand. Bits of ice rattle in the guides like salmon teeth. The fight lasts an eternity but is over in moments, as if it somehow never existed. Finally I see the steelhead, its dark green back darker than the river stones. Its belly like snow. The blush of sunset on its cheeks. At some moment the fish and I agree the fight is done. It yields, is drawn miraculously toward me, an enormous fish of six or seven kilograms, coming without a struggle, its perfectly formed body moving without friction. It seems cut from steel and polished by time. I kneel in the water and draw the steelhead against my legs, not believing a fish so power-ful can suddenly be so submissive.

And then I see that it's bleeding.

As the gill plates move, clouds of rust billow from the fish of steel, ocher threads trail off in the water, marking the hidden currents.

I feel my centre give way.

A fish that bleeds will almost certainly die, for its wound will not congeal in the coldness of the river. I trace my hand up the leader, find the small hook, push it free from where it's embedded, deep in the mouth at the base of the tongue. When the fly comes out it is covered with a dark glob of blood. My hand is red, and later I will realize that I am bleeding too, that I have cut a finger on the steelhead's teeth.

I let the fish go and it rests in the shallows next to me. In that moment I sense the timelessness of nature and the fatalism of the spawning run. I know that the rivers I love are paved with the bones of the fish that I love and by this I am bound to the planet. The dazed steelhead stirs, its tail roiling the surface of the great Bella Coola River, and then it swims out, vanishing under the sheltering forest.

BASIL H. JOHNSTON

Beyond Yonder: Awuss-woodih

BASIL H. JOHNSTON is a celebrated writer and translator and an
Anishinaubae member of the Cape Croker First Nation in Ontario.
He is the author of *The Bearwalker and Other Stories*, *The Manitous:
The Spiritual World of the Ojibway*, *Indian School Days*, *Ojibway
Ceremonies*, *Ojibway Tales*, *The Star Man and Other Tales*, and
Crazy Dave. "Beyond Yonder: Awuss-woodih" appears in *Mermaids
and Medicine Women: Native Myths and Legends*.

THE FOLLOWING does not apply to just one Anishinaubae, but
to all, every single one. There is no question that it is necessary
for them to return to the way that they used to worship, to again
take up their ancient way of believing. At that time they will survive; they will prosper.

For example, I once came upon a story. Exactly where the
story took place is not certain; what is certain is that it was somewhere in Anishinaubae country. It concerns, in particular, the
young, two young men in fact.

These Anishinaubaek despised the district where they lived.
This land was inordinately desolate. It was rocky. There were no
fish and no game. At one point, they voiced their feelings: "It's
hard to imagine how poor we are!" All they had to wear were

deer hides. Their bows and their canoes were plain.

"Look!" said one of these young men. "It is absolutely beautiful beyond there, to the west, where the sun sets in the evening. The land there must be beautiful. We really ought to migrate there. If our parents will not go, we should just leave on our own."

The people decided to leave. But they had no leader. They therefore chose one of the young men. "You will lead the way," his people told him.

"But I don't know the direction we should follow," he replied.

What was to be expected? This young man knew nothing. He was only fifteen years of age. Nevertheless, he was chosen to be their leader.

Because of his uncertainty the young man went to the water's edge to seek guidance. All of a sudden, a fish broke through the surface, a trout. "What is it that you want?" the trout asked.

"Where we live seems so wretched. It seems much fairer on the far shore, to the west."

"As you wish," the trout replied. "I will take you. First gather your canoes, as many of you as there are. Take everything with you."

The young man at once told his fellow Anishinaubaek. As instructed, the people made small canoes, all of them. Finally, they assembled on the shore. The young man prayed. As if in obedience, the trout, it's said, stuck his head out of the water.

The young Anishinaubae then spoke to this trout: "We're ready; would you take us to where we are going, to that land that is beautiful."

"Very well," said the trout, whereupon he summoned his fellow fish to help him lead the Anishinaubaek.

After a time, they arrived in a different land. It looked wretched. There were no berries and the people were hungry. It was obvious that this wasn't the place. The Anishinaubaek were incensed.

Still farther into the distance the land appeared remarkably pleasing to the eye. In anticipation they once again resumed their journey. But this time, it's said, it was a white fish who guided them to Gauminautikawaeyauk, the Land of Berries, Thunder Bay. But still the land looked the same, poor.

Then, it's said, they asked a fox to take them beyond, to the prairie, Kitchi-mishkodaeng, the Great Prairie. That did not suit the Anishinaubaek either.

By chance, a buffalo came along. He led them all the way to the mountains. After that, some say, it was the mountain goat; mountain goats conducted the Anishinaubaek across the mountains, to the Pacific. But even that land did not seem right for the Anishinaubaek.

On they journeyed, toward the north, it's said, where dwell the white bears and where also live the seals. But it was hardly fit. To the sight it was barren.

At last they met Nanabush. "Where are you going?" he asked.

"Oh, we are looking for that beautiful land where the wild animals abound—deer, rabbits, moose, fish—where fish are abundant, and berries as well."

"Why, where you have come from it is thus," said Nanabush.

That being the case, they came back, these people, and when they were once more at home they saw that what Nanabush had said was indeed true. It might seem that it was for nothing that they had wandered so far abroad, but it is said that not until they returned to it did they cherish their own land.

Permissions